SOVEREIGN

THE OWNER'S MANUAL FOR A REMARKABLE LIFE

DAVID ELIKWU

ENDURING BOOKS

ADVANCE READER COPY

Published in the UK in 2025 by
ENDURING BOOKS
email: contact@enduringbooks.com
www.enduringbooks.com

Copyright © 2025 by David Elikwu

The moral right of the author has been asserted.

All rights reserved. Without limiting the rights under copyright reserved above, no part of this publication may be reproduced, stored or introduced into a retrieval system, or transmitted, in any form or by any means—electronic, mechanical, photocopying, recording or otherwise—except for brief quotations in critical reviews or articles, without the prior written permission of both the copyright owner and the publisher of this book.

This book is written as a source of information only. The information contained herein should by no means be considered a substitute for the advice, decisions, or judgement of the reader's professional or financial advisors. As of the date published, all reasonable efforts have been made to ensure the accuracy of the information contained in this book. The author and the publisher disclaim responsibility for any adverse effects arising from the use or application of the information contained in this book.

There exists a myth that destiny falls into the lap of the patient and deserving. That success accrues naturally to the gifted and brave. That all you really need is some elbow grease, pulled bootstraps, and gritted teeth, for life's dice to roll in your favour.

But none of these things, in isolation, is sufficient. Ambition without focus wastes energy. Skill without conviction stalls. Hard knocks without reflection leave scars. This book, *Sovereign*, will show you how ambition, agency, and adversity can propel you forward instead of pulling you apart.

This is the handbook for outsiders ready to bend reality in their favour. If you're looking for tidy clichés, you won't find them here. What follows is a mix of hard history, lived experiments, and practical exercises—designed to help you act before conditions are perfect.

Part narrative, part playbook, this is a practical guide to rewriting the limits of work, wealth, and life. Read on if you'd rather make your own luck than wait for someone to grant it.

Praise for Sovereign

"Sovereign is a passionate call to responsibility and agency. It's packed with helpful principles for shaping a well-lived life, grounded in the real world with brilliant examples from a huge range of fields. David's wealth of experience, his commitment, curiosity and generosity shine through, and getting to know him better is one of the best parts of the journey. Recommended."
 — **Stu Patience, creator of Driverless Crocodile**

"David's approach and writing is thought-provoking, open and most importantly, honest. There are no shortcuts here. It's clear about the effort needed and how to make the most of your time. Pick it up."
 — **Sheree Atcheson, Group Senior Vice President, Valtech**

"David writes with equal parts humility and fire, and it's contagious. This book is both deeply practical and deeply human, and David's stories remind us that agency isn't abstract—it's built one choice at a time."
 — **Kelly Wilde Miller, Author of 'Creative Dysregulation'**

"The internet's latest buzzword is 'agency'. In clear-eyed prose backed by forceful examples, David's Sovereign reveals what it actually means to live a self-authored life without limits. A must read for any ambitious outlier."
— **Jason Shen, 3x Founder & Executive Coach**

"David, a gifted storyteller and keen observer, beautifully weaves stories from historical icons and his own life into *Sovereign*—a powerful guide to living life on your own terms"
— **Arielle Jackson, Marketing Expert in Residence at First Round Capital**

"Elikwu guides you step-by-step toward greatness, your unique target that no one else may see. SOVEREIGN is an invitation to step into your fullest expression, no matter the cards you're dealt along the way."
— **Jenny Blake, author of *Free Time* and *Pivot***

"I wasn't expecting to underline so much. Elikwu's writing is sharp but unpretentious, the kind that stays with you long after you've put the book down."
— **Sulaiman Deka, author of Unscripted Influence**

"So many books like this feel overconfident or overpolished. This one felt honest. I trusted it. I'll be coming back to it again."
— **Emily Rhodes, design lead, Merge Collective**

"A refreshingly sane voice in a space that's become overrun with hacks and shortcuts. Sovereign takes a slower, deeper route, and it works."
— **The Working Mind Journal**

Contents

Dedication	VIII
Preface	XI
Introduction	1
How to Read This Book	

Part I
Ambition

1. Frame Change	11
2. Your Floor and Ceiling	19
3. Desire and Direction	27
4. Find Your Fuel	39
5. The Right Measuring Stick	44
6. Rules Aren't Real	51
7. Finding Your Speed	58
8. Success Can Be Easy	70
9. You're a Luck Magnet	78
10. Keep Your Feet on the Ground	84

Part II
Agency

Confidence — 95

11. Carve a Hole in the Universe	97
12. Break the Box	103
13. Lift the Weight	114

14.	Move the Mean	119
15.	Take Your Seat	126
16.	Bold, Not Blind	132

Competence — 137

17.	Find Something	138
18.	Learn Faster	147
19.	Fail Better	157
20.	Trends Over Streaks	164
21.	The Advice Trap	173

Charisma — 181

22.	The Levels of Charisma	182
23.	Make Friends in the Line	192
24.	Rock the Boat	204
25.	Using your Big Voice	211
26.	Keys to the City	226

Part III
Adversity

27.	Learn to Tread Water	252
28.	Take the Mask Off	255
29.	Keep Your Shoulder Off the Mat	266
30.	Keep Your Wheels Spinning	278
31.	Stay in the Pocket	289
32.	Keep the Dream Alive	297
33.	The Final Chapter	304

    The Illusion of Control
    Navigating Your Nature
    Your Unique Perspective
    The Art of Letting Go
    The Spirit of a Slave
    Make Your Own Music

The Sovereign Choice
Further Reading 317
Acknowledgements 319
About the author 320

To patient friends, without whom I might be consigned to a bleak and lasting solitude.

David Elikwu — Free Flier, 2025

PREFACE

Sovereign *(adj.)*: Possessing supreme power or authority over oneself; free from external control; self-governing in action and decision.

Her first public flight didn't kill her. But it could have. The propeller whacked the air in heated rhythm as Bessie Coleman climbed into the cockpit. The biplane was a Curtiss JN-4 "Jenny" – borrowed for one weekend and insured for none. She would pay it back with history.

Sceptical reporters and curious onlookers crowded the airfield, bracing, on a cool September morning in 1922, for a spectacle: a Black female stunt pilot in an era when neither Black people nor women were supposed to fly.

Bessie cinched her seatbelt. She let her mind drift through the journey that had brought her to this moment. Back to the Texas cotton fields where she'd spent her childhood. As the tenth of thirteen children born to sharecroppers in the late 1800s, there was every expectation that her life would be written for her; dictated by societal pressures and crooked laws. But destiny beckoned.

Life might have been safer, been easier, if she'd accepted her supposed fate—the role society wrote for girls like her. Picking cotton. Cleaning houses. Doing what her parents did, and their parents before them.

She remembered standing in those fields through long Texas summers, back bent from hours of labour. Sweat stinging at her eyes, blisters blooming in her palms. But while her body was in the fields, her mind was in the clouds. She was dreaming of the sky.

The war had been the catalyst. Returning soldiers, her brother included, told wild tales of dogfights and aerial stunts – of pilots who danced through clouds, defying gravity and fear alike. Those stories stoked in Bessie a dream as distant as the stars—to fly.

Her aptitude for maths soon freed her from the fields, and her quest began. First to Oklahoma with just enough money for a single term of college. Then to Chicago where she bunked with her brother while making enquiries – she needed someone who could teach her to fly.

Tampa said no. Tulsa said no. Texas, Ohio, Illinois—NO, NO, NO.

"Coloured?" No.

"Female?" No.

"Next!"

Even flight pioneer Orville Wright rejected all female applicants for training, assuming they were notoriety seekers without the 'mechanical aptitude' to pilot a craft. The message was clear: the skies were not meant for people like her.

For anyone else, the story would end there. A dream broken in the cruel face of reality. But Bessie yearned for a remarkable life – one she could control completely. If America wouldn't teach her to fly, then she'd go somewhere that would.

She started French classes at night, doubling shifts as a manicurist and a restaurant manager to save every coin she could. She convinced two prominent Black businessmen of her potential – Robert Abbott, founder of the Chicago Defender newspaper, and Jesse Binga, a banker. They agreed to contribute to her tuition if she completed those lessons. Soon enough, she was ready. Bessie gathered meagre savings, got herself a passport, and boarded a ship to France.

She may, for a moment, have hoped her trials were over. But the Caudron Brother's School of Aviation wasn't built for shallow stomachs. Thirty hours, thirty stitches, one funeral per month. That seemed to be the curriculum on the wide stretch of beach just outside Le Crotoy, where flights from timber and metal hangars were timed by tide tables.

Bessie watched as fellow students, even those with more experience, washed out or worse. Engines blew back, belching like muskets. Propeller splinters littered the floor. She could either learn quickly or become a statistic.

Seven months—half the standard course—was all she needed. On 15 June 1921 the Fédération Aéronautique Internationale stamped Licence No. 18310. It made Bessie the first Black woman to fly. The first person of Native American descent to fly. One of the first Americans, full stop, to earn French wings. A licence to fly anywhere in the world, including back home in the segregated U.S. One signature unchained an entire hemisphere of sky.

Now, two years later, 29-year-old Bessie Coleman was ready to take to the skies in a borrowed biplane for her American debut. It was a stellar performance. The crowd hooted and hollered, and their excitement sparked a run of booked shows. But Bessie quickly decided that flying wasn't enough. She'd done the first impossible thing. Now, she wanted to change the world.

"No Uncle Tom stuff for me," she said plainly. Her decision to only perform in front of desegregated crowds despite Jim Crow laws made her infamous. After another stint in France and time training with Germany's military aces in Berlin, she returned to newspaper headlines in both White and African American papers calling her 'Brave Bessie'.

She made a small fortune as a speaker when she wasn't flying, drawing audiences of women and other Black folk. She was soon making more money on the ground speaking than in the air flying, but Bessie didn't let fame and wealth distract her. The sky kept calling, and she always answered. On one flight over the hills of California, she fell from the plane during a roll manoeuvre. She broke a leg, cracked some ribs and cut her face.

From her hospital bed she sent this telegram:

"Tell them all that as soon as I can walk I'm going to fly! And my faith in aviation and the use [...] it will serve in fulfilling the destiny of my people isn't shaken at all."

— Bessie Coleman

She was back in the cockpit just a year later. She couldn't be stopped.

Bessie pushed the boundaries of what crowds came to expect. She would fly in figure eights, and upside down, and get people to walk on the wings of her plane mid-air. She once tried to enlist her mother in a stunt, asking her to leap from the plane with a parachute. When her mother said no, Bessie found someone else.

Bessie died doing what she loved, though her life was cut short by tragic accident. She was 3,500 feet in the air on April 30, 1926, practicing for a performance. Bessie let her mechanic pilot the plane while she scanned the ground for a suitable parachute landing site. A loose wrench was knocked. It dropped into the engine. The plane lurched and flipped in a spiralling nosedive. Bessie wasn't wearing a seatbelt and was flung from the craft, perishing on impact with the ground.

Her legacy outlasted her. Bessie was deeply mourned in Texas, Florida, and Chicago, where her body lay in state and thousands gathered in funeral ceremonies that spilled out of churches and into the street. The ceremony was led by prominent civil rights crusader, Ida B. Wells. As fans and supporters gathered below, planes flew overhead, dropping flowers in salute, and flight schools were later developed in her honour.

Bessie Coleman lived a remarkable life. A Sovereign one, marked by a refusal to accept life's default limits. A life only possible because she defied what was expected and dared to reshape her fate. But while rare, Bessie's story isn't unique. Throughout history there have been men and women who, like Bessie, chose to write their own stories rather than accept the ones handed to them.

They come from all walks of life. Some born into privilege, others into poverty. Some facing external battles, others battling personal demons. What unites them is not their circumstances, but their responses to them. This book explores what it means to take control of your life. It's a guide to taking action in the world. A manual for making things happen.

We'll explore what it takes to live a Sovereign life – and the tools you'll need to carve your own path. We'll study stories of those who've done it, extract the principles that guided them, and develop a roadmap for how you can do the same.

Modern life straps you to the jump-seat of a flight outside your control. Algorithms choose the view, adverts choose the meal, deadlines choose the speed. You could accept this reality; sit back, half asleep, choke down microwave gruel and be grateful. Or, grab the yoke, and make this the ride of a lifetime. The Sovereign life isn't given; it can only be claimed through deliberate action. It is a sad irony, on consideration, that Bessie Coleman lost her life on the rare occasion she let someone else pilot her craft. You have to grab the wheel.

You don't need a flight licence to be Sovereign. You don't need to change the world on some grand scale. Sovereignty springs from the choices you make, the challenges you respond to, and the dreams you dare to pursue. Coleman's journey from cotton fields to clouded skies illustrates that for those who walk the Sovereign path, the sky is not the limit.

If you're ready to stop being a passenger and step into the pilot's seat, turn the page, and let's begin.

Introduction

"I was not designed to be forced. I will breathe after my own fashion. Let us see who is the strongest."

— Henry David Thoreau

Eighteen months after dropping out of university, I got an offer to join one of the biggest law firms on the planet. It was my dream firm. One of only a handful at the time that made over a billion dollars a year in revenue. The ground floor had a shoe-shiner. The second had a masseuse, a doctor, and a house chef trained in France. The top floor had views priced at £2,000 an hour.

I joined at age 21—by decent margin the youngest ever first-year, and not only had I not graduated from a prestigious law school, I didn't even have a degree. Stranger still, this wasn't a fluke; it was the culmination of a pattern that had defined my life up to that point.

I'd already had my first graduate job by then. And when I got fired, I walked to a competing firm and interviewed for a better role within 3 hours. Before that, I'd worked as a marketer with clients like Amazon, Credit Suisse, DHL, and Krispy Kreme. Before that, I'd started my first company importing consumer electronics from China.

From selling a computer lab to my school at 15, to landing Adidas commercials at 17, to creating my own positions at Google, I had consistently achieved things that, by all conventional metrics, should have been out of my reach. Not because I was exceptionally talented or uniquely gifted, but because I had stumbled upon a set of principles that allowed me to navigate the world in a fundamentally different way.

These principles—what I've come to call the 'Sovereign Mindset'—are not my invention. They are timeless truths embodied by remarkable individuals throughout history. In this book, we'll explore these principles through the lives of both the layman and the legendary.

We'll learn about ambition from people like Muggsy Bogues, who at 5'3" became the shortest player in NBA history, and from Mary Shelley, who wrote one of the most enduring novels of all time at just 18.

We'll study agency through the lens of Issa Rae, who built a media empire from a web series, and from Elon Musk, who revolutionised multiple industries against all odds, alongside figures in a range of domains from Brandon Sanderson to Venus Williams to Gertrude Stein to Howard Schultz.

We'll discover how to overcome adversity with Tiger Woods, who staged one of the greatest comebacks in sports history, and Barry Marshall, who drank bacteria to prove a medical theory.

We'll learn to navigate our limitations from Ludwig van Beethoven, who composed his greatest works while deaf, and Admiral James Stockdale, who survived years as a prisoner of war through sheer force of will.

These stories, along with many others, will illustrate the core tenets of Sovereignty: nurturing fierce ambition, developing unshakeable agency, overcoming seemingly insurmountable obstacles, and turning perceived limitations into unique strengths.

Throughout this book, you'll learn from Sovereign minds who have achieved impossible feats, and the surprising secrets that make the remarkable commonplace. I am, perhaps, the least remarkable person you'll read about in this book. I only share personal stories to stand in for the average person, because I get a lot of questions about how I've ended up where I am.

I'm not a millionaire, guru, prodigy, or shaman—the kind of person who usually gets paid a six-figure advance to write a book like this. But because of all those things, this book will actually be useful. It's not a puff piece. I'm not an industry plant. You'll get to directly pattern match the traits common to a man on the street with some attainable success, and the stars of legend whose greatness seemed predestined.

Whether you're seeking to break free from golden handcuffs, bridge the gap between your current reality and your potential, or simply craft a life of greater autonomy and fulfilment, the principles of Sovereignty will guide you.

This road won't be easy. It will challenge you to question deeply held beliefs, to confront uncomfortable truths, and to take risks that may seem daunting. But for those willing to embrace it, the rewards are beyond measure.

How to Read This Book

This book is split into three parts, each practical and useful, but with a slightly different structure and focus.

Part one, on **Ambition**, skews toward inspiration. It aims to install a Sovereign mindset, helping you develop the courage to take control, and giving you a lens through which to channel your energy.

Part two, on **Agency**, leans heavily practical. It is structured to help you develop the tools you'll need to take action and actively craft the reality you seek.

Part three, on **Adversity**, is largely driven by narrative, illustrating how Sovereign principles can play out in various contexts, preparing you for whatever obstacles you may face.

I want this book to be true to its subtitle: *the owner's manual for a remarkable life*. Treat it like a manual – keep it somewhere you can continually refer to it. Dip in and out of the chapters you need most. There is a clear narrative structure, and on your first read it would be best to go from cover to cover, but don't be afraid to bounce about and take what you need most.

Make notes, write in the margins, bend the corners and wear the seams. Use it thoroughly, and lend it readily to anyone in your life who might benefit.

— David

Ambition

PART I

Ambition

Everyone's got a secret. Some hidden desire they keep tucked away, far from prying eyes. Maybe it's a business idea that keeps you up at night. Or a novel you've been plotting in your head for years. Perhaps it's a career change that you're hesitant to pursue.

For many, ambition remains a dormant seed, buried beneath layers of doubt, convention, and fear. Society teaches us to temper our dreams, but personal sovereignty only takes root once we wholly reject the limitations that others place upon us, and the ones we place upon ourselves.

Ambition recognises that the status quo is not immutable; that the rules which govern our lives are often more flexible than they appear, and the boundary of what's possible is largely defined by our willingness to push against it.

However, ambition without direction is like a ship without a rudder; powerful but aimless. The art lies in harnessing this force – in channelling it towards meaningful ends. Mastering it requires us to get clear on what we truly want. To distinguish between the dreams that are truly our own and those we've inherited from others.

As we fan the flames of our ambition, we must also learn to keep our feet firmly planted on the ground. Ambition is not a tool for escaping reality, but for reshaping it. Ambition turns abstract visions into concrete plans, and those plans into tangible results.

In embracing our ambition, we take the first step towards sovereignty. We declare that we are not content to be passengers in our lives, but rather the architects of our destinies. In doing so, we open ourselves to a world of possibility limited only by the scope of our imagination and the depth of our resolve.

David Elikwu — The Workers, 2025

1

Frame Change

"The eye sees only what the mind is prepared to comprehend."

— Robertson Davies

Ambition is your evolutionary birthright. It's what dragged us out of caves, sparked revolutions and built cities. But in modern life, we've learned to distrust it. In some circles, ambition has become a naughty word—a dirty curse, marked by association to greed, selfishness and ruthless careerism.

People are warned against being too ambitious – against sharing dreams out loud, or having them at all. We're taught stories, like that of Icarus flying too close to the sun, as a warning against hubris and vain conceit.

We're conditioned to lower our gaze from the skies and humbly accept what we're given. Follow the rules, we're told. Stay in line. Wait patiently. Follow, stay, wait—good dog. That's not me being condescending—the condescension is inherent to that worldview. It's baked into the voice that says you'll get whatever just reward society has predetermined for you, by the luck of your birth; but only if you deserve it. If you get nothing, then that's the way it was always going to be. And if you don't like that, there will always be some invisible spectre to shout at. A vessel to pour your frustrations into. A convenient villain.

You could blame capitalism, bad politics, generational curses, or the greed and excess of a past age.

If you've picked up this book, I think a small part of you knows that you can't accept that.

If those words make you itch with discomfort, you may already have the spark of the Sovereign. You may know, deep down, that cowering suffocates the spirit, and that destiny doesn't fall from the sky—it bursts from the earth—from soil tilled with human hands. You know, or want to believe, that you can make of your life what you wish. And if you haven't figured out exactly how yet, you'll find a roadmap in the pages that follow.

In this part of the book, we'll explore how to awaken and nurture your ambition. Not as a selfish or aimless pursuit, but as a powerful tool for personal growth and positive change. It all starts with how you see the world – your frame.

Your frame determines what you see and how you see it. Imagine looking through a camera's viewfinder. What you see will depend on the lens you have. A macro lens pulls the world within inches. A wide-angle shows you everything, but distorts at the edges. A long zoom compresses distance, smearing sharp lights into the soft blur of bokeh. Change the lens, and the entire picture shifts.

Our mental frames work the same way, shaping our perception of what's possible, what's achievable, and what's worth pursuing. By learning to change our frames, and break limiting ones, we can unlock ambitions we never knew we had, and see paths to possible futures that once seemed fanciful dreams.

Immigrant Superpowers

You need to make or witness one impossible thing happen as early as possible so that you start to believe in magic. Once your 'impossible' frame is broken, you'll realise that most other constraints are either self-imposed, or a mirage of social conditioning. If you still feel a lot of mental blocks around certain outcomes being possible for you, this book will help you to break them.

One of my deep beliefs is that being a first-generation immigrant solved most impostor-syndrome-related issues for me. You get to watch your parents bend reality through sheer force of will, and move you to a place that was only ever a concept beforehand. It's an agency boot camp. Nothing is impossible anymore.

When I was a child, my family moved from Lagos, Nigeria, to London, England. The most vivid embodiment of this transition related to my struggle with severe asthma. In Nigeria, my earliest memories were of being sick. Of visiting hospitals, and getting injections until my bum hurt. Healthcare options were limited, and it was a constant source of anxiety for my parents.

Then you compound that with other societal factors – like being pulled over by armed police that ask who you'll vote for come election day, or the three separate occasions that our cheap car caught on fire. Like the time I burned my finger on a candle because we didn't have constant electricity or a petrol generator, or being beaten by teachers for being naturally left-handed. And you realise, in the midst of these things, that you could only ever make the best of a bad situation. For the record, I still have a small scar on my hand from that burn, and I now write exclusively with my right hand.

After moving to the UK, my health improved dramatically, though I still struggled with asthma. The level of care and resources available were worlds apart. When we first signed up with a local GP, I remember doing tests with the doctor on multiple occasions where they asked me to blow into a tube that would measure my lung capacity. My lungs were so weak that doctors often thought I was only pretending to blow.

I remember a particular day during school, once our family had settled into a neighbourhood after a few moves across London. I'd had a sports day at school, and at the end of the day, I walked home by myself – something that might not have been possible in Nigeria.

At home, on days like this, I had a routine. I'd get down on my knees beside my bed and drag out a heavy machine. It was a nebuliser. There are smaller and fancier ones now, but back then they looked similar to the clunky oxygen machines people used during the COVID-19 pandemic.

I would set up the machine myself, while my parents were still at work. The medication, a liquid called albuterol, came in small plastic ampoules. I'd carefully pour this into the nebuliser cup and attach it to the machine. The nebuliser made a churning, grinding sound, like it was supposed to be making ice cream, but instead of producing sweet treats, it pumped out a stale, medicinal odour.

I'd pull the mask over my face, snapping the elastic against the back of my head. Then roll into bed and lie there for a while, staring up at the ceiling as the nebuliser converted the liquid medication into a fine mist. Inhaling that mist helped open up my airways and make breathing easier. The process wasn't particularly enjoyable, but it was necessary, and represented a form of magic that would never have been available to me had we not moved.

The impact went beyond better healthcare. It demonstrated how dramatically life could change when someone decides to reshape their circumstances. My parents' decision to move—an ambitious leap into the unknown—fundamentally altered the trajectory of our lives.

As I grew older, I realised the principle wasn't limited to moving countries. The message was that boundaries which seem fixed are often illusory. Some obstacles may seem immovable until you reorient yourself. While we can't control everything, we possess more agency over our circumstances than we acknowledge. And progress is often on the other side of a simple frame change.

Frame changes won't always require dramatic changes in geography, either. They can happen right where you are, through a simple yet profound shift in perspective.

The World's Fastest Mile

For decades, running a mile in under four minutes was considered not just unlikely, but physically impossible. Scientists believed the human body couldn't move that fast over such a distance. The four-minute barrier had become a physical and psychological wall that seemed unbreakable.

Yet on May 6, 1954, a British runner named Roger Bannister shattered that illusion. Bannister wasn't even a full-time athlete; he was a neurology student who squeezed training into short, intense sessions between classes. His accomplishment didn't come from an overbearing training schedule or cutting-edge technology – but from his ability to reframe the problem.

Instead of accepting the common belief that the four-minute mile was impossible, Bannister approached the challenge with a different mindset. He saw the barrier for what it was – a psychological hurdle more than a physical one. Bannister understood that the limitations were largely a result of collective belief, rather than physiological science.

So on that fateful day at the Iffley Road track in Oxford, with about 3,000 spectators watching, Bannister ran the mile in 3 minutes and 59.4 seconds. The crowd erupted in astonishment. The BBC interrupted its broadcast to share the news. The impossible had become possible. And once the barrier was broken, it opened the floodgates for others. Bannister broke a world record that had stood for almost a decade, but his own would only last for 46 days. Within two months, John Landy, an Australian runner, clocked 3:58:0. Another sub-four-minute mile. Within the next three years, 16 more runners achieved the same feat.

What changed? Every runner likes to credit their unique regimen and 'special scientific method', but the physical capabilities of runners didn't suddenly improve overnight. All that changed was their frame of reference. Once Bannister proved it was possible, the psychological barrier was shattered. What was once seen as an immutable limit became a benchmark to surpass.

This pattern of reframing leading to subsequent breakthroughs isn't unique to running. It's a recurring theme across various fields.

Jumping Backwards

In the 1960s, high jumping was dominated by the straddle technique, where jumpers would clear the bar face down, as if leaping over a fence. The form was considered optimal for years, with its mechanics honed and perfected by athletes around the world. And then one day a young man from Oregon did something bizarre.

Dick Fosbury had trouble mastering the straddling technique and decided to train a completely different way, simply because it felt easier to him. He launched into the air, leaned back, kicked his legs up, and arched over the bar head-first, landing on his shoulders.

This backward dive looked ridiculous, and many dismissed it as an awkward fluke. His coach at the University of Oregon tried to train it out of him. However, in 1968, Fosbury took his unconventional style to the world stage at the Mexico City Olympics. Not only did he win gold, but he set a new Olympic record by clearing 2.24 metres (7 feet 4¼ inches). His victory stunned the world, and his backward approach—later dubbed the "Fosbury Flop"—permanently changed the sport.

The key to Fosbury's breakthrough wasn't raw athleticism, it was actually the opposite. It was a reimagining of how the human body could engage with the mechanics of the high jump. Fosbury reframed the problem from "How do I jump over the bar?" to "How do I clear the bar with the least resistance?"

By turning his body in a way that seemed counterintuitive to the traditionalists, but easier to him, he reduced his centre of mass and made it easier to clear heights. In retrospect, it seems obvious, but no one could see it that way at the time. Within a few years, however, the Fosbury Flop became the dominant technique in high jumping, and it remains so to this day.

Frames Change Everything

Sometimes, frame changes in one area unlock possibilities in another. For example, Johannes Gutenberg's invention of the printing press in the mid-15th century dramatically increased the speed and efficiency of reproducing written material, but the ripple effects had groundbreaking impacts in two completely different domains: biology, and physics.

With the advent of the printing press, books—once luxuries only accessible to the wealthy and powerful—became widely available to the public. The printing press didn't just democratise knowledge – it reframed society's relationship with information and literacy. But the revolution didn't stop there.

As more people began to read, many of them encountered an unexpected problem: their near-field eyesight was terrible. They had never known how bad their eyesight was because nothing else required such close and constant inspection. But as soon as they tried reading more frequently, the pain point was obvious.

Once people began noticing issues with their vision, there was a surge in demand for something to aid their eyesight: reading glasses. This new awareness of visual limitations encouraged innovations in lens-making, so society got better and better at making glass lenses for reading. But they didn't stop there – people kept experimenting. As artisans refined this booming craft, they inadvertently laid the groundwork for two of the most important scientific inventions in history: the microscope and the telescope.

These instruments, both relying on advanced lenses, opened up entirely new worlds of discovery. The microscope allowed scientists to observe life forms invisible to the naked eye, while the telescope revealed the vast expanse of the universe. What began as a simple solution to the problem of reading text eventually led to revolutionary breakthroughs in biology and astronomy.

Once you change your frame and start seeing the world differently, new opportunities emerge everywhere. These examples illustrate a crucial point: many of the limits we perceive are not physical constraints, but mental ones. Our aspirations are often limited by what we believe to be possible, and the boundaries we inherit from those around us. By changing our frame of reference—our perspective on a problem or situation—we can unlock new possibilities and ignite ambitions we had never previously considered.

Five Ways to Break Your Frames

1. **Name the frame.** Most people don't realise they're looking through a lens until someone shows them the distortions. Ask yourself: What am I assuming is true in a given situation? Whose definition of success, safety, or possibility am I using?

2. **Borrow belief.** If you've never seen something done, find someone who has. Let their example fracture your inherited limits. Bannister ran so others could. Fosbury jumped backwards so others might leap further. Look for your own precedents.

3. **Stack impossible wins.** Seek one tangible "impossible" win early. It rewires your expectations permanently. Immigrants, founders, athletes—many develop confidence not from pep talks but from seeing the world yield to their effort at least once. Make the world blink.

4. **Switch contexts.** Frames harden in familiar environments. Travel, change rooms, talk to people outside your industry or culture. Read outside your usual zone. Changing your context changes your constraints, and reveals which ones were never real.

5. **Build a new normal.** Once a limiting frame cracks, don't stop. Shatter it. Make the new frame your default. A sub-four-minute mile was once a miracle. Now it's a benchmark. Take your new frame and build systems, habits, and standards that keep it alive.

2

Your Floor and Ceiling

"Whether you think you can, or you think you can't—you're right."

— Henry Ford

As you grow up, you are surrounded by people and environments that shape what you believe is possible. These early signals set your frame, giving you a script that could either supercharge or shortchange your beliefs about the world, your place in it, and the extent to which you believe you can act on it.

Everywhere you go in life, you'll come across guidelines and best practices – guardrails and rules to keep you on the right track. But not all of those rules will enable your success. The ultra-successful Sovereign minds become so by learning to tell the difference between two sets of rules: ceiling rules and floor rules. One set limits you from above, and the other supports you from below.

I'll illustrate this with some examples from the world of basketball.

Jump Like You Mean It

Ceiling rules are internal – they're the self-limiting beliefs that cap your growth. We accumulate many of these rules as we grow up; they're frequently imposed on us by parents, teachers, and peers. Until you learn to discard them, there will always be a limit to how high you can fly. It's like driving with the clutch down or sailing without material to catch and harness the wind.

The problem is that ceiling rules are usually obvious to anyone except you and people like you. You can easily notice this blind spot when you consider how easy it is to give better advice to friends than you would give to yourself. When you see your friend in deflated spirits, failing to see what they're capable of, you often know exactly what to say. But when you're in that position yourself, the weight of the thoughts inside your head can feel crushing.

Something exciting happened to me a few years ago, and it was exciting specifically because of how little I had to do with it.

Some friends and I had just wrapped up a game of pickleball, and as we packed away, local teens had come in to play basketball. There were some spare balls in the storeroom, so I joined in. On the far side of the hall, one kid and I were casually draining shots into an empty hoop. At one point I saw him practising layups and called over to him.

"Yo. Can you dunk?"

He stared back somewhat blankly, hesitating. He was young, maybe 16 or 17.

"I don't think so," he said.

But I'd already seen him jump – the kid had hops. It had been over 10 years since I'd played basketball competitively, and I'd put on about 30kg since the last time I was able to dunk or even grab the rim. In fairness to me, I'd put on the first 15kg intentionally when I switched from basketball to American football during university. The rest came from sitting at my desk too long cranking out billable hours in corporate law.

But there was one thing I still knew for sure – if you could get your fingers about two inches above the rim, you could dunk. And that's what I told the kid.

"Try and grab the rim," I said. He did it—barely. Now that he was consciously aware of his actions, he was more restrained. He certainly wasn't jumping as high as I'd seen him get before.

"Can you get higher?" I asked. He tried again. He was definitely close enough.

I nodded. "You can dunk. Try it."

He grabbed the ball and took another run up. He missed, but I think he was surprised at how high he got. He was finally awake. He ran over to his bag and got out his phone, propping it up to record. I could see the twinkle in his eye. He was starting to believe it.

He tried again. Another miss. Another attempt. Same result.

"You're almost there," I said encouragingly. There wasn't much additional coaching I could provide. I didn't need to.

He tried again. Boom. He hadn't even realised that the ball went in. He hung his head, collecting the ball, bracing himself for another attempt. But he turned around and saw me grinning.

"You did it!" I said. For a second I'm not sure he believed me.

"Did it go in?"

"Yep," I nodded, bumping fists with him.

He ran over to his phone excitedly. He still couldn't believe it. He played the video back and saw it in high-definition. His first dunk. He looked up at me beaming. I laughed. I'd contributed nothing except confirming that he was perfectly capable of something he'd dreamed of but never attempted. All it took was a different frame, a dose of borrowed belief, and I watched him break his own ceiling right there.

He did another two dunks right afterwards. It's incredible that for many of us, we never even realise what we're capable of because we're not earnestly trying. Why would you bother attempting something you don't think is possible?

Our perceived limitations are often uncorrelated to our true maximum capacity. They're just what remains of the assumptions we've never thought to question. By challenging these assumptions—whether through our own efforts or with the help of others—we can break through self-imposed ceilings and unlock potential we never knew we had.

Stand on Solid Ground

Ceiling rules are mental blocks – internal limits that hamper your development. Floor rules, on the other hand, are external. They're your proof, your skin in the game; the manifestation of potential. Floor rules are the beliefs and behaviours that you must have to achieve extraordinary success. If you don't have them, don't even bother getting on the court. You're genuinely wasting your time. No amount of self-belief will help you overcome them. You can't be a top player without them.

Kobe Bryant was one of the greatest players in basketball history. In a 20-year career with the Los Angeles Lakers, he won five championships, led the league in scoring twice, scored the second-highest number of points in a single game in NBA history (81), and won two Olympic gold medals.

But when Kobe was 12, he almost gave up basketball forever. His family had returned to the US from Italy to give him a better shot at basketball, but that summer he burned out of a basketball summer league in Philadelphia, playing against some of the best young talents in the country. And for 25 straight games, Kobe couldn't score a single point. Not a jumper. Not a layup. Not even a free throw.

Young Kobe was so demoralised that he considered switching sports to soccer, until he read about one of his heroes, Michael Jordan, who didn't quit after being cut from his high school basketball team. It lit a fire under Kobe, changing his frame. If Michael never quit, Kobe couldn't either.

This eventually became known as his "Mamba mentality". Kobe refused to leave anything on the floor. He wouldn't just turn up early to practice. He made his own sessions. He'd shoot 400 shots per practice and challenge teammates to play him up to 100 points.

Kobe became obsessed with improving his game. He wasn't just relying on natural talent or self-belief. He was establishing floor rules, setting a baseline of competence that would propel him to greatness.

Six years later, he was drafted into the NBA as the 13th overall pick. In Kobe's NBA debut for the Lakers, he played six minutes off the bench and scored zero points. But that setback wouldn't deter him. He kept working, kept improving, kept raising his floor.

Eighteen years after that scoreless NBA debut, Kobe Bryant passed Michael Jordan on the NBA's all-time scoring list.

Other people will lie to you and pretend self-belief is the only factor that matters. It's a major one, but you must marry it with a baseline level of genuine competence. If you don't have that, you're just setting yourself up for a premature failure, after which you'll hang your head and doubt yourself.

In the first story I told, the floor for being able to dunk was getting your knuckles above the rim. If you're not at that level yet, no amount of self belief will give you wings.

If you can't hit a shot, can't make a pass, and can't defend, don't bother lacing up your shoes. You won't even get a spot on the bench. You'll only be playing pretend. But just because your skills don't yet meet the baseline standards for game time, that doesn't mean giving up completely. Work on your jump shot at home. Put on some weight. Hit the gym. This is what it takes. Find the floor, then raise it.

Before becoming the bestselling author of Atomic Habits, James Clear spent years honing his writing skills. He committed to publishing two articles every week on his blog, rain or shine. This consistent practice—a floor rule he set for himself—allowed him to improve his writing, build an audience, and eventually secure a book deal. The source of Clear's success wasn't just believing he could write. It was a direct consequence of putting in the work to become a writer (the floor rule) combined with believing in the book's potential to become a bestseller (breaking a ceiling rule) and planning accordingly.

Between Earth and Sky

Despite what I've said so far, there's a crucial secret to understand here – many of the things people will tell you are floor rules, the minimum requirements for entry, are actually ceiling rules, an illusory block that people only imagine exists. Let's stick with our basketball theme for a moment and consider Muggsy Bogues, the shortest NBA player in history.

Many people might tell you that someone shorter than 5'10" has no place in the NBA. Common sense might tell you that for someone under 5'5", playing in the NBA would be impossible. The lowest benchmark possible. But standing at only 5'3", Muggsy Bogues made it into a league where the average height was 6'6", joining the Charlotte Hornets in the same era that giants like Shaquille O'Neal, Karl Malone and Hakeem Olajuwon dominated. And if that wasn't enough, he went on to lead his team to the playoffs three times in six years, and was one of the top ten players in assists for six straight seasons, only once finishing worse than fourth.

There are plenty of fake obstacles people will put up to gatekeep their spaces. The only way to find out which rules are real is to test them. Test them by being good enough. Break them by being audacious enough.

Not meeting floor rules will keep you out of the game. Not breaking ceiling rules will keep you from dominating it.

There's no point being talented and confident if you're not actively working on your game. How much can you lift? How hard can you hit? If you're an entrepreneur, which ideas have you brought to market? If you're an artist, where are your sketches? You can't be conceptually great—the seed of your greatness must germinate physically in habits and behaviours before it can be fully realised.

Delusional self-belief without the right habits and behaviours to accompany it is useless. You must find the balance between these two things – the inner game and the outer game. Internal confidence and external competence.

Call Your Shot

Once you know you meet the bare minimum of skill, keep raising your floor. Raise the baseline of what you expect for yourself, and simultaneously clear the skies for your growth.

YOUR FLOOR AND CEILING

Decide who you want to be and claim it. Don't wait for a statue to be built in your image. Build the statue of the person you will become, and grow into its likeness.

Howard Stern called himself the king of all media, and then people started calling him that. LeBron James dubbed himself 'the king' and 'the chosen one' and got that tattooed on himself as a kid. He grew up to be the NBA's all-time leading scorer and arguably the greatest player to ever live.

Joan of Arc was a young shepherdess who convinced a prince to let her lead an army. When Muhammad Ali said, "I am the greatest," he wasn't predicting history; he was crafting it.

The easy out here is to call these examples of *survivorship bias*. You never hear about the people who thought they were called to greatness yet amounted to nothing. **But survivorship itself is inherently biased towards those with the will to survive.**

> Very often we're too shy to call our own shot—especially to say it out loud. We're scared of failing in public. Scared of putting a commitment out into the void and having the void stare back at us blankly. Afraid that we may eventually be unmasked and deemed unremarkable. But calling your shot with conviction changes the way you approach the game. It changes your confidence, your effort, and your certainty.

When you believe that you have the mandate of heaven, you'll ride into battle with the wind at your back. You must put your truth out there and wait for the world to catch up. People won't see the full picture immediately – they won't see the potential you can see in yourself. But to see it in yourself, you must search for it and call it forth.

If you wait to believe in yourself until believing in you is inevitable, you have waited far too long. All the alpha lies in the gap between truth and discovery. **Plant a flag on your greatness and start building a moat around it before people are even aware the landmass** exists. By the time they discover it, the fortress you've built there will be unassailable.

The Floor and Ceiling Rule Checklist

1. **Name your ceiling rules.** What have you decided isn't for you? Where have you silently accepted limits? Identify beliefs you've inherited rather than earned.

2. **Test your assumptions.** Treat every "rule" as a hypothesis. Can you jump higher than you think? Apply for a job above your pay grade? Try, and see what breaks.

3. **Establish your floor.** What's the *bare minimum* you need in order to show up? Build that. Improve it. Don't chase mastery before you've earned competence.

4. **Raise your floor over time.** Once your baseline is solid, start demanding more from yourself. Increase your reps. Ship faster. Stretch the definition of what "normal" is for you.

5. **Call your shot.** Decide who you are and declare it. Speak it before others see it. Your confidence will grow to meet your commitment.

3

DESIRE AND DIRECTION

"All men should strive to learn befre they die; what they are running from, and to, and why."

— James Thurber

Talent is a double-edged sword. The same qualities that make you exceptional at one thing usually make you capable of many things. And that's where the trouble starts.

Joseph Plateau's mind was a factory of ideas, spinning out innovations across physics, mathematics, and art. In 1832 he invented the phenakistiscope, a spinning disc device that produced the illusion of motion – essentially the earliest form of animation. It was revolutionary. But instead of pushing this breakthrough to its limits, he was already moving on to study fluid dynamics, visual perception, and mathematical problems.

Each pursuit was fascinating. Each study was valuable. But imagine if he'd given that animation device his full attention. Imagine if he'd focused all his brilliant energy on developing what could have become the foundation of modern cinema. We might have had movies half a century earlier.

> This is the curse of the capable—the more you can do, the more you try to do. And with each new venture, each new interest, each new "opportunity", your impact gets diluted. Like light through a prism, your talent splits into a rainbow of possibilities – beautiful, yes, but weaker than the focused beam it could have been.

Robert Hooke knew this feeling. For a time, in the late 1600s, he was probably the most broadly talented scientist alive. He made notable contributions to physics (e.g., Hooke's Law of elasticity), biology (coining the term "cell" in Micrographia, 1665), astronomy (observing Mars, suggesting planetary gravity), and more.

After the Great Fire of London in 1666, Hooke was appointed Surveyor of London and 'chief assistant to Christopher Wren', playing a key role in urban rebuilding and even co-designing the Monument to the Fire. He also invented instruments like the spring balance for watches and improved microscopes.

Around the same period, however, another great scientific mind focused narrowly. A young Isaac Newton went into near-total isolation during the Cambridge plague closure of 1665–1667 and emerged having quietly rewritten the laws of reality.

In just a few years, Newton formulated the law of universal gravitation and cracked the hidden physics behind white light. When asked why the planets in his calculations orbited in ellipses rather than circles, Newton invented entirely new mathematical tools—differential and integral calculus—to find the answer, allowing us to describe planetary motion accurately. Impressive. And then you realise he did all of that before turning 26. This is the power of obsessive focus.

While Hooke spread his efforts across dozens of fields and public projects, Newton poured himself into a few fundamental questions. And for a time, that gap in focus made all the difference. Newton's breakthroughs didn't just contribute to science, they reshaped it entirely. He became a singular force. Hooke's position in popular consciousness, despite his talent and industriousness, was gradually overshadowed, remembered more for his quarrels with Newton than for any single defining achievement.

But the story doesn't end there.

After his incandescent early burst, Newton's focus began to drift. He became consumed with alchemy and religious prophecy—pursuits that would dominate the second half of his life. By the end of his days, Newton had written far more about mysticism and scriptural chronology than about physics or maths.

Some of this was private obsession. Some, like his delay in publishing his magnum opus, *Principia*, was driven by paranoia and perfectionism. Newton spent decades engaged in intellectual turf wars, fiercely defending his legacy rather than extending it.

In the end, the man who had once revealed the mechanics of the universe spent his final years chasing hidden messages in the Bible and guarding the Royal Mint from counterfeiters. He never again reached the heights of his youth.

So while Newton and Hooke may seem like opposites—one scattered, the other focused—the truth is more fragile. Focus isn't a fixed trait. It's a choice you make, and have to keep making. Even the sharpest mind can lose its edge.

The world loves to celebrate Renaissance people—those brilliant minds who excel in multiple fields. But even Leonardo da Vinci, the ultimate Renaissance man, has a lesson for us here.

Giorgio Vasari, Leonardo's earliest biographer, wrote that as he lay dying, Leonardo "lamented that he had offended God and mankind in not having worked at his art as he should have." He was famously distracted, and died with many works left unfinished.

Leonardo's notebooks and letters show chronic procrastination – he would conceive grand engineering or artistic projects, then abandon them when novelty wore off. His very first commissioned work, an altarpiece for the Chapel of San Bernardo, went undelivered. He started an enormous bronze horse statue, "Gran Cavallo", for the Duke of Milan but never completed it. He left paintings like The Adoration of the Magi and Saint Jerome in the Wilderness incomplete. Even the great Mona Lisa portrait was never delivered to its patron—Leonardo kept tinkering with it for over a decade, returning to it intermittently until he died.

Leonardo's notebooks overflow with incredible ideas: flying machines, armoured vehicles, automated looms. But how many of these ideas were fully realised? How many revolutionary innovations remained as sketches because he was already moving on to the next fascinating problem?

None of the things Leonardo studied were inherently unreasonable. It's largely due to cross-pollinating his breadth of interests that he was able to produce such great work. But the opportunity cost of reasonable choices only becomes clear in retrospect. Ambition needs direction. It must be channelled in order to be fulfilled.

> The trap isn't in being capable of many things. The trap is in trying to do them all at once, without prioritisation. In letting your talents draw you in so many directions that you never go far enough in any single one. In making the reasonable choice to pursue every interesting opportunity, only to find that you've let the tug of the reasonable pull you from the orbit of the remarkable.

This pattern of diluted greatness isn't an accident. It's built into how we develop our ambitions in the first place. We inherit our desires from the people around us, absorbing them via osmosis. A French philosopher named René Girard called this "mimetic desire" – the idea that we want things because other people want them or have them.

The Inheritance of Want

Think about the last time you scrolled through Instagram or LinkedIn. Each post is a window into someone else's desires – their career moves, their lifestyle choices, their definitions of success. With each scroll, you're not just seeing what others have achieved. You're absorbing their wants, their ambitions, and their models of what matters.

We see someone quit their job to start a company, and suddenly entrepreneurship feels like our calling. We watch a colleague pivot into tech, and suddenly coding bootcamps start appearing in our search history. We notice someone building a personal brand, and suddenly we're thinking about our own "platform."

Girard argued that this copying of desires is fundamental to human nature. We learn what to want by watching what others want. A child doesn't inherently know that certain toys or games are desirable. They want what they see other children wanting. A teenager doesn't naturally know which brands are cool. They want what their peers value.

Oscar Wilde put it like this:

> *"Most people are other people. Their thoughts are someone else's opinions, their lives a mimicry, their passions a quotation."*

> — Oscar Wilde

It's a pattern you can trace back to the dawn of mankind in most schools of thought. In the biblical garden of Eden, Eve only yearned to taste the forbidden fruit after seeing this desire modelled to her by the serpent. And Eve, in turn, modelled that same desire to Adam.

This mimetic effect doesn't stop in adulthood, it just gets more sophisticated. The young lawyer gunning for partner isn't just chasing success; they're chasing a specific vision of success they've absorbed from their environment. The entrepreneur working 80-hour weeks isn't just building a business; they're pursuing a model of achievement they've seen celebrated by others.

The problem isn't that these desires are fake. They're very real, and they can drive real achievement. The problem is that they're often borrowed without examination. We inherit ambitions like we inherit old furniture, taking them into our lives without asking if they truly fit our space.

This inheritance of want creates a peculiar paradox: the more ambitious and capable you are, the more vulnerable you become to borrowed desires. Ambition opens many doors—the secret is knowing which paths are worth following. When you're good at many things, you start to want many things. Every achievement exposes new doors of possibility, and behind each door is a new set of desires waiting to be absorbed. Before you know it, you're chasing ten different versions of success, each borrowed from someone else's playbook.

Borrowed desires rarely lead to lasting fulfilment. They're like borrowed clothes – hand-me-downs that never quite fit right. You can wear them, you might even look good in them, but they'll never feel truly yours. You can't stop wanting things entirely, but you can begin to examine where your wants come from and whether they truly align with your direction.

Navigating Borrowed Desires

When you realise that your desires have fingerprints on them, the natural response is to try and wipe them clean; to search for some pure, untainted want that's completely your own. But that's missing the point entirely. Rather than aiming to eliminate unconscious, mimetic desire, become intentional instead about what you borrow and from whom.

Think of desires like seeds. Some fall on your soil by chance—carried by the wind of social media, dropped by the birds of peer pressure, scattered by the storms of cultural expectations. Others you deliberately plant after seeing them flourish in someone else's garden. The source of the seed matters less than what you choose to water.

This is where most advice about "following your passion" or "finding your authentic self" falls short. They assume there's some pure, original version of you waiting to be discovered, untouched by outside influence. There isn't. All of us are walking gardens of borrowed desires. The trick is to become a better gardener.

Here's what that looks like in practice. When you feel the pull of a new ambition, a new goal, a new definition of success, pause and ask yourself three questions:

First, *what's the real game being played?*

Often, we adopt desires not because we want the thing itself, but because we want what it represents. The entrepreneur chasing a billion-dollar exit might really be seeking validation. The lawyer gunning for partner might be trying to prove something to their parents. These aren't invalid desires, but you should know what game you're really playing.

Second, *who are you in competition with?*

Mimetic desire inevitably leads to mimetic rivalry. We don't just copy wants; we copy the entire structure of wanting. You begin by pursuing a goal, but soon you're trying to beat others to it. Sometimes this competition is healthy, driving you to greater heights. Other times it's a trap, pushing you to play games you never actually wanted to win.

Third, and most importantly, *does this desire have depth?*

Surface-level wants come and go with the seasons, shifting with whatever's currently being celebrated in your circle. Deep desires, conversely, have roots. They connect to multiple areas of your life. They energise rather than drain you. They feel less like chasing something external and more like becoming more fully yourself.

Early enough in Warren Buffett's investing career, he noticed everyone around him trying to make clever trades, timing the market, playing the short game. The mimetic desire in financial circles was for quick wins and smart plays. But Buffett chose to copy a different model—Benjamin Graham's value investing approach. He didn't reject mimetic desire; he was just selective about which desires he adopted.

Crucially, Buffett didn't copy blindly. He examined Graham's model, tested it against his own insights and interests, and eventually transformed it into something he could make his own. The seed was borrowed, but the garden it grew into, when transplanted to Buffett's soil, and watered with his own thoughts and ideas, was unique.

Likewise, Jerry Seinfeld watched his fellow comedians chase acting roles, TV hosting gigs, and movie careers. The mimetic pull of Hollywood was strong, but Seinfeld knew that his deep desire was for the craft of comedy itself.

Even after his show became the biggest thing on television, Seinfeld maintained his identity as a stand-up, often performing at clubs between TV tapings. After his show *Seinfeld* ended, instead of staying in Los Angeles to pursue a career as a leading man, he moved right back to New York to keep doing stand-up. Seinfeld borrowed the desire for excellence in comedy, but rejected the usual desire for Hollywood diversification.

Then look at Virgil Abloh. He was a trained architect who frequently borrowed inspiration from art, music, and street fashion. But Abloh didn't accumulate these ideas randomly. He carefully chose which desires to nurture. The ones which aligned with his vision. The ones which could grow together into something new.

In 2012 he launched an experimental streetwear fashion line called Pyrex Vision, known for remixing athletic wear with high-concept graphics. A year later after running into legal issues around the Pyrex name, Abloh transformed the brand into Off-White, a Milan-based luxury streetwear label that combined elements from all his passions into something authentically his own.

Off-White quickly drew the eyes of celebrities and bent the ears of the major fashion houses. In March 2018, just five years after creating the Off-White brand, Louis Vuitton tapped Abloh to become their Artistic Director of Menswear, making him the first Black designer to lead a major French luxury house.

Louis Vuitton, at the pinnacle of luxury, is exactly where mimetic desire might have drawn Abloh from the start. It is the trophy that the distraction of competition could have compelled him to chase. But by taking the time to nurture his ambition, by training his taste through traction with his own brand, Virgil Abloh was able to take Louis Vuitton in a different and more unique direction, free from the shackles of expectation.

This selective borrowing of desires is crucial because it sets up everything that follows. Before you can channel your ambition effectively, before you can decide what to prioritise, you need to know which desires are worth pursuing in the first place.

This is where talent becomes tricky. When you're good at something, people will tell you what you should want. They'll show you paths you could take, opportunities you shouldn't waste, positions you'd be crazy not to pursue. And because you're capable, because you could succeed in those directions, the desires can feel natural, even inevitable.

But being able to do something isn't the same as wanting to do it. Being good at something isn't the same as being called to it. **The most successful people aren't just good at saying no to opportunities – they're good at saying no to entire sets of desires that don't align with their deeper direction.**

The Map and the Compass

Well-worn paths are often the most crowded. Common success paths exist for a reason—they work, sometimes. But they work precisely because they're designed for the average case, based on the most common variables.

It is easy to default to looking for maps. You see someone achieve something remarkable and immediately start looking for the breadcrumb trail. What university did they attend? Which career moves did they make? What habits did they develop?

The problem with maps is that they're historical documents. They show you where someone else has been, not necessarily where you should go. And they certainly won't show you where no one has gone before.

The fashion industry thought that upstart designer Ralph Lauren was making a terrible mistake; He had no formal design training. He didn't apprentice under the right people. He wasn't playing the haute couture game. Instead of seasonal collections and runway shows, he was obsessed with polo shirts and casual wear. What those around him didn't understand at the time, was that Lauren had already committed to a Sovereign path.

Born Ralph Lifshitz in 1939, he legally changed his last name to "Lauren" at age 16, partly to escape childhood bullying and assumptions of his social class. This name change was his first step in crafting a personal brand identity on his own terms. Lauren began his fashion career as a salesman for a necktie company in the 1960s. In 1967, with a $50,000 loan note in hand, he boldly began making his own ties under the brand name "Polo", expanding into a full line of menswear a year later.

Lauren did not "fit" the typical mould. He was a Bronx-born son of immigrants with an unfashionable surname. But those humble, self-driven beginnings gave rise to a $17 billion fashion empire.

Lauren understood something crucial. The traditional path to fashion success was optimised for a different kind of designer, with different goals. The established route—from fashion school to apprenticeships to prestigious houses—was perfect if you wanted to be the next Yves Saint Laurent. But Lauren didn't want to be the next anyone. He wanted to build something of his own.

This exemplifies why, on a day-to-day level, copying successful people's habits or routines often leads nowhere. Someone might suggest that you should wake up at 4 am because Tim Cook does. But Cook's schedule is optimised for running Apple, not for running your life. Unless you're also managing a trillion-dollar company with operations across every time zone, you'd be copying the wrong variable.

The same goes for any prescribed path to success. Law firms have their lockstep progression to partner. Tech has its startup playbook. Academia has its publish-or-perish pipeline. These paths aren't wrong; they're just optimised for specific outcomes that may not match your actual goals.

Asking *"What should I do?"* is less useful than *"What am I optimising for?"* The first question leads you to look for maps. The second helps you calibrate your compass.

> The map obsesses over the beaten path, but the compass hunts for hidden opportunity. Its job is to show you the direction, not to order your steps.

Dame Stephanie Shirley was born Vera Buchthal in Dortmund, Germany. Evacuated from danger with thousands of other Jewish children, she boarded a Kindertransport train from Vienna to London in 1939 without her parents. She was five years old and clutching the hand of her nine-year-old sister.

As an adult, finding her path, she would eventually start a software company in 1962 staffed entirely by women working from home. The concept was so radical at the time that Stephanie had to sign her business letters as "Steve" to get responses. The technology industry had a very clear map for success, and it didn't include flexible working or female programmers. Luckily, Shirley wasn't following their map. She was following her conviction that talent was being wasted by conventional workplace structures.

The industry thought she was daft. Programming was serious work that needed to be done in proper offices by men in proper suits. It couldn't be done by women working from home between household tasks. Yet Shirley's company went on to develop the black box flight recorder for Concorde and eventually made millionaires of 70 of her early employees; all while pioneering flexible work practices that wouldn't become mainstream for another 50 years.

This is what happens when you follow your compass instead of someone else's map. The map shows you where others have gone before. The compass shows you where you need to go next.

The map wants you to follow. The compass wants you to lead.

How to Protect Your Focus and Reclaim Your Ambition

1. **Talent is a trap—unless you prioritise.** Capable minds often fall into the trap of doing too many things. Impact requires subtraction. Combining depth and breadth can work in the long run, but not if you never go deep enough for your efforts to compound.

2. **Watch where your desires come from.** You inherit more than genetics. You absorb goals, ambitions, and status markers from the world around you. Most of them aren't yours – choose wisely.

3. **Don't copy the outcome. Copy the direction.** Success isn't a function of waking up at 4am or using someone else's planner. Borrow principles, not playbooks. Use your own metrics.

4. **Use your compass, not their map.** Maps show old roads. Compasses reveal new terrain. The Sovereign path isn't prescribed – it's chosen, tested, and walked.

5. **Plant selectively. Water intentionally.** You can't escape borrowed desires, but you *can* become a better gardener. Choose which ambitions to cultivate and which to let die.

4

FIND YOUR FUEL

"The mind is it's own place, and in itself can make a heaven of hell, a hell of heaven."

— John Milton

At the best of times, aspiration alone is enough to fuel our ambitions—when our desires have enough depth that making progress towards them feels effortless and inevitable. Deep desires can feel like a fountain of boundless energy – a source of permanent motivation. However, there comes a time when these deep desires become depleted.

You see, desire is just the starting point. As crucial as it is to begin by nurturing deep and enduring desires as a foundation to build your ambitions on, desire needs drive to be functional. **Want without will is worthless.**

Eventually, your determination may waver. When life's turbulence overwhelms you. When the hand you're dealt seems wild and wicked and manifestly unfair. In those moments, it becomes even more crucial that you're able to harness alternative sources of fuel.

Fuel, in this context, isn't just motivation – it's any force that propels you forward when the path gets tough, doubts creep in, and the finish line seems impossibly far.

Marvin Gaye wrote one of the best albums of all time (Here, My Dear) because he didn't want to pay a divorce settlement. During his divorce proceedings, he was ordered to pay more money than he actually had on hand as alimony. So a deal was arranged—50% of the royalties from his next album would go to his ex-wife.

Marvin was incensed. He didn't want her to get a penny. In his anger, he decided to throw out a quick album that critics would hate and no one would buy so that the album would flop.

He didn't usually write his own lyrics for his albums, but he wasn't usually consumed by fury either. So this time he did. He wrote and he wrote. He poured more of his heart and soul into this album than any before it, laying bare the full complexity of his emotions. And in the process, he became strangely fascinated with it.

The outpouring of his anger developed a life of its own. He wrote all his own lyrics and penned all the piano chords. And finally, it was finished. He titled it appropriately—Here, My Dear. A complex ode to life and love and bittersweet endings.

Ironically, the album was snubbed at the time as he had originally intended, but it's been loved by critics since. Rolling Stone has consistently listed it as one of the best 500 albums ever made.

It was the kind of album Gaye might never have written were he still flying high, with life going smoothly. But by diving into the depths of his hard-worn emotions and embracing them, Marvin Gaye produced not just one of his own best works, but one of the best works of all time.

In the absence of an enemy, every potential hero is just an ordinary and often unremarkable citizen. It's often only when the antagonist enters the scene that the protagonist can step up and become a hero. The antagonist may not take on a physical form—it may not even exist outside of the protagonist's mind—but acknowledging something, not just to fight for, but to rally against, can be powerful. Adversity itself can become a wellspring of power.

An underrated amount of success is fuelled by spite. Every great entrepreneur imagines themselves as the underdog. Sometimes you need the haters, the doubters, and detractors. The people around you who can't see what you're building towards. A chip on your shoulder that can drive you to heights you may never otherwise reach.

But there's a second lesson in the story of Marvin Gaye. He had that album in him all along. He was always capable of producing the work; he just lacked the right type of motivation.

Once you find your fire, you can raise your expectations.

The DeLorean Mindset

In the epic film trilogy 'Back to the Future', Doc Brown's time-travelling DeLorean occasionally ran out of fuel. With any other car, he would've been stranded, but he'd re-engineered this vehicle to be ultra-resilient. It didn't just run on diesel, or ultra-refined petroleum – its flux capacitor could run on anything. Doc grabbed a can of garbage from the side of the street and started emptying it into the car's fuel compartment. He dumped in banana skins and rotten fruit, leftover beer and other bits of trash. Anything he could grab. And the car jumped back to life.

It's easy to get comfortable in cruise control when the going is good. But when the tide turns, you'll need to harness whatever you can find. You need to develop a DeLorean mindset. Turn anything into fuel – the good, the bad, and the ugly.

Some people wait until they can get the perfect fuel at the perfect price. If there's no good fuel available, they won't drive. They can't. They stay pulled up by the side of the road, waiting. They won't put their emergency lights on because they don't think there's an emergency. *"Any minute now..."* they say, when you ask why they haven't made any progress. They'll wait forever for the stars to align.

The Sovereign re-engineer their minds to be hyper-resilient. They don't only flourish in kind and pleasant environments. They take whatever fuel they can get their hands on. Anger, pain, spite, hunger.

Every experience can become powerful fuel if you choose to harness it.

But here's the thing. Trash fuel is still trash. If you just set it on fire and sit there with your car idling, you'll choke on toxic fumes. Don't stew in those feelings for the sake of it. Instead, you must use them to propel you forward.

Those fuels won't always burn clean. And you can't run on them forever. But when you're stuck in a rut by the roadside, fresh out of gas, fuel is fuel. Take what life gives you. Intense emotions can give you intense energy. Don't let it go to waste.

You can download the Four Types of Fuel worksheet to develop a personal strategy for channelling your energy at:
tools.becomesovereign.com/fuel

Turn Trash Fuel Into Productive Energy

1. **Acknowledge your emotion.** Don't hide from the heat. Start by recognising and naming what you're feeling. Feel your emotions deeply and fully, embrace them for what they are, so that you can then channel them when needed.

2. **Find an outlet.** Instead of letting negative feelings fester and stewing in them, reframe your pain, spite, or frustration—don't waste the energy they can bring. Let them fuel action instead

of angst and anxiety.

3. **Run short, not long.** Volatile fuel burns hot and fast. Use it to launch something, but not to sustain it. Set tight deadlines and channel it into immediate output.

4. **Build rituals for ignition.** Know your emergency protocols. Write, train, ship—whatever gives form to your fire. Channel emotion into effort, not indulgence.

5. **Redirect and refuel.** After the fire, return to sustainable energy: purpose, joy, discipline. Don't get addicted to chaos. Burn wisely. Reflect on the feeling – where it came from – and have a longer-term plan for dealing with it.

5

THE RIGHT MEASURING STICK

"Not everything that can be counted counts. Not everything that counts can be counted."

— William Bruce Cameron

It's easy to fall into the trap of measuring the wrong things. Society trains us to chase easy metrics: job titles, follower counts, annual salaries, magazine covers. But these numbers don't account for direction, depth, or fulfilment. And if you measure the wrong thing for long enough, you can end up winning a game you never meant to play.

Sovereign thinkers don't just ask, "What do I want?" They ask, "How will I measure progress, and will that measurement stand the test of time?"

The Three-Body Test

To answer that question well, you need perspective. Here's a powerful tool to help.

Consult three versions of yourself:

1. *Your present self*

2. *You in three years*

3. *Your 80-year-old self*

This approach acknowledges an important truth: your values change as you age. The future you might be unrecognisable to your current self. That can be positive, but it also means we risk discarding the hard-won insights of our former selves. Blinded by life's complexity, we can lose important truths we once held dear.

Start with today. ***What am I optimising for right now?*** Skill growth? Novel experiences? Stability? Career positioning?

Now step three years ahead. It's not so much time that you're an entirely different person, but it's enough to be a little older and wiser. ***What will future me (in ~3 years) be grateful I did today?***

There is a spectrum of choices that compound over the course of your life. What you read, how you eat, who you talk to, and what you do with your money. These decisions are investments that pay continual dividends.

Luck can strike at any time, but you can certainly be the architect of your own serendipity. Choosing where to live, where to work, and where to spend time online can be a crucial part of that. Each of these decisions sends ripples into the future, opening some doors and closing others.

Which path leaves you with the largest number of high-quality future paths? And which path might be dark and fraught with danger, but offers a reward or experience that you wouldn't trade for anything? You don't need to become a slave to chasing optionality, but you don't want to find yourself constrained by the shadow of your past self.

If you find yourself at a crossroads and you've already asked yourself those first two questions, it's time to get in the time machine.

How would I answer the rocking chair test?

This is the third question. Project yourself to age 80, looking back on a life well-lived. From this vantage point, taking the long-term view of how well the decisions in front of you aligned with your values, what would you regret more in retrospect?

People respond to risk differently—it's important to understand and appreciate where you fall on the spectrum. Do you feel more pain considering the opportunities missed by playing it safe, or the risks taken that didn't pan out? The time invested in relationships, or the adventures not pursued?

If you still find yourself stuck, there's another way to frame it: Imagine you're 80, looking back on a specific decision you're facing now. You've passed the crossroads. You've made the choice. You already know how this pans out. In retrospect, you are absolutely certain that you made the right decision.

- Imagine you chose path A, and it was undeniably the right decision. What happened?

- Now, imagine you chose path B, and *that* was the right decision. What happened then?

What would have happened in either scenario that would absolutely convince you that you made the right choice? Which narrative, which future outcome, resonates more deeply?

This is the Three-Body Test. Use it whenever you're stuck or at a crossroads. It balances short-term realism with long-term alignment. It makes your goals elastic enough to grow with you, but grounded enough to act on now.

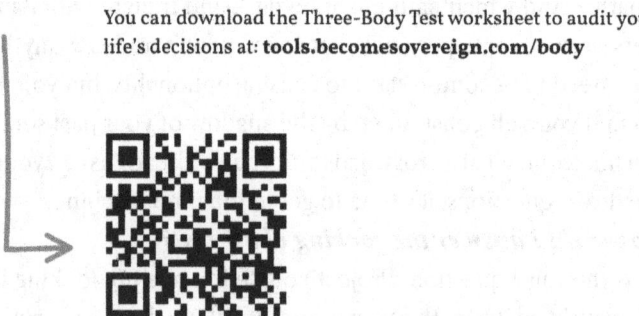

You can download the Three-Body Test worksheet to audit your life's decisions at: **tools.becomesovereign.com/body**

Measure by Progress

Even with better goals, we still need better benchmarks.

It's easy to measure success based on outcomes. The trophy, the tangible end product, the smiles on faces, the money in the bank account. Measuring by outcomes can make us feel stagnant if we fail to achieve the singular goal we earmark as the benchmark of success. Anything short of that absolute goal sounds like failure.

There's an obvious problem here. If you had a goal of losing 30 pounds and you lost 28, you may have failed to hit the arbitrary target, but clearly, you've also achieved something monumental. The trajectory of your failures is a far better indicator than crossing some imaginary threshold.

For over a decade, I've participated in NaNoWriMo – a 30-day challenge to write 50,000 words of fiction in November. I have failed more times than I've succeeded. Here were my first five years:

- 2013: 22,758 words
- 2014: 37,569 words
- 2015: 54,350 words (win)
- 2016: 50,583 words (win)
- 2017: 29,870 words

For what it's worth, the year I ruined my potential three-peat, my law firm's clock claimed 95 hours a week on average. That includes at least three days where I was at my desk for over 20 straight hours apiece, faithfully billing time in 6-minute increments. I ended up sick for a few days after trying to do both, and bowed out of the writing challenge after 20 gruelling days. I was left with a trophy of 36 empty energy drink cans piled high on my shelf.

In nine years of attempts, including numerous failures, I wrote nearly 400,000 words. My consistency improved. My quality improved. My thinking sharpened. If I'd only measured success by 50,000-word trophies, I'd have become disillusioned long ago.

Progress is a trendline, not a scoreboard.

And for anyone curious, I failed in 2018, quit in 2019, failed in 2020 (do I get a pass for COVID?), skipped 2021, then won in 2022, 2023, and 2024. The key is to make your benchmark of success the opportunities you create and the progress you make, rather than binary outcomes.

This principle applies broadly. If, while pursuing a career change, you enter the interview process for 5 roles and get 0 offers, that might indicate you're not cut out for the job. But if your first failure was in the initial phone screening where you were describing your background and the last was a final interview delivering a pitch, then your trajectory should tell you that you're on the right track. Refining your process is more important than counting your wins.

In the words of Jeff Bezos:

"Be stubborn on vision. Flexible on details."

— Jeff Bezos

Forget About the Outcome

Outcomes can be deceiving. Take Super Bowl 49. The Seattle Seahawks had it all to play for. 26 seconds left on the clock. One timeout remaining. One yard from glory. Destiny was in their hands. Their coach, Pete Carroll, made an ambitious call.

They had a monster on their side—Marshawn Lynch—one of the most feared running backs in the league. But Carroll knew that a handoff play is what everyone would expect. He called a *slant* play instead—a short pass. In those conditions, the play would have a 98% success rate. But on the night, it was 0%. The pass was intercepted, and the Seahawks lost.

Everyone blamed Carroll. He was lambasted by every broadcaster. There's just one problem – statistically, his decision made sense. Short-pass interceptions happen less than 2% of the time, and an incomplete pass would've stopped the clock. His decision increased their chances of winning, even though luck didn't go his way in the end.

The result was bad, but the decision was good. It's a mistake to let an unlucky outcome convince you otherwise. Sometimes all you can do is focus on maximising your odds.

Don't let shiny outcomes become your primary benchmark. Ignore the vanity of mimesis and aspirations of accolades—feedback that colludes with ego to quell your ambition. Look for clear, tangible progress. Signal among the noise.

Ask: *Did I make the best decision available, with the information I had? Did I learn something? Did I move forward?*

Aim to fail on bigger stages. Break new ground with each mistake. Accepting that failure is a prerequisite for growth is just the first step. Understanding how to intentionally plan for the best possible failures is a next-level skill. We'll cover that in detail in part two of this book.

Build Your Own Scoreboard

1. **Use the Three-Body Test.** Check your decisions with three perspectives:
   - Present You: *What's your ultimate objective right now?*
   - Future You (three years): *What seeds can you plant today?*
   - 80-Year-Old You: *What will you regret not doing?*

2. **Track progress, not perfection.** Judge success by movement, not finish lines. Aim to *fail forward*—each failure should happen further down the track.

3. **Focus on decisions, not outcomes.** Don't fall into "resulting". Good outcomes don't always follow good decisions. But good decisions compound. Optimise for repeatability, not headlines.

4. **Design better postmortems.** After a project or choice, ask:
   - *Was the process sound?*
   - *Did I act in line with my values?*

— Was more information available that would have helped me, had I looked for it?

5. **Ignore borrowed benchmarks.** Vanity metrics—titles, likes, prestige—aren't Sovereign metrics. Build a scoreboard that reflects your values, goals, and definition of progress.

Stop worshipping outcomes. Build momentum. Measure what matters. Trust your process.

6

Rules Aren't Real

"The opposite of courage is not cowardice — it's conformity. After all, even a dead fish can go with the flow."

— Jim Hightower (adapted from Rollo May)

There are rules for everything. Rules for how to dress, how to behave, and how to think. Most people go through life following the rules without thinking about them. But what if breaking the rules is the necessary precondition for creating anything extraordinary?

Often, dispensing with the status quo is the key to escaping mediocrity.

Rules are selfish. They exist to perpetuate themselves. They care only for the efficiency of the system, not the autonomy of the people within it. You need to decide if you're just along for the ride or if you have someplace to be. If you have ambition, you must go against the grain.

Here's a well-kept secret I've been exploiting for over a decade; feel free to use it if you're ever taking the metro (known locally as 'the tube') in London. At London Bridge station, the fastest way to switch trains from the Jubilee line to the Northern line is to ignore the signs. There's a tunnel labelled 'Northern Line', and another unmarked tunnel right next to it. Whenever I take people to the unmarked tunnel, they hesitate. They stare at the signs, confused, and say, *"But it says that way."* And I hold out my hand like Aladdin and say, *"Do you trust me?"*

The signs aren't telling you where to go to reach your destination quickly. They're telling you where to go to cause the least commotion. The rules dictate you must travel in a way that minimises risk to the system.

Here's another quirk. At stations like Bank, there are several signs on the train platform that say 'way out'. You'd think that because they all say the same thing, they'd all take you the same way. They don't. They're designed to reduce congestion. On one platform, the exit at the back lets you transfer lines fastest. The one at the front helps you leave the station fastest. The one in the middle takes you in a loop, adding an extra four minutes to your journey. With any luck, say the system engineers, you'll miss the next train and voilà—less congestion on the line.

Sometimes that's fine. If you're in an orderly queue, follow the rules. But sometimes you need to decide if the rules are intentionally taking you far from your individual goals in the name of system efficiency.

Sometimes the rules aren't rules at all. They're just illusory swim lanes designed to corral you. Use the compass, not the map, and you'll find the fastest way.

The fastest way isn't necessarily the easiest, and there's no guarantee that you'll make it to where you're going. That's the risk of breaking the rules. But deviating from the path is the only way to make a new one.

Paved Roads and Desire Paths

If you've ever come across a trodden dirt path through a park, you've seen a desire path. As the name suggests, desire paths are unofficial paths made by walkers, bikers, and animals who carve out routes that travellers find more appealing than what the route planners had in mind.

Desire paths are what happen when people break the rules—they follow curiosity and either discover new things, or a more direct route.

And then others see the new trail and follow suit. But then something funny happens. The desire path becomes the path. In some cases, city planners will come and pave the new path to make it official. And thus the result of initial creativity becomes the new constraint.

There was a time when deep scholarship was entirely optional. Everyone else had a trade or enough money to busy themselves with political chit-chat. Those who chased the desire paths of continued study made unusual discoveries which changed society. Then, school became popular, and everyone did it. The desire path became the path. Now, there are people with multiple degrees who can't get jobs working for people who left school at 16.

The new desire paths are in fields like crypto, AI, and frontier tech. The internet, at first, was largely ignored. Then a few people went deep. They strayed from convention. They found the magic. Suddenly, people were claiming plumbers must "learn to code or die". By 2020 it became vogue to say you had dropped out of Stanford to pursue a startup. The desire path has become the path. And the truly curious minds must find another way.

> There are two ways to look at this. The first is that we've become a society of lemmings, all going the same way because it's the path of least resistance. And there's some truth to that. But there's another way to look at it: maybe the desire path has always been the path, and societal progression relies on people brave enough to leave the comforting safety of the known path behind, and show us the way to something better.

Escaping the Mundane

Mediocrity is the enemy of progress. It stifles originality and breeds conformity. To be creative, you must be willing to challenge the rules.

You must be willing to take risks. And you must be willing to embrace the power of asymmetry.

The moments I feel most stagnant in my life are the ones where I forget a fundamental truth: rules aren't real.

I usually don't talk about my age, and occasionally refuse to answer when asked. The reason is simple. People typically use age as a heuristic—a way to measure what you have and haven't done. It works well because age has a linear progression. The number goes up by one every 365 days. You tell me your age, and then I'll tell you if you look young or old, healthy or unhealthy, beautiful or haggard. The expectation is that your level of success should track similarly. And if you haven't achieved thing X by age Y, you're in big trouble.

I once found success by being precocious, and seeming wise beyond my years. I then found success via ignorance, when people assumed I was much older and thus gave me more responsibility automatically. Once I realised that telling people your age was a shell game of poor inferences, I just stopped doing it. I don't care if I'm successful for my age; neither should you. That kind of comparison is a fool's errand. You can judge me by my work, by my physique, and by the bags under my eyes (an undesirable sign of poor sleep and skincare). At times I might seem weak, fat and haggard. At others, I will seem quick, strong, and whip-smart. My habits, work ethic and ambition will, over time, speak for themselves.

If you are young, old, or anything in between, let me give you a simple razor—one that favours the Sovereign path:

Unless you aspire to be absolutely mediocre in every respect, never get caught doing exactly what people expect you to be doing.

Sometimes that means going above and beyond. Sometimes it means foregoing an exercise entirely. Why? Because most of the time, expectations are a trap. The rules are a snare. A sham. They're designed to draw you into the alluring grip of fitting in.

The average life, statistically, sucks. The average marriage ends in divorce. The average savings rate is next to nothing. The average person feels lost and unfulfilled. I hope one day that these things change, but until then, you should do whatever it takes to escape that cohort. I don't say this to be disparaging—I say it to remind you that it only takes the tiniest nudge to move your mean; the smallest bump to move slightly to the right of the distribution curve.

The average person gets average results. You don't need to inherit transcendent brilliance to be above average; just do one thing slightly differently from the way you see most people do it. If everyone around you reads five pages a day, read 6. If they save £10 a week, save £12. If they spend 20 minutes exercising, spend 25. The simplest edge compounds in remarkable ways—across domains, and over time.

In your career, as in creative pursuits, fitting in is dangerous. Complicity leads to commodity. Following the status quo leads to comfortable complacency. And worse than that, it's boring. In my view, there's no greater sin.

If Frodo and Bilbo never left the Shire, The Lord of the Rings would be a Hobbit cookbook.

If Luke Skywalker never left Tatooine, Star Wars would be a horticultural digest.

Doing the expected is what kept Harry Potter in a cupboard and Neo in an office cubicle. The magic only comes when you break out. So does the risk, the danger, the adventure. All the hidden treasures are buried on the road less travelled.

Rules are designed to corral the outliers. They optimise for status quo. Rules are selfish. They prioritise their own longevity. They stave away risk, variety, and anything novel. Rules maintain a stasis of replicable simplicity.

There is a time for rules. There is a time to build well-oiled machines and conform for their assemblage. Sometimes the best way to drive results is to become a nondescript cog in a beautiful machine. At other times, it is best to become a lynchpin. And on occasion, we must dispense with machinery altogether and make art.

> *"Art begins with resistance — at the point where resistance is overcome. No human masterpiece has ever been created without great labour."*

— André Gide

Seven Tips for Thinking Like a Rule-breaker

1. Question everything.

The first step to breaking the rules is to question why they exist in the first place. Why do we dress a certain way? Why do we behave a certain way? Why do we think a certain way? There are usually underlying assumptions that govern group behaviour. Which of those assumptions might be outdated? How can you take advantage of that?

2. Expose your biases.

We all have biases that influence our thinking. It's important to identify these biases so that you can recognise and correct for them. Learn to recognise the narratives you're already incentivised to believe.

3. Be open to new ideas.

Scott Fitzgerald famously wrote, *"The test of a first-rate intelligence is the ability to hold two opposing ideas in mind at the same time."* Actively seek out and understand what drives dissenting opinion. The better you get at discovering where you're wrong, the more frequently you'll end up being right.

4. Be willing to take risks.

To be creative, you must be willing to take risks. This means being open to failure. Not every risk will pay off, but it's important to try new things if you want to create something extraordinary.

5. Hunt asymmetry.

Asymmetry is one of the most powerful tools in the creative toolbox. Investigate ideas that have asymmetric outcomes—where the range of potential outcomes is greater than the initial input. An asymmetric mindset will lead you to things that are both new and unexpected.

6. Be persistent.

Sometimes the fastest way to an outsized result is to stick with a common thing for an uncommon length of time. Most people give up or wear out before the real game begins. They're tearing ACLs during practice. The longer you stick with a skill or craft, the more you open yourself up to unusual outcomes.

7. Embrace chaos.

Many productivity systems are a bit like 'tidying up' when guests come by throwing all the mess in your cupboard. One solution to clutter is buying all the organising widgets that IKEA has to offer. Another is sitting with the mess and truly observing it. Decide what needs a home and what doesn't. Do the same with mental clutter. Don't just file it away; sit with it and prune.

The next time you're feeling stuck, remember that the best way out is often through the side door. Sometimes, the only way to create something remarkable is to break the rules.

7

FINDING YOUR SPEED

"If you hang around the barbershop long enough, sooner or later you're going to get a haircut."

— Denzel Washington

You may have heard this phrase before: *"You're the sum of the five people you spend the most time with."* It's cliché, but usually true – birds of a feather flock together. Our environment shapes us in ways we often fail to recognise.

We pick up habits and behaviours via osmosis – through the energy in the air of the places we inhabit. The fastest way to learn a language is the same as the fastest way to build any habit or skill: immersion. Surround yourself with Spanish speakers, and your Spanish will improve. Surround yourself with productive people, and your productivity will increase.

The people you spend the most time with will influence the habits you develop, the ideas you sit with, and the products you buy. This phenomenon isn't limited to just the people you directly interact with. Nicholas Christakis and James Fowler's research on social networks found that the behaviours of people in our social circles—including habits like smoking or obesity—extend well beyond our immediate circle. Their Framingham Heart Study was a longitudinal medical investigation tracking health choices in networks of people over the course of 32 years. Results showed that health choices, like smoking or weight gain, can be influenced by people you don't even know – up to three degrees of separation. Meaning your friend's friend's friend could affect your choices without you ever realising it.

For instance, in their 2007 study on obesity, they found that if someone in your social network becomes obese, your chances of becoming obese increase by 57%. This happens even if your direct relationship with them is minimal. Other lifestyle habits followed similar patterns. When one person in a group quits smoking, their decision ripples through the network, encouraging others to do the same, whether they're close friends or several degrees removed.

Show me your friends, and I'll show you your future.

Set the Right Baseline

To understand the power of environment, I'll take you back to 1816. To a dark and stormy night at Villa Diodati, a mansion on Lake Geneva.

A group of friends were cooped up inside, sheltering from the elements. Lord Byron was there, and his doctor, John Polidori. So were Mary Shelley, her lover Percy Shelley, and her stepsister Claire Clairmont who was pregnant with Byron's child. A rather circular affair.

It was pretty miserable being stuck indoors during a storm. They coped by writing horror stories. Polidori wrote The Vampyre, the first work of fiction to include a blood-sucking hero (rumoured to be based on his friend and patient Lord Byron), which laid the groundwork for modern vampire mythos. Mary Shelley wrote Frankenstein, which became a cornerstone of both horror and science fiction.

None of this was a coincidence; the magic came from the inspiration they fed each other. From their competitive spirit and the unique combination of minds present. Seemingly overnight, they set a new baseline for literature. People love horror stories, but most people have no idea that some of the most iconic characters in the genre were born on the same night because four writers were sharing a cabin.

We see similar dynamics throughout history. Would the personal computer revolution have unfolded in the same way without the rivalry and mutual admiration between Bill Gates and Steve Jobs? Would modern fantasy literature look the same without the creative exchanges between C.S. Lewis and J.R.R. Tolkien in their writing club, The Inklings?

Your circle doesn't just influence you – it defines your sense of normal and can push you to greater heights than you might ever have imagined on your own.

How Circles Shape You

You may have come across the popular Ebbinghaus optical illusion featuring two orange circles. They're identical in size, but appear dramatically different. One seems large, the other small. The difference is in what surrounds them.

The first orange circle sits among large grey circles. By comparison, it looks tiny. The second sits among small grey circles, making it appear enormous. The same circle in a different context creates a completely different perception.

This is how easily context can shape reality. A famous photograph from the 1927 Solvay Conference illustrates how a similar illusion plays out in our lives. The photograph shows 29 physicists and chemists, many of whom would later become household names. Einstein. Curie. Heisenberg. Schrödinger. Planck. Of the 29 people in that room, 17 would go on to win Nobel Prizes. But, crucially, they didn't have them at the time this picture was taken.

This lays bare the concept of 'scenius' coined by Brian Eno. Scenius is emergent, collective intelligence – the energy in the air when like minds gather, which can amplify individual talent through exchanged ideas and incremental development.

In the case of the 1927 Solvay Conference, you didn't win the Nobel Prize because you happened to be in that room. You were in that room because you were the kind of person who wins Nobel Prizes. Being surrounded by other future Nobel laureates undoubtedly reinforced that identity. The room was full of people thinking at the highest level, treating groundbreaking discoveries as normal Tuesday conversations.

Imagine being Marie Curie—the only woman present, among giants of science. But in that room, they were peers. Her context made her achievements seem almost routine, which likely made her next breakthrough feel not just possible, but inevitable.

This is the power of high-expectation environments. Not the false encouragement of participation trophies, but the quiet assumption of excellence as a standard operating procedure.

There's a group of old colleagues who came to be known as the Paypal Mafia. The early employees at PayPal—including Elon Musk, Peter Thiel, David Sacks, and Reid Hoffman—went on to fund, found, or lead Facebook, Tesla, SpaceX, LinkedIn, YouTube, Yelp, Yammer and countless other billion-dollar companies. They didn't become successful entrepreneurs solely by virtue of working at PayPal. But working alongside other ambitious, capable people normalised the idea of starting world-changing companies. There was something in the water.

When Circles Become Ceilings

The reverse is equally true. Surround yourself with people who treat mediocrity as acceptable, and mediocrity becomes your ceiling. Spend time in environments where small thinking is the norm, and your ambitions unconsciously contract to fit. **Live among settling souls, and you'll start to settle, too.**

Your context isn't a neutral, passive thing – it's an active force in your life. The circles around you are constantly sending signals about what's normal, what's possible, what's expected.

Which circles are you choosing?

Are you the smartest person in your peer group? The most ambitious in your social circle? The most successful in your professional network? If so, you might be surrounded by small grey circles that make you feel bigger than you are, while limiting how much you actually grow.

> Aim to be in rooms where the conversation assumes a level of capability you're still reaching toward. Read publications that stretch your thinking. Attend conferences where you're among the least experienced in each room. Follow thinkers whose ideas challenge your assumptions.

Then you'll see the true illusion in action – because by virtue of being in the room, everyone will *perceive your potential at their level.* They'll recognise the successes you diminish and the skills you might ignore. They'll be just as eager to learn from you as you are from them.

The discomfort of feeling like the smallest circle is the price of growth. It's the psychological tax you pay to expand your sense of what's possible.

What the optical illusion teaches us is that size isn't absolute. Potential isn't fixed. Your sense of what you can achieve is largely determined by what surrounds you.

Choosing your circle is choosing your perceived ceiling.

How Fast Do You Drive?

Tell a friend they drive slowly, and they may think you're bananas. *"I'm always driving fast,"* they say. *"The normal driving speed is 30mph. I'm usually at 32-35mph."*

But is 35mph fast? If you're accustomed to the quiet and slow-paced driving of the suburbs, 40mph might seem like a wicked speed. But drive at that same speed on a highway, and people will think you're asleep at the wheel.

Speed is relative, and most people judge their pace compared only to those immediately around them. If everyone around you is driving at 30mph you'll look crazy driving at 40. Driving at 40 in an area where everyone else is much slower can trick you into thinking you're a speed demon. But once you get out of the suburbs, your baseline resets.

On the highway, nobody drives under 40. You'll need to be at 50 just to keep up. Most people are touching 70. If you don't have much practice driving at these speeds, suddenly things might feel a little too fast. You'll do your best to keep up, but your discomfort will be obvious, and any hesitation is more likely to lead to an accident.

But is 70mph really that fast? Get onto a racetrack. Formula 1 cars have an average speed of 138mph and have been known to reach a top speed of 223mph. Their drivers move so fast that they have to train like astronauts so their necks don't snap and their bodies don't crumple.

Most people have no idea what their top speed is. They stop trying once they overtake a few cars. This applies as equally to your life as it does to your motor vehicle. You could easily spend your whole life in first gear, with no idea what you're capable of, satisfied to keep pace with the people on your left and right.

> If you really want to know how fast you can go, find people who make your current speed look pedestrian. This doesn't mean abandoning your current friends or constantly comparing yourself to others. Instead, strategically expand your circle to include people who can push you to new levels.

Look for people who have an abundance of the traits that you're looking to develop. If you're an entrepreneur, seek out founders a few steps ahead of you. If you're a creative, find artists who are pushing boundaries in ways you aspire to.

But don't just seek out those ahead of you. Real growth comes from a diversity of influences:

1. **Those slightly behind you** – not just to remind you of how far you've come, but because supporting and teaching them will solidify your own knowledge and understanding of what you've learned.

2. **Those at your level** – they provide camaraderie and understanding of your current challenges. Any of you might help the

others make a dozen small breakthroughs, which cumulatively represent great shifts forward.

3. **Those far ahead** – they show you what's possible and pull you towards greater heights.

That said, find a balance—life isn't a constant sprint. You can't stay on the highway forever. Formula 1 drivers, for all their speed, eventually have to pull over and change tyres before they melt the rubber off their wheels. And they've got a full team behind them checking diagnostics at all times. Different phases of your journey will require different paces. The key is learning to shift gears appropriately.

Most people find one gear and stay in it. They work like this; they play like that. Gear 1 people burn out on the highway. Gear 5 people can't make it up a hill. You must learn to modulate your speed based on the terrain you're navigating.

It's crucial to diversify your experiences, switch lanes, and explore new contexts to avoid becoming trapped in a singular, limiting perspective. Learning to oscillate between different speeds will help you become more resilient in the long run. The key is knowing when to shift and how to maintain relationships across different speeds.

Audit your current circle: Who are the five people you spend the most time with? What speed are they operating at?

Identify the gaps: In what areas of life do you want to accelerate? Who do you know that excels in these areas?

Expand strategically: Attend events, join communities, or reach out to individuals who seem to be operating with ease at a speed you're not used to.

It's useful to identify at least one friend who drives a little slower than you, one about the same, and another, much faster. All of them should be of admirable character. There will be seasons when you learn predominantly from each of them: The friend that can help you wind down, diagnose issues, and modulate. The friend on equal footing that keeps your foot on the gas, even if you're on different paths. The friend that motivates you to keep pushing, because they seem to have cracked something you're still wrapping your head around. If you don't have at least one of each yet, figure out where you can go to make that new friend.

There are a few different frameworks for defining your circle. The one I've referred to above aligns well with the 'Plus, Minus, Equals' strategy coined by MMA fighter and trainer Frank Shamrock. Shamrock advocated, in his coaching philosophy, that fighters should have three types of sparring partner in order to stay sharp: plus—a partner on a higher level, minus—a partner you can teach, and equals—a peer on your level.

In my professional life I broke this down further into a framework I dubbed TEMPO, and challenged myself to identify, and regularly meet with, people in these categories:

- Team – direct, professional colleagues
- Executive Mentors – trailblazers who know the way ahead
- Mentees – people you're proactively supporting
- Personal Advisory Board – adept thinkers who bring clarity
- Operators – contemporaries you can learn from and share knowledge with

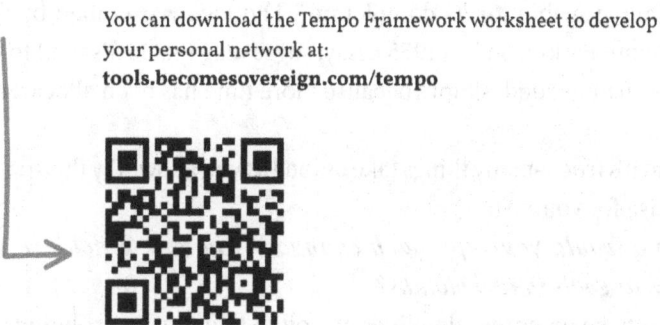

You can download the Tempo Framework worksheet to develop your personal network at:
tools.becomesovereign.com/tempo

Identify these archetypes in your life, and you'll be well on your way to having a broad, fulfilling, and challenging circle.

Two Months or Two Years

When I first transitioned from corporate law to technology, I spent time working with a range of startups. At one, where I reported directly to the CEO, we were discussing an upcoming project I'd be driving forward.

"How long do you think this will take?" He asked. I thought about it for a moment, pattern-matching against my most recent experiences driving cross-functional projects in a law firm.

"Probably about two months," I said, weighing up the amount of time it would take for VPs to buy into the plan, and then the time to roll out and iterate. "Why not two weeks?" He asked. I resisted my initial urge to reject this suggestion immediately. CEOs loved setting unrealistic deadlines that they could later flog you for when you naïvely committed to them—but in this case, I thought about it. Did it need to take two months, or was that just the default number I threw out to give everything enough time to fall into place, risk-free?

After that day, I realised this was a useful thought exercise. The truth is that most timelines, whether too short or too long, are entirely arbitrary.

Parkinson's Law is the oft-quoted adage that "work expands to fill the time available for its completion." The idea was coined by Cyril Northcote Parkinson in a 1955 essay, suggesting that tasks tend to take longer than needed, simply because more time has been allocated for them.

And it's true—many things take as long as you allow. Try this thought exercise for yourself:

How would your approach change if you had to achieve your two-year goals in two months?

When we compress timelines, we often find creative solutions and efficiencies we wouldn't have discovered otherwise. This approach:

- Forces us to prioritise and focus on what's truly essential

- Encourages rapid prototyping and iteration

- Helps us avoid perfectionism and overthinking

This is not an exhortation to rush or cut corners. Undue haste has a heavy cost. Instead, this thought exercise will help break limiting frames around what is possible in a short space of time. And if you end up choosing a longer timeframe, you can make those decisions consciously rather than by default, with a full understanding of the intentional tradeoffs you're making.

Here are some strategies to adopt a "two-month" mindset:

- **Ruthless prioritisation:** Identify the 20% of actions that will yield 80% of the results. Focus on these relentlessly.

- **Rapid prototyping:** Instead of planning extensively, create quick, imperfect versions of your idea. Iterate based on real feedback.

- **Parallel processing:** Look for ways to work on multiple aspects of your goal simultaneously, rather than in sequence.

- **Leverage:** Identify tools, technologies, or people that can dramatically speed up your progress.

- **Constraint as a catalyst:** Use tight deadlines and limited resources as a force for creativity and efficiency. Often, limitations breed innovation.

- **Regular reality checks:** Frequently ask yourself, "If I had to launch/finish/achieve this next week, what would I do differently?"

Take a Long Look

Speaking of undue haste, the converse can also be true. Many of the things we desperately wish could take two months would be better off considered on a two-year horizon.

We want to make money fast, lose weight quick, and find happiness in a hurry. The problem is that searching for ease can lead to more hardship. The crash diet leads to piling on weight. The get-rich-quick scheme turns into a gaping hole in your savings, pension, and your child's college fund.

When you find yourself compelled towards a short cut or quick win, try this thought exercise:

What approach would guarantee this outcome over the next two years?

This changes our frame again, and the wording is specific. If you need to lose 10kg in two months, you'll dive deep into the latest ridiculous fad. But to guarantee that you lose that amount in two years wouldn't require anything drastic. To be absolutely certain it happened, you only need to make small, consistent contributions over a long period of time.

It could be as easy as dropping sugar from your coffee or walking an extra mile on your commute each day. The same applies to wealth: you could leap into the latest pump-and-dump stock hoping you're not left holding the bag, or you could guarantee a long-term win by slightly increasing (or starting) your monthly ETF investment. Surety in the long term rarely requires massive and wholesale shifts. It only asks for usual effort over an unusual period of time.

Here are some strategies to adopt a "two-year" mindset:

- **Sustainable habits:** Focus on developing routines and behaviours that you can maintain consistently over a long period. Small, daily actions compound over time.

- **Systems over goals:** Instead of fixating on end results, design systems that naturally lead to desired outcomes. This shifts focus from short-term achievements to long-term progress.

- **Resilience planning:** Anticipate obstacles and setbacks. Build in redundancies and contingencies to ensure your progress isn't derailed by unexpected challenges.

- **Incremental improvement:** Embrace the power of marginal gains. Seek to improve by just 1% regularly, knowing these small improvements compound dramatically over time.

- **Strategic patience:** Resist the urge for immediate results.

Learn to find satisfaction in the process and small wins along the way.

- **Regular reflection:** Set aside time periodically to review progress, reassess goals, and adjust your approach. This ensures you stay on track without becoming rigid.

Remember, the goal isn't just to move fast—it's to move at the right speed for each situation, always pushing the boundaries of what you believe is possible.

8

SUCCESS CAN BE EASY

"In the confrontation between the stream and the rock, the stream always wins- not through strength but by perseverance."

— H. Jackson Brown

Life is hard in the same way that the ocean is strong—it's an unquenchable force of nature—you can't contain or control it with your bare hands. It can't be wrestled or wrangled. Can't be stopped. Life seems wild and uncontrollable. But that shouldn't stop you from plotting a course and getting to where you need to go.

The popular narrative is that success only comes through relentless struggle, that every achievement must be paid for in blood, sweat, and tears. As we discussed in the chapter on changing frames, these are the kind of narratives that immigrants, outsiders and underdogs often thrive on. However, the opposite is also true: life can be easy, if you let it be. But you'll need to learn to surf. Easy doesn't mean smooth or effortless. The ease comes from the way in which you approach it.

You're more likely to stay afloat by lying flat than by thrashing wildly. Success might not come while you lay on your back, and challenges won't magically disappear while you sleep, but you'll learn it's easier to move with the tide than to stubbornly struggle against it.

Surfers know that they can't control the ocean. They can't change the size of the waves, stop the winds, or smooth the currents. What they can do is read the water and position themselves to ride an oncoming wave before it fully emerges. Mastering surfing requires you to learn when to paddle, when to conserve energy, and when to climb up into the rush of the water.

The novice fights the water, wearing out their body by trying to assert themselves against the tide. But the experienced surfer lets the waves do the work, and collaborates with the flow of the water, maximising their use of energy.

Laziness as a Lever

Growing up, my mother always had a biblical quote up her sleeve about the dangers of laziness. Any signs of excess leisure were met with some quip from the book of Proverbs. *"Go to the ant, you sluggard!"*

In the Bible, laziness is typically construed as causing futility and ruin—procrastination and death. The opposite case, would be advocating for laziness as tactical resource allocation. The problem is that this argument is typically invoked in jest, or as a way to shirk responsibility and hide from hard work. You may hear "I'm just resting my eyes so I can be more focused later" from the habitual napper, or "If I try too hard, the creative muse won't come to me" from the chronic procrastinator. Renowned author Steven Pressfield, like my mother, is keen to disabuse us of such notions.

Pressfield preaches that the artist, writer, and all who seek to create are infantrymen. Progress is measured in yards of dirt and paid for in blood. The muse favours working stiffs and hates prima donnas. To the gods, the biggest sin is pride and preciousness. The muse only rewards those who show up and work daily.

But I think there's a line between laziness as a crutch and laziness as a lever. The goal is to conserve energy where it counts so you can maximise impact when it matters.

In the words of Robert A. Heinlein:

"Progress isn't made by early risers. It's made by lazy men trying to find easier ways to do something."

— Robert A. Heinlein

As a junior in a corporate law firm, you may often be tasked with any manner of mundane activities in the spirit of getting the deal done. I remember one of the first simple but deceptively brain-numbing tasks I was given was cross-referencing and sorting data across multiple spreadsheets. I was given a three-week deadline. I'd rather have spent the three weeks like Prometheus, chained to a rock, letting birds peck out my eyes.

So in a typical slothful fashion, instead of doing the work, I spent three days researching easier ways to accomplish the task. On the fourth day, armed with my research, I was able to cobble together a VBA macro in Microsoft Excel. It was a hot Thursday afternoon, and autumn had yet to make way for winter. I finished my code and hit 'run'. Twenty minutes later the work was done. The script had done it for me. I packed my bag and went to the park.

Addition by Subtraction

Working for longer doesn't mean you're producing more value. People commonly refer to this concept as 'working smart instead of working hard'. But an even greater unlock is figuring out whether you need to do any work in the first place.

Leidy Klotz, an engineer and behavioural scientist at the University of Virginia, has conducted extensive research on the power of subtraction. In one study, participants were given an unstable structure made of Lego blocks, with the goal of making it more stable. Most people's first instinct was to add more blocks to reinforce the structure. The participants in the study sat there stacking new pieces, thinking that increasing complexity would strengthen the Lego bridge. This additive approach was natural to them. It aligned with how we often think about solving problems: adding resources, tools, and effort.

What the participants missed was that the bridge could be stabilised more effectively by removing one single block rather than adding any more. Less than half of the participants even considered subtraction as a solution. It wasn't until later in the experiment, when subtraction was explicitly suggested, that participants began to realise its potential.

We default to thinking the only way to improve is by addition—more hours, more features, more steps. But in many cases, the most efficient solution is to go the opposite way: doing less, not more.

> Adding feels like progress. Effort feels like value. But the paradox of efficiency is that sometimes, the harder you try, the less you achieve. Effortful work may feel rigorous, but as far as output is concerned, it may often be the equivalent of being stuck in quicksand: the more you struggle, the faster you sink.

The Messi Method

Lionel Messi is arguably the most talented football player in history. His nicknames include La Pulga (little flea), the Wizard, the Lion, the King, the Golden Boy, and the Messiah. When you watch his highlights, you see his fluid motion and effortless touch as he guides the ball softly between opponents and into the net. But what you see in the highlights isn't the full picture. What's most remarkable about Messi is what he does when the camera isn't on him.

It turns out that Messi's brilliance on the football pitch doesn't come from constant motion or tireless running. If you were to watch one of his games in person, you would notice that he spends most of the game walking or standing still, meandering around the pitch and watching the play evolve.

He doesn't press or chase after every ball. He doesn't engage in fruitless runs. Instead, Messi conserves his energy, reading the game like a chess master anticipating his opponent's next move. Then, when he sniffs out a moment—when the right opportunity strikes—he accelerates with laser focus, creating space, beating defenders, and capitalising with his minimal but precise movements.

This approach allows Messi to be at his absolute best when it matters most. By not exhausting himself with constant movement when there are only low-stakes rewards to be had, he ensures he has the energy reserves to capitalise on those crucial, game-changing moments.

Sometimes, doing less in the short term allows you to do more when it truly counts. It's a matter of recognising when to conserve your resources and when to go all out.

But this isn't the only way to manage your effort. The Messi method is diametrically opposed to the Jason Bourne blueprint.

The Bourne Blueprint

On the flip side of Messi, we have the Jason Bourne approach. In the Bourne film series, the titular character is always running, always pushing his limits. Jason Bourne runs so much that even when he lost his memory and couldn't remember his own name, he still knew exactly how far he could run while maintaining top speed. He knew what his body was capable of. He knew it in his bones, because he'd spent so long testing the limits of his capabilities.

Bourne is never idle—always scanning, always prepared for the next threat or opportunity. From the moment Bourne steps into a room, he's mentally mapping exits, observing people, and calculating his next move. His edge comes not from resting or waiting, but from constantly staying sharp, pushing his limits, and ensuring he's ready for anything at any time.

Bourne's method is about constant preparation, always operating at the brink of your power. By consistently pushing himself to understand and expand his limits, Bourne ensures that when crunch time arrives and he has no choice but to use every resource possible, he can instantly level up. By testing himself before he's tested by fate, he can kick into maximum gear when the moment requires it.

If you have a central heating system in your house, you might realise that your boiler runs the same way. It's easy to assume, in the dead of winter, that the best way to save money is to turn the heating off when it's not as cold. The problem is that the most expensive part of heating a house is kicking the boiler up from zero. If instead you kept it on, at a consistent rate for most of the day, you'd actually save money because you never need the effortful burst.

Bourne keeps his engine warm through consistent training. As General Norman Schwarzkopf once said to the 1991 batch of US Naval Academy graduates, "The more you sweat in peace, the less you bleed in war." By maintaining a state of readiness, Bourne handles complex, high-stakes situations effortlessly because he's already conditioned himself for chaos. Life can be easy if you're always prepared for the hard parts.

Both Messi and Bourne represent different but equally valid approaches to making life easier. Messi's path relies on strategic effort and energy conservation, while Bourne's philosophy centres on being ever-ready for the toughest challenges. I'd make the case that you can do both. Conserve your energy for key moments, but keep your mind at peak readiness. Don't wait until you're tested—proactively take opportunities to operate at your best and show yourself what you're capable of. Push yourself to find your limits, even when the situation doesn't require it.

Take the Stairs

The more you run from hardship, the weaker you become. Embraced difficulty can be a path to ease, and the quest to avoid pain at all costs can be recursive. It's easy to get stuck in a doom loop of running from pain and then being crushed by it, because the more you flee the worse it gets.

On the London metro system you can navigate most stations using the lift, the escalators, or the stairs. But if there's a closed stairwell, they'll typically put a sign by it telling you exactly how many stairs there are, especially if it's going to be a long one. That warning has to be there so people know what they're signing up for before they start taking the stairs.

The funny thing is that when you are forced to take the stairs, either in an emergency or when the lift is out of service, you naturally end up hating it. It's arduous, strenuous, and you're panting after the first two flights. But the reason you hate it in an emergency, is because you ignore the small, hard thing that you could have done every day, which is taking more stairs.

People often avoid the small inconvenience of taking the stairs on a regular day, even though incrementally, day to day, it's not that bad. Then on the one day that you actually need to take the stairs, it feels like the worst thing in the world.

In the process, you learn the wrong lesson. After being forced to take the stairs, you think, "Oh gosh, that was terrible; I'm not going to do that again." And so from that point on, you continue to avoid the stairs because you remember how hard it was. Until you're forced to take the stairs again, and the cycle continues.

It is easier to take 50 stairs ten times than 500 stairs once. That seems obvious, even though it's the same number of stairs. But most people pick the latter in their regular lives, because taking zero stairs on nine of ten days feels better than taking some stairs on ten of ten days. What seems easier up front sets you up for a harder task later. The easy path becomes the hard path. The hard path eventually feels easy.

> Hardship is objective; difficulty is subjective. The more you run from difficulty, the more you will encounter it. The more you embrace it, the more it disappears.

Don't do hard things solely because they're hard. Don't struggle because you think you must struggle. Do hard things because they will eventually make everything else easier. And then you won't need to struggle, grind, or grit your teeth through force of exertion. The weight is easier to lift when you welcome it.

Turning Hardship Into Ease

1. **Read your environment, don't fight it.** Just like surfers who work with the tide rather than against it, learn to read the conditions you're navigating. When resistance is unavoidable, find ways to redirect the energy around you rather than waste your own.

2. **Save energy for the moments that matter.** Don't waste your best effort on low-stakes tasks. Learn from Messi: keep your head up, observe, and wait for the moments that truly count – then attack them with everything you've got.

3. **Use subtraction as a first principle.** Don't default to adding more work, more steps, or more complexity when faced with a challenge. Ask, "What could I remove to make this easier?"

4. **Test your limits deliberately.** The easiest way to make hard things feel easier is to do them in small doses, consistently. Take the stairs daily, not because they're easy, but because they're hard enough to build resilience without overwhelming you. The key is to treat hardship as training rather than as punishment.

9

YOU'RE A LUCK MAGNET

Life can only be understood backwards; but it must be lived forwards."

— Søren Kierkegaard

Throughout this book you'll see stories of me and others achieving wild and crazy things—taking shots in the dark and pulling off the impossible. And there will be many calls to action where I encourage you to do the same.

You might feel an instinctive urge to reject the call. It comes from the tug of the dark inside you, which prefers to wallow in timid helplessness. It's that safety-seeking, self-preserving voice in the back of your head telling you to turn away and dismiss the potential that these things are equally possible for you. Please don't.

Don't flinch because you think I might be smarter than you, or more competent than you, or more fortunate in some other dimension. I promise you, it doesn't matter. None of the things that happened for me in my life should prevent you having similar or far greater success in yours.

Don't be tempted to give yourself excuses like "This wouldn't work for me" or "You just got lucky".

Of course I got lucky. That's actually the secret. I'm always lucky. I'm the equivalent of a two-tonne luck magnet in a field full of luck.

Luck finds its way to me the same way birds navigate south for the winter. Luck's emergence in my life now feels as inevitable as the laws of physics.

I will never stop being lucky. Not because I was born lucky, but because I actively court luck. I cultivate it. And if you take this book seriously, it will make you a luck magnet too. In fact, it's already working.

Only a tiny fraction of the world's population will ever discover this book. And here you are reading it. What are the odds? *Aren't you lucky?* You're going to get even luckier with every chapter you finish. Keep going.

7:15 in Nebraska

I'm not sure if you believe in miracles, luck, or serendipity, but all three of them struck one Sunday in a tiny Nebraska church in 1950.

It's a cold March in Nebraska. We're at the West Side Baptist Church. Choir practice starts at 7:15. The Reverend comes in a few hours early to put the furnace on so it's not cold when everyone arrives. He sets everything up and goes home for dinner.

Choir practice starts at 7:15. At 7:25, a gas leak causes an explosion. The blast demolishes the church, destroys the windows of nearby buildings, and takes a local radio station off the air.

Every single one of the 15 choir members survived. It turns out they were all running late. And each choir member had a different excuse. One was napping. Some were still eating dinner. One was waiting in the car to pick up another. One couple had to change their kids' diapers.

This is the kind of miracle most people anticipate when they imagine luck. And yes, sometimes luck strikes like lightning. But most of the time, luck is like oil.

Luck is more accessible than you think. While the Nebraska church story might seem like a once-in-a-lifetime occurrence, research suggests that such "lucky" connections are everywhere.

In 1967, Stanley Milgram, a social psychologist, set out to investigate just how interconnected our world really is. He devised an experiment that would later be known as the "Small World Experiment." Milgram randomly selected people from Omaha, Nebraska, and Wichita, Kansas, and gave them a seemingly impossible task: get a package to a named stranger in Massachusetts.

The rules were simple. Each person could only send the package to someone they knew on a first-name basis. That person would then do the same, passing the package along through a chain of personal acquaintances until it reached its final destination: a stockbroker working in Boston and living in Sharon, Massachusetts.

The results were astounding. Of the 160 packages that began the journey, 44 actually made it to the target. Even more surprising was the number of steps it took. On average, the packages that arrived successfully had passed through just six people. This experiment gave birth to the famous concept of "six degrees of separation"—the idea that any two people in the world are connected through a chain of about six acquaintances.

Blessed Are the Believers

A British variation of that study controlled for self-perceived luck. They took all the same steps, but participants were split into people who believed they were naturally lucky, and people who believed they were naturally unlucky. The results were massively skewed towards those who believed in their own luck for one major reason: many of the participants who believed themselves unlucky hadn't bothered sending their packages in the first place.

In life, this plays out in myriad ways. People manifest their own demise. They opt out of success because of fear, shame, and lack of confidence. They self-sabotage at every opportunity to reinforce the narrative of their natural misfortune. Meanwhile, those who believe in their luck move with confidence and stumble into it everywhere.

A good example of why this occurs can be found in the Birthday Paradox. In a group of just over 20 people, there's a >50% chance that two of them share the same birthday. At first glance that sounds bizarre. You might think, "There are 365 days in a year. The odds of someone matching my birthday exactly are 1/365 – that's tiny!"

But what matters isn't how likely it is for someone to share *your* birthday—it's how many pairs of people exist who could share a birthday with each other. In a room of 23 people, there are 253 possible pairs (23 × 22 / 2). That's 253 chances for a match, and their individual probabilities add up, making it more likely than not in aggregate. Increase the number to 57 people, and the chance of a match is over 99%.

Coincidences are far more common than we intuitively believe. We're surrounded by hidden probabilities that only seem improbable because we're thinking in the wrong frame. Serendipity is not rare; it's simply under-recognised. But the more you're aware of the prevalence of luck, the more you can make it work for you.

> *"Life is what happens when you're busy making other plans."*
>
> — John Lennon

Humans are wired to seek stories, not stats. We like clear chains of cause and effect more than hidden phenomena unfolding behind the scenes. That's why luck feels like magic—it seems disconnected from effort. But in reality, chance events emerge far more frequently once you increase your surface area for luck. **A lot of what we think is magic is really just math, and probabilities can easily be shifted in your favour through your volume of attempts.**

Consider how many people met their husband or wife by simply being in the right place at the right time. And then think of all the people who stayed at home. Or who kept their mouth shut. Or who never called, and called again. Luck favours the persistent and reveals itself to those who pay attention.

Don't underestimate the power of putting things out into the world.

There's a phrase online that proliferated until it became a meme, but its truth is no less potent: *"You can just do things."* When I quit my job in corporate law, I'd been dabbling with a few different half-baked businesses on the side for months. I was organising group trips and honeymoons for strangers. I'd do design work for small brands. I'd give marketing and growth strategy advice to fledgling startups. I'd taught myself photography and started taking photos for events. But a single stroke of luck catapulted me to another level of notoriety.

The firm had given me gardening leave, but on my last day in the office, I'd called in sick. I could've spent it anxiously pacing the floors and saying awkward goodbyes, but instead I was catching a flight to New York. I was on my way to my first New York Fashion Week—or so I hoped. The trouble is, my friends and I didn't have invites for any shows, beyond a few random after-parties. The day we landed, I yanked the tags off a few items I'd bought from Calvin Klein for the trip and self-directed a mini street shoot, modelling the items while my friend held the camera. I edited a selection of the photos on my phone while we sat in a cafe and then uploaded them to Instagram, tagging the brand. Before I'd finished my coffee, someone had reached out via DM.

Within a few hours, I'd been emailed and signed a release contract. Calvin Klein wanted my photos. The pictures I had taken myself, spontaneously, on the same day I arrived in New York, would soon be featured on their social media page and website. My friends and I hustled for invites with the same enthusiasm, quickly filling our days with fashion week events. At parties we made new friends; I leveraged my work with Calvin Klein to get influencer campaigns, consulting gigs, and media work. London Fashion Week came the week after, and we ran the same playbook. I pounded the streets and partied enough to make myself sick, but in just two weeks I'd built the foundation for a growth strategy and media consultancy in the fashion industry.

A half-decade of detours later, I became co-founder of a luxury fashion e-commerce platform. By now I'd attended London, New York, and Paris Fashion Weeks several times apiece (though sadly never Milan). Instead of sneaking into shows, I was now being dressed by brands and featured in media publications. I'd met industry legends, global superstars, and partied with everyone from Kanye West to Bella

Hadid. None of this happens without luck. But you don't get the luck without inertia—without turning your life into a game of pinball and propelling yourself towards nascent opportunity.

Luck is something you can invite. The key is increasing your exposure to randomness. Meet more people. Try more things. Say yes more often. Each new conversation, project, or interaction adds another "pairing" to your Birthday Paradox; another invisible string connecting you to something unexpected.

> I can't promise you'll ever have a single stroke of luck comparable to the choir members of the West Side Baptist Church, or even my stunt with Calvin Klein. But in aggregate, in compounding doses, you certainly could. Luck typically lies dormant, waiting to be encountered. If you spent your whole life poking about in the ground nonchalantly, you might find very little or enough to last a lifetime. What makes the difference, is consistency and intentionality.

At scale, and over time, getting lucky is a skill. Make the decision to get lucky today.

10

KEEP YOUR FEET ON THE GROUND

"All men dream, but not equally. Those who dream by night in the dusty recesses of their minds wake in the day to find that it was vanity; but the dreamers of the day are dangerous men, for they may act on their dreams with open eyes, to make them possible"

— T.E. Lawrence (Lawrence of Arabia)

Deep down, everyone has some change they'd like to make in the world—some quiet ambition. They just may not frame it in such grand terms.

What are your dreams? If you knew failure was impossible, what would you hope to accomplish someday? Seriously – email me (david@theknowledge.io) and let me know.

If you say you don't have any ambitions, that's fine. I won't think you're lying to me. I'll know you're lying to yourself. And the worst part is, you're probably doing it by accident.

The problem is that most people don't spend enough time getting clarity on their dreams – they don't give themselves the room, or grace, to ruminate on what they really want. Dreams become something you think about occasionally but never invest any time or effort into. You've got enough on your plate without worrying about your highfaluting future plans, right?

Dreams are accelerants, not ornaments. The Wright brothers looked at gulls and saw engines. Marie Curie stared at glowing glassware and saw medicine. Martin Luther King Jr. went from pulpit to podium and rewrote American society. Each started with an 'impossible' fancy—some deep desire—and dragged it into daylight.

> Unfortunately, many people treat their dreams the way they treat money – like it's something valuable you can shove in your back pocket for a rainy day. The problem is that, just like money, dreams suffer from inflation. The longer you hold on to a dream without investing in it, the less valuable it becomes. You can't keep your dreams under your mattress and expect them to retain their value until you're ready to return to them.

So, here's what I want you to do: Pick one of the dreams you've shoved between the couch cushions. Identify three steps you could take to bring it into reality. Make sure one of those steps can be achieved in the next 24-48 hours. Make your first investment.

You Can't Dream Forever

Everyone dreams, even if they don't remember them. But not all those who dream are 'dreamers'. Ambition doesn't require you to be a dreamer, and that's a good thing. Many habitual dreamers are dangerous because they're only powerful inside their dream, and so they avoid encounters with reality.

Chronic dreamers promise riches they haven't earned, spend cheques that haven't cleared, chant *"any day now"* as another year evaporates.

Don't sacrifice reality for the world inside your head, as alluring as it may be—keep your feet on the ground.

Real power is dream alchemy: learning to bring dreams out of your head and into concrete reality. That's the part most people baulk at.

Because dream alchemy is hard. It's a lot easier to stick your head in the sand and pretend that you're flying, than it is to envision and build a small flying machine.

A lot of people use dreams the same way addicts use drugs—a warm shot of tranquil, regularly revisited, to pacify any anxiety around your lack of progress. You close your eyes and make a wish and click your heels three times—but now you're stuck—if you open your eyes and see nothing has changed, you'll be devastated. But, the dream-voice whispers... If you keep your eyes shut for long enough, then eventually one day things will happen exactly the way you imagined, and you can finally open your eyes and shout, *"I told you so."*

I'm sorry to burst your bubble, but life rarely works that way. Most dreamers end up having to keep their eyes closed forever. They commit spiritual seppuku to stay alive in a limbic daydream rather than coming out to face the barbs of reality.

When you imagine yourself as Dorothy embarking on a magical adventure that only exists in your head, everyone else just sees someone wandering aimlessly, lost in their own thoughts.

Sometimes when it feels like it's you against the world, it's because you're the only one who refuses to live in it. I know I sound harsh, but you need to hear this: your dreams don't have to stay figments of your imagination. If you open your eyes, everything will be okay.

The real world will occasionally be harder and tougher and nastier. You may get cut and bruised and endure highs and lows. But it will be so much sweeter because you'll realise that magic is possible here; dreams don't have to stay dreams. You can bend reality to your will without blinking. You have the power to bring about all the circumstances you wish existed.

You'll find all the tools you need in the chapters that follow: confidence, competence, charisma, resilience, and the ability to embrace chaos.

The writer Philip K. Dick defined an era of science fiction with works like *'Do Androids Dream of Electric Sheep?'* and *'The Man in the High Castle'*. In opening a 1978 speech, he recalled an encounter with a college student in Canada who had asked him to define reality. He said:

> *"Reality is that which, when you stop believing in it, doesn't go away."*
> — Philip K. Dick

Some people spend so long anticipating great things that they start acting like great things are already happening. And the longer they spend dreaming, the stronger these hallucinations become. Until one day, while skipping down the yellow brick road you've concocted in your head, you'll be shaken from your stupor as the path fades and you find yourself falling. Then, eyes finally open, you'll realise you were on a cliff edge the whole time and just couldn't see it.

Don't buy into your own delusions. Don't lose touch with reality, mistaking a rich inner world for actual progress, while those around you wonder why you're struggling against unseen forces. The longer you remain in a dream, the more disconnected you become, and the more time you'll spend fighting your shadow.

The sleeper must awaken. Get your head out of the clouds and see the world for what it is. Become a dream alchemist. Pull fleeting thoughts into concrete reality. Count your chickens and make them hatch. Embrace Sovereignty.

Agency

PART II

Agency

A world that prizes scale requires order and compliance. So our systems are designed for control and conformity. Outliers are scorned, but they win in the end.

Society creates containers to sort personality, capability, and potential. It's easy to hyperfocus on the gap between those that *have* things and those that don't. But to do so is to neglect the growing chasm between those that *do* things and those that don't. Between those who create, and those who consume.

Most people sleepwalk through life, following predetermined paths laid out by others. They accept the rules of the game without questioning who wrote them. Agency is the difference between passenger and pilot. Agency is realising that you're not just a product of your circumstances but a force capable of shaping them.

Those that do, those that act, have true power. Agency is the force that transforms thought into deed, and dream into reality. It's the difference between being swept along by currents of life and charting your own course through its waters.

Agency isn't a default. It's forged through self-belief, honed through skill, and wielded through influence. Some mistakenly reduce agency to 'ruthless individualism'; to a boundless yearning to get what you want, at any cost. But agency built at the expense of others doesn't last.

True agency is the product of three ingredients: the **confidence** to take action, the **competence** to enact your will, and make a vision concrete, and the **charisma** to enlist and recruit co-conspirators; to bring others to your side.

These three elements—confidence, competence, and charisma—form the triad of personal power.

To shape your reality, you must reject the notion of immutable circumstances. You must look at the world not as it is, but as it could be. This perspective shift is the first step on the path from passive observer to conjurer, alchemist, hero, sovereign.

In the end, agency grants you more than just personal gain. It allows you to contribute to the world in a meaningful way. Because once you fully realise your own power to act and create change, you become a catalyst for transformation far beyond yourself.

David Elikwu — Warring Queen, 2025

Confidence

At the core of every great achievement lies an unshakeable self-belief. Not the brash overconfidence that crumbles at the first sign of adversity, but a deep-seated certainty in one's own capacity to learn, grow, and overcome.

Confidence is often misunderstood because it is crassly mimicked. In its true form, confidence is quiet. It has no need to announce itself, because it's present in every action, every decision, every step forward in the face of uncertainty. It's the voice in the darkness. The whisper daring you to believe when the world suggests otherwise.

Building this kind of confidence doesn't require eliminating fear or doubt. Real confidence acknowledges those feelings and moves forward anyway. It's a confidence that trusts in your ability to handle whatever comes your way, not because you're certain of the outcome, but because you're certain of your capabilities and your capacity to carve a path when the known road seems untenable.

Confidence enables us to take calculated risks, to push beyond our comfort zones, to persist when others would quit. It's the foundation upon which all other aspects of personal power are built. Without it, skills lie dormant and charisma falls flat.

But with it, we become unstoppable forces. We carve our own paths where none existed before. We break through the ceilings others accept as fixed. We create momentum that propels us forward, stacking small wins into monumental achievements.

As we cultivate this inner strength, we learn to fully inhabit our potential. We claim our rightful seat at any table, not out of arrogance, but out of a clear-eyed assessment of our worth and capabilities.

In the end, confidence is living up to our own standards, not anyone else's. It's becoming the fullest, most authentic version of ourselves. And in doing so, we unlock the power to truly shape our reality.

11

CARVE A HOLE IN THE UNIVERSE

"For of all sad words of tongue or pen, The saddest are these: 'It might have been!'"

— John Greenleaf Whittier

The word 'decide' comes from two Latin words: *de-* 'off' and *caedere* 'cut', which, taken together, mean 'to cut off'. When you make a decision, you're not just choosing one path; you're cutting off the others.

Each time you make a decision, you plunge a knife into the heart of the universe and cut yourself off from a dozen future paths. All the possible future versions of you that did that other thing and lived with the consequences are dead. But this act is only as powerful as your intentions. The more decisively you cut, the more powerful your decisions will become. Confidence, then, is the key. The more confident the cut, the clearer the path to the outcome.

When, subconsciously, you are always checking over your shoulder for an escape hatch, or to monitor the progress of those on the path you didn't take, you signal to yourself that you don't trust your own judgement. Your hesitance in pursuing the path you're on can lead you to the worst of both worlds: failing to make sufficient progress, while persistently aware of the alternate reality.

You see this in the queue at the supermarket when someone is torn between two checkout aisles. They switch lines and switch again. They're constantly double-checking to see if they made the right choice. And often, in their hesitance, caught between two lanes, others join the queue, leaving them further behind than they otherwise could have been, or at best in the same place, though infinitely more weary.

You see this in careers, and in relationships. The colleague who laments the acting career that never happened. The friend who can never confirm they intend to marry their partner of six years. We pretend to choose and make half-choices. We watch ourselves dither, and we doubt.

But when you cut decisively—when you commit fully to a path—you build evidence of your own capability to choose well.

The Power of Decisions

When you make a decision, big or small, you decide which version of you remains canon. You decide which version of you will get to tell your story, looking back on a lifetime of choices.

If you think decision-making is mundane, your life will be mundane. Decision-making is the kind of superpower that lies dormant until you're worthy. Until you're ready to take it seriously. Until you realise that you can use your decisions to time travel, lift heavy objects, and bend reality around you.

You make a few hundred tiny decisions each day, thousands per week, and multiples more each month. There are just a handful of decisions you'll make in any given decade that dramatically alter the course of your life.

One decision to pursue higher education spawns countless smaller choices—which school, what major, which classes to take—each shaping your knowledge, network, and future opportunities. And going deeper, on any given day, you'll decide how late to sleep, which classes to attend, how long to study, which friendships to maintain, and more.

While the large decisions seem to carry the most weight, it's a mistake to discount all the tiny decisions along the way. The error is assuming that they each exist in isolation. They don't. They add up and coalesce, aggregating into a landslide of behaviour.

Those tiny decisions become your habits and ingrained beliefs about how the world works. This avalanche of past behaviours drives your actions every day, and has a massive influence on your ability to make the few large decisions that shift your world on its axis.

There is no way to avoid this compounding. Decision becomes behaviour. Behaviour becomes life. There is an allure to the idea we can shy away from hard choices; to put them off and to the side, and buy ourselves time to be bolder. But passiveness is only pretence. Inaction is, itself, action. You *choose* to delay, choose to stall, choose to procrastinate, and put off the good you know you ought to do. These things may seem to just 'happen', but you actively create the circumstances for them. The status quo is not a perpetual force – it is something you rebuild and reinforce daily through action and inaction.

To use the words of philosopher and psychologist William James:

> *"When you have to make a choice and don't make it, that is in itself a choice."*
>
> — William James

The die is not cast – your past doesn't bind your future in perpetuity. Failing to choose, is choosing to fail. It is never too late to take a new path.

Hunt Your Alts

I teach a course called Decision Hacker, which helps driven people to transform their lives and work through decision-making. One of the patterns I've seen most often, whether in coaching startup founders, training management consultants, or in counselling fledgling artists, is an inability to let go of the people they might otherwise have been.

The path you choose is just as significant as the paths you ignore. Most people settle for a shadow career and are haunted by ghosts of themselves in possible alternate timelines. The versions of you that took that other path and did that other thing. The version who was brave when you weren't. The version that paid attention when you failed to. The version who was on time to that event, or talked to that girl. The afterimage of that person—the life you might have lived given the chance to do things over—it burns into the back of your brain, when you fail to cut with confidence.

Your decisions determine your destiny. Versions of you in every possible alternate universe are fighting for survival, for canon, for control of your immortal soul. You decide which path you take, which version of you survives. But to avoid being haunted by the shadow of regret, you need to hunt your alts and kill them.

In the wacky show Rick and Morty, there's a memorable arc where Rick battles an alternate version of himself from a parallel reality, a version that has been introducing unplanned chaos to his timeline. The same thing happens in your life when you hang on to paths not taken. You allow the downstream possibilities of actions you didn't take to become seeds of doubt that corrupt the path you're on.

This haunting by alternate selves is one of the greatest destroyers of confidence. When you're constantly second-guessing past choices, you undermine your ability to make future ones with conviction. The person still wondering, 'What if I'd taken that job?' can't fully commit to excelling in their current role. But when you successfully hunt your alts—when you fully own your choices—you free up mental energy to pour into your chosen path. This commitment creates a feedback loop: better results from full commitment lead to greater confidence in your decision-making ability.

Every decision you face creates multiple possible futures. When you only focus on a single possible outcome, you can easily fall victim to a series of events you never planned for. Carefully considering the range and variance of all potential outcomes allows us to hunt down alternate versions of ourselves that could be roaming wild and causing chaos in a future beyond our contemplation.

You should think well enough, in advance, about what lies on the other side of each decision you make, to ensure you're happy with the reality you choose to live in.

> In the fabric of the universe lies all the fantastic lives you could possibly live. It's not too late to claim them. If you don't like the timeline you're in right now, you can change that. One decision at a time. One confident cut after another. Slicing away the strands of time and chance between the version of you that exists right now and the people you could become. Shifting timelines is not easy. Nor is it quick. But the possibility is the point.

There is no conclusion you will ever be forced to accept, except the final rest of death. Everything else is negotiable. It's entirely in your hands. You get to decide. You get to choose. Accept the path you're on, or fight your way to a better timeline.

Learning to make confident decisions is like building any other skill – it requires practice and progressive challenges. Each decisive cut you make strengthens your capacity for the next one. Start with smaller decisions where the stakes are manageable, but practice making them cleanly and without regret. This builds the confidence muscle you'll need when facing the handful of decisions each decade that truly alter your life's trajectory.

Practising Decisive Action:

1. Before any decision, big or small, pause and consider its potential ripple effects. Not just the immediate consequences, but the possible consequences of those consequences. Which doors does this decision open? Which does it close? How concrete or reversible are those possible outcomes? What is

the cost of reversing course if needed?

2. Visualise multiple outcomes, both positive and negative. How would it feel to inhabit that timeline? Which possible futures are best avoided, and how can you hedge against them in advance? Which possible futures hold the potential of great value? How can you optimise for ending up, and remaining, on that timeline?

3. Once you've decided, commit fully. Don't waste energy second-guessing. But make note of your original assumptions, and revisit the decision as soon as those assumptions change. Now that you know what you know, how should that impact your approach moving forward? You don't need to dwell on the past, but you also don't need to hang onto sunk costs once you've already realised you've made a misstep.

4. Regularly review your decisions and their consequences. Use this information to refine your decisions, allowing you to pattern-match and cut even more decisively in the future.

5. Celebrate the path you've chosen, rather than mourning those you've left behind. Commit to making the best of the path you're on, and continually pruning the timeline, slowly moving yourself to the best possible path.

12

BREAK THE BOX

"You cannot swim for new horizons until you have courage to lose sight of the shore."

— William Faulkner

The world is full of containers. Categories, schemas, and tidy little boxes to put people in. Categorisation makes the world seem neater and more digestible. But you don't want to be eaten, do you?

Most of the pain you'll feel in your professional life will come from taking one of three paths:

1. You fit seamlessly into at least one box, and under clearly defined labels in most areas of your life. The type-A student. The athlete. The kid who's good with numbers. The artist. You were easily accepted by the in-group, so you accepted the titles with gratitude. You followed all the rules until you realised that every layer of acceptance was a subtle and elaborate trap. You now want something more, but have no way to break free. You've fused your identity to the title already.

You realise now that the boxes you previously welcomed now define you and entirely contain your identity and sense of self. You slam your hands against the walls until your knuckles bleed, but the walls don't budge; they only increase your discomfort. You're wedged in so tightly that abandoning the box would feel like the death of your identity, and the image you have spent your whole life perfecting.

2. You hardly fit into any boxes. The labels you see tossed around often seem appropriate, but they're still not quite right. You're so close to fitting in but you never really do, and your attempts to go along smoothly with everyone else just result in nicks and bruises as you bump up against the edges and sharp corners of the box that everyone else easily navigates.

You break your own legs, contort your identity and cut off parts of your true self, trying to wedge yourself in and be palatable, but it still doesn't quite work. Maybe you're not destined to be a well-paid cog in the accolade-fuelled machine after all.

3. You don't fit into any boxes. You know it. Everyone knows it. And it hurts. The prospect of having to figure everything out on your own feels hauntingly isolating, without the guiding comfort of a group around you. All you can do is sit on the sidelines and watch everyone else live perfectly coordinated lives, doing the right thing at the right time, and reminding you simultaneously of how awkward and unconventional you are.

Those sound like three different problems, but they're not. Here's the simple truth: all boxes, on some level, are a trap. Seeking the mollifying comfort of fitting into some broader category will either be a trap when you change your mind, or a constant source of anxiety while you try and find your place in the world.

The one thing you want to avoid at all costs is being put in a box that you didn't build yourself, or being arbitrarily assigned a label.

This is harder and more counter-intuitive than it sounds. People secretly covet labels. Some people would like to think of themselves as original, counter-cultural rebels, but they only rebel against labels they don't like. All labels are a trap. Labels create assumptions which either make you predictable and docile, or dangerous.

> *"Labels are for filing. Labels are for clothing. Labels are not for people."*

— Martina Navratilova

Once you find yourself snugly aligned with any label, be it your political affiliation, your style and aesthetic sensibilities, or your membership in any subculture, sit up and be wary. It may be an early sign that you're no longer thinking or acting uniquely, and your sovereignty is slipping away.

In-groups may be comforting, but maintaining membership of a group identity can easily, over time, become a force that erodes your individual thoughts, your voice, and your self-knowledge.

A Box of One's Own

The year I broke into Biglaw, the odds of being selected at my firm were 1500:1. Maybe if I had known that number I would have hesitated. But ultimately it wouldn't have mattered. This was the only thing in the world that mattered to me.

I knew it would be hard. Everyone around me kept telling me that. I knew people like me didn't belong in places like that. I told my mentor, a war veteran with the scars to prove it, that I wanted to apply to my dream law firm. He sat me down on a park bench and told me not to waste my time. And he would've been right if it wasn't for one small revelation: when you don't fit neatly into a box, you can just make your own.

I got invited to open days and evening events at about a dozen top law firms, and at every single one, I saw the same group of people. It's a bit like the dating market—every firm wants the best they can get, so as long as you fit the criteria, you're quite likely to run into the same batch of people at firms of a similar calibre. But for me, there was an obvious problem. I knew it from the very first time I stepped foot in a law firm.

The first corporate law firm I ever visited was exquisite—aesthetically overwhelming and part of the elusive 'Magic Circle' of top law firms headquartered in London.

The morning began with a series of talks by associates and partners at the firm. I sat near the front and took copious notes—I still have them. I was a first-year undergrad, and I felt honoured to be there, in this room full of supposed peers.

When the morning sessions ended, we networked over lunch. Everyone I spoke to already had an incredible resume. This wasn't the first law firm they'd been to. It was at least their fifth or sixth. And in fact, the decor here was relatively drab in comparison to those swankier firms. I couldn't argue—the only law firm I'd been to before this was a criminal law firm above a Burger King in North London.

We were about to make our way to another room for the afternoon sessions, and just as we stepped out, I noticed one of my new friends was going the wrong way. She was one of the few other ethnic minority students so we'd stuck together during the break.

"Hey!" I called out. "The negotiation session is this way."

Her laugh seemed to bounce off the marble walls. "It's okay, I'm just going upstairs to see my uncle."

That's when it hit me. She wasn't my peer. None of them were. Everyone here was well-groomed and well-connected. I wasn't in that box.

I had plenty of similar encounters at similar firms. On one hand, I was always 'just happy to be here'. On the other hand, I was constantly reminded of how subpar I was, how behind I was, and how brilliant everyone else seemed in comparison.

And then one day a revelation came to me like a gift from the stars—a truth I would need to accept if I wanted to make any progress. A single thought that would change my frame completely.

Firms like these only hire brilliant people. There were no exceptions to that rule. Meaning if I were to ever end up working here, I would need to be brilliant. It was a prerequisite. They would need to be convinced that I was brilliant. That's what the interviews were for.

This thought came to me while sitting in the boardroom of a US law firm. And I looked around the room at all the other students. Each of them was indeed brilliant, and you knew that because they fit the criteria. Excellent grades, strong backgrounds, great commercial awareness. It was already obvious that I wouldn't fit the criteria in the same way they did. And that meant if I was going to end up at a firm like this, I'd need to be brilliant in some other way—dramatically different, yet equally valuable.

That revelation led to me dropping out of school and, eventually, to a job at my dream firm.

Different is Better Than Good

I remember crying after my second final interview at the law firm I would later join. I had two final interviews because it was that close. My first 'final' interview went great, but apparently, they still couldn't decide. So I had to come back.

My second set of interviewers were senior partners with stern faces. They asked how I had managed to get my first graduate consulting job without actually graduating, so I told them—it was quite simple, really: when you're taking big swings, be ready to knock the ball out of the park. When you're going against the grain, nothing short of a home run will do. I'd finally learned to be myself, even if that meant being drastically different.

Initially, they'd headhunted me for that graduate role. The recruiter saw I'd spent some time at Google, and I was just returning from Shanghai, having spent some time at a pan-Asian law firm during what should have been my final year at university. I clarified over the phone that I hadn't actually completed my degree but convinced them to let me through to the next stage of interviews anyway.

After a second interview and a packed assessment day, my last task was a presentation to the directors. I was shown to a spare desk and given 45 minutes to cobble together a 10-minute presentation answering the question: 'How did bankers' bonuses lead to the credit crunch?'

I didn't bother turning on the provided computer. Being a perfectionist by nature, I could easily have spent five hours crafting the 'perfect' PowerPoint. There wasn't enough time. Instead, I took a notepad from my bag and wrote down everything I knew about the financial crisis. Then, with five minutes to go, after being given a warning to get ready, I wrote my headings in large font horizontally across spare notebook pages.

When I was called upon to present, there were no slides to fiddle with and no notes to read from. I just tore the heading pages out of my notebook and held them up one at a time as I talked freely for ten minutes about how the financial crisis in 2008 was caused by the fall of the Berlin Wall almost 20 years prior.

Without a global antagonist to balance against, I explained, capitalism had proliferated unchecked. I talked about how collateralised debt obligations emerged during the same period and how their use became continually abstracted from the underlying debt as financial instruments became more sophisticated.

You get the idea. I sounded pretty smart. Films like The Big Short hadn't come out yet, and there weren't many kids who could talk through financial instruments in depth and spin webs between finance and geopolitics.

The less glamorous secret was that I happened to live across the road from a library. I squatted there most schooldays if I didn't have detention, making sure to arrive home at the same late hour each day regardless so my parents couldn't tell the difference when I *did* have detention. It was the place I hid when I had nothing to do, and I happened to have read several books on finance because I'd decided that finance law was the only thing I wanted to do. All I needed was an original angle.

I'd presented to five directors. Four said yes. The one that said no ended up being my boss.

When the time came, I took a similar approach with that second 'final interview' with the law firm. The thesis I'd developed by this point was that the more audacious it was for me to be in the interview room in the first place, the more outrageous I'd have to be to pull it off.

So when the senior partner asked me to propose a solution to speculation that Greece might leave the Eurozone and revert to the Drachma (a hypothetical event fondly referred to as 'Grexit' before

Brexit was within the realm of contemplation), I told him that the real solution was for Germany to leave the EU instead and revert to the Deutsche Mark. Germany was the only country in the EU at the time with a budget surplus, and the wealthiest EU countries wasted too many resources, propping up the rest. Take out Germany, and the Eurozone could reset at a lower baseline, which suited the average of the remaining struggling economies.

I remember leaving that interview having no idea how it went. I had thought on my feet and defended my ideas well, but the stone faces on the other side of the table gave me no clues about how my performance went over. After I walked out, I sat in the courtyard in the shadow of the building and shed a tear or six. This was my dream firm, and all my hopes hung on that singular opportunity.

Almost every morning for the next five years I had the good fortune to walk past that spot where I'd cried, as an occasional reminder that the 'impossible' in 'impossible dream' is a figment of your imagination.

The secret isn't being ridiculous for the sake of being ridiculous. It's ignoring the boxes everyone else is trying to check and pouring all your energy into the one thing you can be better at than anyone else. I can read a lot, quite quickly, and make interesting connections between ideas. It's a simple edge, but it's served me well. It's the exact same thing I do with my newsletter today, which is read by legions of strangers and now helps pay my bills.

If you don't know what that superpower is for you yet, mess around and find out. Try things. Find what feels like fun to you but feels like work to others, and camp out on that competitive advantage while building up ancillary skills.

Remember, there are only two interview strategies: fit the criteria precisely or prove the criteria wrong. Pick one route and max out on it. If you're an unconventional candidate, don't waste time proving you can fit conventionally. Show them why convention sucks. This applies equally to work, dating, and anything else you have to put yourself forward for.

Win the Small Hill

There are two ways to be successful: winning small, and winning big. The easiest way to win big is to be the best. But you might not always be the smartest, fastest, or strongest. If you're not born within touching distance of the top, you'll likely have to find another path. Fortunately, there is one. When you can't easily dominate the big hill, you should find a smaller one to conquer. Often, you can leverage each small win for a larger one. Instead of focusing on the big box like everyone else, find a niche to corner, an intersection to master, or a category to create.

Faheem Najm, aka T-Pain, is better known as the king of Auto-Tune. He blew up in the mid-2000s with hits like Buy U a Drank, Kiss Kiss feat. Chris Brown, Good Life feat. Kanye West, and Low feat. Flo Rida. It's a strong discography, and he's been able to maintain a cult following despite not having been at the forefront of popular music in the decades since.

The rise of autotune made it possible for artists to perform believable melodies without having natural singing talent. And because T-Pain made Auto-Tune popular, a lot of people came to assume that he couldn't sing. They were wrong.

T-Pain has a great singing voice. He can probably sing better than 75% of comparable musicians. But singing 'pretty good' won't get you to the top of the charts. T-Pain can sing, rap, and produce, but ultimately made his name with the unmistakable warble of digitally altered vocals. Now he's a legend.

Here's the thing. If T-Pain rapped and sang in his natural voice, his songs would still pop, but they wouldn't be hits. When he rapped, he'd have to compete with Kanye West. When he sang, he'd have to compete with Chris Brown. But by using Autotune, he escaped those comparisons completely. His potential enemies became his allies. Those other artists were happy to feature on his tracks because his style was complementary rather than competitive.

By defining the game he chose to play, and winning on a smaller hill, T-Pain was able to win the bigger prizes by creating and dominating a unique category first.

Josh Peck did something similar, but it almost crushed him.

Get Big or Go Home

Drake and Josh was one of Nickelodeon's most popular shows, and it put Josh Peck on the map. Peck himself admits in retrospect that he only got his first headline role in part because he was the fun, lovable, chunky guy. It's the same role he had played on almost anything he featured in before then, and it was a beloved Hollywood archetype.

Before Drake & Josh came out in 2004, Josh Peck had played three different characters called 'Fat Boy' and one called 'Slim'—an ironic joke. He was knee-deep in a single lane. There was already a category carved out for people who looked and sounded like him, and he fit right in.

As he grew older, however, Peck realised the problem with being sorted neatly into a pre-labelled box. The cold reality, several roles into his career, was that his weight was no longer just an internal psychological battle. Losing weight could fix his health and self-esteem, but it might also doom his career.

As a bigger guy, you could get big-guy roles. Showing up fat, with piles of charisma, when you audition for roles labelled 'fat boy' is guaranteed to be the easiest money you'll ever make. It was a smaller hill—one he was skilled enough to conquer. But losing weight meant he could no longer fit the big guy archetype. He tried to take care of his health, lost a tonne of weight, and suddenly he was having to audition for the same roles as Marvel heartthrob Chris Hemsworth.

The benefits of puberty were also an obstacle. Now taller and slimmer, Josh was quickly sizing out of slam-dunk roles and suddenly had to fight for any opportunity. His pants got slimmer, his parts got smaller, and his addiction to drugs grew deeper. So even when he got jobs, he'd fizzle out on set and be a pain to work with.

Peck didn't go out without a fight. He would still fight for solid roles but decided to find another game he could win—a box that he could put his own label on. By being one of the first stars to pivot to social media, Josh Peck was able to build a secure lifestyle as a creator through YouTube and sponsorships, which he could leverage to get himself back into global headlights.

Winning the small game is only a route to success if you can leverage each position for the next. If you can't find a way to exploit the system, the system will exploit you. Containers for your identity become constraints if you can't find a new way to define yourself.

There are better singers and rappers than T-Pain who never charted. There are more talented child actors than Josh Peck who faded into obscurity. Sometimes, to win the game you're optimising for in the long run, you must be willing to lose the ones you've been told were important. Find games you can win and tune out the rest.

If a map you can follow doesn't exist, create your own. Chart a course you can conquer; find a hill you can dominate. If you can beat them on the hill, you will crush it on the mountain.

How to Forge Your Own Path

1. Recognise the comfort and risk of boxes: labels and categories can feel safe, but they often become cages that limit your growth. Don't blindly accept any label—even flattering ones—without understanding the tradeoffs they demand.

2. Design your own container: If you don't naturally fit into an existing path, create a box of your own making. Craft an identity around your unique strengths and passions. The edges may be rough at first, but it's the only box that can grow with you.

3. Choose originality over conformity: When you realise that you don't fit the typical mould, resist the urge to contort yourself to fit. Difference is your edge. Show why convention is limiting, not why you can measure up to it.

4. Win the small hill first: Don't obsess over the biggest prizes from the outset. Conquer a niche, a smaller domain where your talents shine brightest. Use it as a launchpad to tackle bigger opportunities on your terms.

5. Leverage your differences: The traits that make you an outsider in one context can make you a pioneer in another. Like T-Pain's autotune, find a way to reframe your supposed weakness into an undeniable asset.

6. Refuse to be defined by others: Sovereignty requires owning your narrative. When you let others dictate your box, you surrender your agency. Craft your story so it reflects who you are, and what you aim to become.

7. Stay fluid, stay ready: Even the best-built box can become a new trap. Keep an eye on evolving opportunities and be ready to break out or pivot. Like Josh Peck, keep redefining yourself rather than letting old labels limit your future.

13

LIFT THE WEIGHT

"In theory there is no difference between theory and practice. In practice there is."

— Benjamin Brewster

The heaviest weight a person can lift isn't forged from iron or steel. It's the unbearable lightness of potential—a weight that can be everything and nothing at once.

Many of us carry a comforting delusion that we could conquer the world if we actually decided to try one day. It's that honey-sweet lie you sell yourself as you scroll through success stories, nodding sagely. *"I could do that,"* you say, *"if I really wanted to."*

There's a secret comfort in not trying things. We cradle our potential like a precious egg, terrified it might crack if we dare to hatch it. Untested potential is a paralytic force. It keeps you frozen, afraid to move, lest you shatter the illusion of your imagined greatness.

Your perceived potential grows bigger as expectations are stacked onto it, like an invisible weight attached to you at all times. But eventually, you've got to lift that weight. The longer you leave it hanging there without harnessing it, the more it will weigh you down.

At first, it feels great. You may look at the growing weight of your potential and say "Wow, look what I could lift". The people around you, at every stage of your early life and career, might look at you and say

"Wow, I can't believe she can lift that". And in the process, expectation grows, pressure mounts, the weight accumulates.

The longer you leave your potential untested, the more it swells, and the heavier it gets. But as time passes—when no one actually sees you pick up the weight—the thing that could have made you feel superhuman will eventually make you feel fragile.

To quote British writer Cyril Connolly in his riff on an old Roman idiom:

> "Whom the gods wish to destroy, they first call promising."
>
> — Cyril Connolly

Potential without proof is just a comforting myth. Potential holds you back until you actually attempt to utilise it. But lifting the weight requires confronting reality, testing your limits, and transforming potential into actual ability.

The Venus Trap

For a moment, imagine being Venus Williams. You're fourteen years old. Your father has been telling you, and anyone with ears to listen, that you're destined to be a tennis champion. An all-time great. But unlike other tennis prodigies, you haven't actually played in any junior tournaments. Your father wanted to protect you from burnout on the junior circuit, but now people are starting to wonder if there's fire behind the smoke. Your potential is untested, existing only in the dreams of your father and the confines of your practice court.

Then comes the moment of truth. It's 1994, and you're making your professional debut at the Bank of the West Classic in Oakland, California. The world is watching, eager to see if the hype matches reality. This is where the rubber meets the road, where potential transforms into performance or evaporates into disappointment.

In your first match, you face Shaun Stafford, ranked 59th in the world. You win in straight sets, 6-3, 6-4. The victory seems to confirm everything your father has been saying. Everything you've been waiting to validate. You really are the next big thing in tennis. The weight of potential feels lighter than ever.

But tennis tournaments don't end after one match. In the second round, you face Arantxa Sánchez Vicario, the World No. 2; the elite level of tennis personified. The weight of your potential suddenly feels much heavier.

This match is a brutal reality check. After a fast start winning the first set 6–2, Vicario dismantles your game, beating you 6-3, 6-0. It's not even close. In the span of two days, you've experienced both the intoxicating high of living up to your potential and the sobering low of realising just how far you still have to go.

This is what it means to lift the weight. Not simply trying to prove you're the best, but honestly assessing where you stand. Lifting the weight means transforming the nebulous but comforting "what if" into a concrete "what is."

Venus Williams didn't crumble after that big, public defeat. Instead, she used it as a benchmark. A clear indicator of the work ahead. Over the next few years, she honed her skills, improved her game, and eventually became the champion she (and her father) had always dreamt of.

But none of that would have been possible if she had remained in the safe cocoon of the training ground. By stepping onto that court, Venus replaced soothing illusions with hard truths. And those truths, however uncomfortable, became the foundation of her future success.

This is the paradox of potential: failure can be more valuable than success. A win might temporarily validate your potential, but a loss gives you a roadmap for improvement. Both outcomes are infinitely more useful than the paralysing comfort of unused ability.

Success isn't always guaranteed. Developing a mindset of trying regardless of the odds can allow us to lift weights heavier than we could ever imagine.

For George Dantzig, approaching the problem with an open mind allowed him to solve what was thought to be impossible.

The Dantzig Dilemma

Sometimes things are only as hard as you expect them to be. While Venus Williams knew she was stepping into the arena, George Dantzig's story shows us that ignorance, at times, can be a *superpower*.

In 1939, Dantzig was a doctoral candidate at the University of California, Berkeley. One day, he arrived late to his graduate statistics class. Scribbled on the blackboard were two problems. Assuming they were homework, Dantzig jotted them down.

He found the problems unusually difficult, but after several days of intense work, he solved them. When he finally turned them in, he apologised to his professor for taking so long.

The professor was stunned. Those "homework" problems were actually two famous unsolved problems in statistics. Problems that had stumped mathematicians for years, Dantzig had solved in days, simply because he didn't know he couldn't.

Dantzig's story underscores the weight of perception itself. While Venus had to shoulder immense expectations, Dantzig bypassed that weight entirely by not realising how impossible the problems were supposed to be.

Your frame of what's possible changes when you approach challenges with an open mind and a willingness to try. Attempting the lift not because you're sure you can, but because you're curious to see what happens if you do.

Identify one area in your life where you've been relying on the comfort of potential rather than the reality of action. It could be a skill you think you could master, a project you've been putting off, or a change you've been contemplating. Commit to lifting that weight; trying regardless of the outcome. Set a concrete goal and a deadline. Take that first step, however small.

How to Manage Your Burden

1. Test your potential in the real world. Don't let the comfort of "what if" keep you in stasis. Even a small attempt will give you clarity.

2. Approach challenges with fresh eyes. Like Dantzig, tackle new problems as if they're solvable. Forget how "hard" they're supposed to be.

3. Learn from the first attempt. Don't be afraid of falling short. Venus didn't let an early loss define her; she used it to map her future training.

4. Set a clear challenge for yourself. Pick one area you've been avoiding and set a specific, measurable goal with a short timeline.

5. Treat your potential like a muscle. Muscles grow by repeated stress and adaptation. So does potential—by lifting heavier each time.

6. Separate potential from perfection. Don't wait to be "ready." Perfection is an illusion. Progress comes from acting before you feel prepared.

14

MOVE THE MEAN

"There is only one way to avoid criticism: do nothing, say nothing, and be nothing."

— Elbert Hubbard

Confidence compounds through iterative effort. The easiest way to build it isn't with big swings. It's by taking enough swings to nudge your average outcome upwards.

In baseball, a player's batting average is a key measure of their offensive success. It's calculated by dividing the number of hits by the number of at-bats. The crucial note is that you can't have a batting average after just one swing. You need multiple attempts. Some will be hits, some will be misses, but over time, you establish a baseline—your average performance.

Life works the same way. You can't judge your capabilities, your potential, or your progress based on a single attempt. You must step up to the plate again and again, establishing your baseline and then working to improve it. To achieve sustained success, you'll have to move your mean.

A Cold Night in Hamburg

We're in a grimy club in Hamburg's red-light district. It's 1960. Cigarette butts dance like shrivelling fireflies through the musk of fresh smoke and stale beer. On stage, four lads from Liverpool are playing their hearts out, sweat dripping from their brows as they power through their third hour of performance. This isn't a special night. It's just Tuesday. They'll come back to the club and do it all again tomorrow, and the next day, and the day after that.

This punishing schedule wasn't a choice – it was a necessity. 'The Beatles', still unknown and unpolished, were paying their dues in the most literal sense. They played for hours on end, night after night, for two years straight. Why? Because they had to eat. Because they had nowhere else to go. And because, whether they realised it or not, they were slowly but surely moving their mean.

John, Paul, George, and Pete (yes, Pete – Ringo wasn't in the picture yet) lived in a cramped room behind a cinema screen, sleeping on bunk beds and subsisting on not much more than beer and pretzels. Each night was a swing of the bat, an opportunity to refine their craft, expand their repertoire, and hone their stage presence. They weren't hitting home runs every night – far from it. But with each performance, they were getting a step closer to 'overnight success'.

Over the slow course of 300 nights, their performances got a little tighter, a little more confident, a little more "Beatles-esque". But here's the magic: if you happened to show up at a club in Hamburg one cold night in the early '60s, you'd never know it was their 217th night performing, but your experience of watching them was infinitely better than if you'd shown up just a few months earlier. Each rep vanished into myth as soon as the sun came up, and The Beatles were better for it.

The Writing Wizard of Utah

Brandon Sanderson is, quite likely, the most prolific and popular writer you've never heard of. Unless, like me, you're into fantasy novels, in which case he's your LeBron James.

While most fantasy authors dream of signing books at Comic-Con, Sanderson has an entire convention each year, Dragonsteel, dedicated solely to the lore of his books. He's responsible for the biggest Kickstarter crowdfund in history simply because one year, outside of the books he was already contracted to write, he wrote an extra four 'secret projects' and his fans paid $42 million in pre-orders to get their hands on copies.

These fans didn't know the names of the books or what they would be about. All they knew was that one night an author they loved had uploaded an unexpected YouTube video with the promise of new writing, and within 48 hours they'd already forked over $18 million.

Knowing now that he's reached this level of success—enough that he could afford to build an underground lair to work in, with 20-foot-high ceilings and a private cinema—it's hard to believe that Sanderson's story started with crushing rejection. But it did. Lots of it. Sanderson's first novel, written at 19, was turned down by every publisher he approached. His second met the same fate. And his third. And fourth. And fifth.

Imagine writing a full-length novel, and nobody seems to care. Now imagine doing it 12 more times, knowing that not a single one will ever see the light of day. This was Brandon Sanderson's early career. Before becoming a fantasy powerhouse, Sanderson wrote *thirteen* novels that went nowhere. But "nowhere" is relative. While these books never made it to bookstore shelves, they took Sanderson exactly where he needed to go.

In 2005, the fantasy world was introduced to a "new" author named Brandon Sanderson. His debut novel, "Elantris", was met with critical acclaim. But it wasn't really his debut. It was his sixth novel. The sixth of thirteen. He was already seven books better than his breakout debut by the time anyone even knew his name.

When success finally came, Sanderson wasn't scrambling to deliver a follow-up. He was ready with a backlog of completed works and a well-honed writing process. He'd turned himself into a one-man publishing powerhouse, not overnight, but over years of dedicated practice. And now the spotlight can barely keep up.

With each of those early books, Sanderson moved his mean, improving his confidence through steady incremental improvement. By the time he "arrived" on the scene, he had far more writing experience than many published authors.

Stack the Bricks

Much like the floor and ceiling rules we discussed earlier, the Beatles and Sanderson raised their floor through private practice. They incubated their talent, moving their mean by refining their craft before emerging to a broader audience. But confidence can equally be built in public by slowly stacking small bricks of proof until you have a tower that's undeniable and unassailable. Issa Rae built her foundation like this, in the spotlight.

In 2011, Issa Rae was just another college graduate with big dreams and an empty résumé. But she had something that would prove more valuable than any fancy degree – a laptop, a camera, and an idea.

That idea was "Awkward Black Girl", a web series she wrote, produced, and starred in, uploading episodes to YouTube. The show, which followed the cringe-worthy adventures of "J", resonated with a set of viewers who rarely saw themselves represented on screen.

The first episode was 3 minutes and 40 seconds, and the production quality was utterly unremarkable. Just a shaky, handheld vlog with blown-out highlights and occasionally garbled audio. But she clearly cared about story, craft, and communicating something people immediately understood. Issa wasn't waiting for permission or validation from traditional gatekeepers. She was building her own foundation, one awkward moment at a time.

As the series gained traction, 30,000 views became 60,000, then 100,000. Each episode released was a brick of solid proof. Proof of effort. Proof of work. Proof of her ability to show up, and do the thing she said she was going to do. And Issa's stack of bricks was growing taller week by week. A loyal fanbase. Press coverage. Awards for web content. Each achievement, no matter how small, added to her growing credibility.

Issa didn't rest on her laurels when the first season ended. She launched a Kickstarter campaign to fund a second, raising over $56,000. Another brick in her wall of proof that she could create content people wanted to see. Issa's consistent output and growing fanbase eventually caught the eye of Pharrell Williams, who offered her a platform on his YouTube channel for season two. Her stack of bricks was now tall enough to be noticed by industry heavyweights.

By 2013, "Awkward Black Girl" had amassed millions of views and won a Shorty Award for Best Web Show. Many in her position would accept this as comforting validation. But the Sovereign mindset sees wins and reframes them as compounding leverage. Issa used this success to pitch a book deal, adding another significant brick to her stack. The resulting book became a best-selling memoir, giving her the momentum and leverage to pitch her show to HBO. The network saw her body of work—her tower of bricks—and green-lit "Insecure".

"Insecure" debuted in 2016, five years after that first shaky YouTube video. It wasn't an overnight success story. Issa had built a body of work that made her value and capabilities hard to question. And she'd done it all without permission, without accreditation, without waiting.

Over the next six years, Issa racked up two Golden Globe awards for Best Actress, three Emmy nominations for Best Actress, and an Emmy award. Today, Issa Rae is a household name, with multiple shows, a production company, and a string of accolades to her name. She did it the Sovereign way, on her own steam, one brick at a time.

Whether you build in public or in private in the early days, the lesson is the same: you don't need to wait for gatekeepers. You don't need to rely on self-belief. You don't need to wait for respect, approval or validation. If you want to be a writer, write. If you want to be an actor, act. If you want to be a dealmaker, source deals. Not having access to the final version of what you want shouldn't stop you from intentionally developing the skills you'll need in advance. Start early.

> *"Start where you are. Use what you have. Do what you can"*

Arthur Ashe

Starting small doesn't mean you need to stay small. Your attempts don't need to follow a linear progression. You can stack them in a way that allows you to continually level up and leverage yourself to new heights.

> The evidence is in your actions. Put down one brick at a time, and build an undeniable stack of proof that you are who you say you are.

Update Your Machine

Fear and ego are the twin enemies of progress.

Fear tells you not to try because you might fail. Ego tells you not to try because you're already good enough. Both keep you stagnant, trapped in a comfort zone that feels safe but is actually suffocating your potential.

Moving the mean requires that you silence both these voices. It demands that you embrace discomfort, and actively seek out situations where you might fail. Because the path to mastery is paved with failures.

Neuroscience confirms this. Each time you push past your comfort zone, you're rewiring your brain, creating new neural pathways that make future attempts easier. It's how the impossible becomes possible, then routine.

Here's how you start moving your mean today:

1. **Set a baseline:** You can't improve what you don't measure. Whatever skill you're working on, find a way to quantify it. Words written per day. Sales calls made. Problems solved. This is your starting point.

2. **Embrace volume:** Forget perfection. Aim for quantity over

quality, at least at first. Don't be afraid to try 100 things that don't work, as long as the average quality of your output keeps ticking upwards. Volume is the secret sauce of improvement.

3. **Build in public:** Even if your early output feels clumsy, share some version of your work. Each artefact builds credibility. Publish drafts. Share learnings. Document progress. Create feedback loops that give you information after each attempt.

4. **Challenge your mean:** Routinely step slightly outside your comfort zone. Push your baseline upwards by deliberately attempting harder things. Don't just practice—progress.

5. **Celebrate small wins:** Track visible improvement. Not milestones, but movement. Confidence is built by seeing yourself grow. Proof compounds, and so does self-trust.

15

TAKE YOUR SEAT

"The day came when the risk to remain tight in a bud was more painful than the risk it took to blossom."

— Anaïs Nin

Success is a shape-shifter. It transforms the moment you grasp it, morphing from a clear, tangible goal into a complex and unwieldy beast—the often overwhelming reality that lurks behind an alluring idea:

You want to be the boss until you have to make the tough calls. You dream of being a parent until you have to wake up at 3am and deal with self-doubt about how badly you're messing up your kid.

There's an old Haitian proverb which says, *"Behind mountains are more mountains."* This is the paradox of achievement. You scale the mountain expecting a resplendent view, only to find another peak looming in the distance. Or worse, you reach the summit and find it didn't look like what you expected, and you have no idea what comes next.

Reaching a goal is just the beginning. The real test isn't in getting the position, it's in rising to its demands. It's in the daily choice to step up, to lean in, to fully embrace the role you've worked so hard to attain.

For many, this is where the journey stalls. We find ourselves standing at the threshold of our achievements, one foot in and one foot out, grappling with the weight of expectations – both external and self-imposed. This liminal space between accomplishment and ownership is where your real work begins.

It's easy to falter in this moment, disorientated by dissonance. You achieve the position but struggle to inhabit it. You have the title but not the confidence. The role, but not the readiness. This seemingly bottomless valley between external success and internal alignment is where impostor syndrome thrives and emerging greatness retreats.

Executive coach Andy Christinger calls this 'taking your seat': the transformation required for a founder to grow into being the CEO that their company needs. But it applies far more broadly, to the necessary evolution of your self-identity.

The Fangless Spider

A common theme in superhero origin stories is the try-fail cycle where the hero struggles to accept their new identity.

One of my favourite such arcs was in Spiderman 2 (2004) specifically because it happens long after Peter Parker has taken on the Spiderman mantle. He's already got the powers. Made the costume. Kissed the girl. But deep down, he still hadn't stepped into the role required of him. He still wasn't ready for what it takes. He wanted the highs he'd dreamt of, without the difficulties that came with it.

Peter Parker didn't wake up one day and decide to quit being Spider-Man. It was a slow, creeping realisation that being a hero was costing him everything else.

Two years into his double life, Peter was drowning. His grades were in freefall, his boss at the Daily Bugle was one missed deadline away from firing him, and the girl he loved was slipping away. Every time he put on the Spiderman mask, a little piece of Peter Parker disappeared.

So he did what any rational person would do. He quit. Threw his costume in the trash and walked away. And for a moment, I'm sure it felt like freedom.

But the city didn't stop needing Spider-Man just because Peter Parker needed a break. Him not doing the job didn't mean the job didn't need doing. Crime rates soared. A new villain, Doc Ock, emerged. And Peter found himself watching helplessly as the city he'd sworn to protect crumbled around him.

It wasn't until a heart-to-heart with Aunt May about the nature of heroism that Peter realised the truth. Being Spider-Man wasn't a job he could clock in and out of. It was who he was. Who he would need to become. Putting on the mask wasn't enough. He couldn't just pretend. If he was going to be Spider-Man, he would need to *be* Spider-Man. Peter needed to take his seat.

This doesn't just happen to comic book characters. In many of our lives, reaching that first piece of success won't be the end of the road. But you'll never be able to move beyond that first mountain if you don't realise that each level of success requires an evolution in your identity. Each rung you climb will require you to grow – to internalise the requirements of your new baseline.

Even when great power falls into your lap, you won't be able to wield it effectively until you accept the requisite level of responsibility.

The Virgin Queen

Elizabeth Tudor wasn't born to rule. Seen by many as the illegitimate child of an unlawful marriage, Henry VIII's second daughter had a tragic path to the throne. When she finally ascended at 25, few expected the redheaded girl to last long in the cutthroat world of 16th-century politics.

She was young, untested, and facing a nation in crisis. The treasury was empty, religious tensions were at a boiling point, and every European power was eyeing England like vultures circling a wounded animal.

For a while, it seemed the sceptics might be right. The young queen hesitated. She wavered on key decisions. She danced around marriage proposals, deflected inquisitions about bearing an heir, and procrastinated on religious reforms. Elizabeth had the crown, though she hadn't mentally claimed the throne.

But slowly, then quickly, something changed. She found her voice and crafted her image. The hesitant girl became the "Virgin Queen", married to her country.

Her crucible was facing the Spanish Armada in 1588. As the greatest naval force in Europe bore down on English shores, Elizabeth couldn't afford to falter. Thirty thousand men and some 2000 cannon crossed the ocean towards her, with the express intent of removing her from power and bringing England back under Catholic rule. The chips were down. The enemy was at the gate. The survival of her nation depended on how ready she was to commit to the role she had inherited.

Refusing to cower in the comfort of her castle, Elizabeth resolved to join her men, mounting a white horse and riding out to Tilbury, the coast of the battle. It was here that she made her most famous speech, as much a call to arms as it was a moment of self-ascendance. It was Elizabeth's public declaration that she was done second-guessing herself:

> *"I know I have the body of a weak and feeble woman, but I have the heart and stomach of a king [...] I myself will take up arms, I myself will be your general, judge, and rewarder of every one of your virtues in the field. [...] by your obedience to my general, by your concord in the camp, and your valour in the field, we shall shortly have a famous victory over these enemies of my God, of my kingdom, and of my people."*
>
> — Queen Elizabeth I

In the moment of delivering that address, Elizabeth finally stepped into her power. The crown, no longer a burden, was an extension of herself. Elizabeth had taken her seat, transforming from an uncertain heir into "Gloriana", the monarch who would define an entire era of history – the Elizabethan age.

Lean Into Greatness

We're all familiar with the concept of 'faking it till you make it.' But what happens when you've made it, and you're still faking it?

This is the heart of the psychological battle in taking your seat. It's dealing with the disconnect between external achievement and internal alignment. You've got the job title, the corner office, the accolades – but your brain hasn't caught up yet.

When I first realised I was making six figures independently, I felt on the verge of a breakdown. It manifested as a gnawing, destabilising, internally chaotic crisis of identity. It was hard to wrap my head around the amount coming into my account each month. I still remembered being in my first year of university, walking 45 minutes to the supermarket to save 4p on a pack of 29p crackers. That's mostly what I subsisted on at the time, while studying law and working part-time in private security.

In the neighbourhood I would walk to, which was slightly cheaper than my own, £2.50 could buy me 10 packs of crackers instead of 8, and I'd make the extra packs last. Twice in that period, I remember seeing my bank account in single decimal place figures: £0.06, and £0.08. No crackers that week, unless a friend could bail me out. And now, years later, I'd gotten so used to the assumed identity of being 'poor' that I had no idea how to cope with the ways my life was already changing.

I would walk around my new neighbourhood, looking at the occasional Range Rover or BMW and lament the fact that I couldn't afford one. And then I remembered that inside each of those houses was an entire family – with two people, likely in their 50s, who had worked for a very long time to afford that house and car. Meanwhile I, still in my 20s, lived in one of the most expensive houses on the street, and my household income had only one contributor.

I still had a full-time job, but I made more money outside that job than I made in it. I was just showing up because I wanted the psychological safety of a monthly paycheck. At first, I was saving 30% of my job's take-home pay. Then 50%. Then I was saving my entire paycheck. Eventually, I was saving more each month than my pre-tax income. It was mind-boggling, and I was scared. I was living in a dream and a voice in my head was telling me the walls could cave in at any second. It was insane. I felt insane. I wasn't rich—but I wasn't poor anymore either. The only demons left to slay were the ones inside my head.

Psychologists call this cognitive dissonance; the mental gymnastics your brain does when your self-image doesn't match your reality. And it's exhausting. But this discomfort isn't a sign that you don't belong. They're growing pains. Your brain is rewiring itself, adjusting to your new reality. It's uncomfortable, sure. But it's also necessary.

Taking your seat means pushing through this discomfort, actively working to align your self-perception with your achievements. It means accepting not just the privileges of your position, but the weight. Once you stop fighting your own success, you can finally wield it.

> The seat doesn't make the leader. The leader makes the seat.

Once you anchor yourself in confidence, you can sift out arrogance and ego. You can accurately assess your abilities and position. You can show up fully, not just for yourself, but for those who depend on you.

16

BOLD, NOT BLIND

"Katte kabuto no o wo shime yo" /
"After victory, tighten your helmet."

— Japanese proverb (oft. attributed to Tokugawa Ieyasu)

In 1988, Michael Spinks walked into a boxing ring undefeated. His record was perfect: 31-0. He'd never even been knocked down once in his professional career. He was the golden boy who'd moved up from light heavyweight to claim heavyweight gold, outfoxing every opponent he'd faced.

91 seconds later, for all his confidence, Spinks was on his back, staring at the ceiling. He would never fight again.

It's a powerful reminder of what can happen when our internal narratives collide with reality. In Spinks' case, reality took the form of a 21-year-old Mike Tyson.

Spinks wasn't delusional. He was legitimately great – an Olympic gold medallist who had successfully moved up from light heavyweight to become a heavyweight champion. His confidence was built on a foundation of real achievement. A record built brick by brick. He had solved every problem the ring had presented him. Until he couldn't.

Confidence, when misplaced, can be dangerous. When earned through consistent success, your confidence can feel unshakeable. Each victory becomes evidence of invincibility. Each problem solved becomes proof that all problems are solvable. But reality doesn't care about your track record. Sometimes, everything you know still won't prepare you for the one thing you don't. As Mike Tyson would later famously quip:

> *"Everyone has a plan until they get punched in the face."*
>
> — Mike Tyson

> As much as you know, remember there will still be things you don't. As competent as you are, understand that you may eventually run into a problem you're not yet equipped to solve. The trick is not losing composure completely when reality strikes.

The fascinating thing about the Spinks-Tyson fight isn't simply that Spinks lost. It's that his entire framework for understanding reality collapsed in less than two minutes. All his skill, all his experience, all his previous solutions — none of it survived contact with Tyson's first punch.

After the first hit, fear set in. It camped out in his hippocampus and slowly spread through his body. It sank into his bones, making him slower and weaker. It cemented his defeat. And the fear didn't leave his mind once the bout ended — it drove him into immediate retirement.

It's easy to spin elaborate theories about why we're different, why our approach is special, why the rules don't apply to us. We mistake our streaks of success for laws of nature. But reality comes for us all eventually. The question isn't whether you'll have your own 91-second reality check. It's whether you'll learn from a hard knock and adapt, or allow it to crush you.

Confidence should make you bold, but not blind. Your expertise should make you effective, but not invincible.

The Best Time to Lose

You're most vulnerable to a loss after a big win. Sports analysts call this phenomenon the "hangover effect." Teams that dominate one week often stumble the next. Boxers who demolish opponents sometimes get their world rocked in the following fight. Stock traders who hit massive gains frequently throw them away in subsequent trades.

Success can make you complacent.

To quote the war-weary ronin, Kambei Shimada, in Akira Kurosawa's 1954 classic film 'Seven Samurai':

> *"When you think you're safe is precisely when you're most vulnerable."*
>
> — Kambei Shimada (Seven Samurai)

You see this when the company known for past innovation doesn't maintain its rate of development. When the founder who raises a massive round of funding burns through it faster than peers on shoestring budgets. When students who learn they can ace tests without studying eventually bomb hard.

The psychology behind this is predictable. Victory breeds overconfidence. Success reduces vigilance. Winning feels like validation that you've cracked the code, that the hard work is over, that you can now coast on talent and the compounding returns of prior success.

This also plays out in more subtle ways. In the UK, over 60% of car accidents occur within 7 miles of the driver's home. In the US, it's nearly 80% within 10 miles. The easy answer is that most car rides are short-distance and local. But a substantial factor nonetheless is the lull of the familiar. The complacency of comfort. You drive a long way home and switch your mind off with the finish line in sight, believing you no longer need to concentrate.

The mechanism behind the hangover effect also works in reverse. Counterintuitively, you're also more likely to win after taking a pounding.

The fighter who fights her way out of the corner begins the next round stronger. The startup that escapes bankruptcy in its first year eventually outlasts better-funded competitors. The driver who survives a near miss keeps his eyes on a swivel.

A hard loss navigated early helps strip away illusions. It forces you to confront reality. It eliminates the luxury of half-measures and demands your full attention. When your back is against the wall, you stop taking success for granted and start fighting for it.

This truth, once acknowledged, becomes a powerful weapon.

The Romans had a specific ritual during triumphant parades. As victorious generals rode through the streets receiving adulation, a slave would stand behind them whispering, "Memento mori"—remember you will die.

While morbid on the surface, it served a practical purpose. To remind those with power that victory is the most dangerous moment, when hubris can destroy what competence has built. When hard-won efforts can be snatched away in an instant.

"Pride leads to destruction, and arrogance to downfall," goes the biblical proverb.

In the words of Seneca:

> *"Let us prepare our minds as if we'd come to the very end of life. Let us postpone nothing. Let us balance life's books each day... The one who puts the finishing touches on their life each day is never short of time."*
>
> — Lucius Annaeus Seneca

Stress-test your strategies when things are going well. Assume competitors are gaining ground, even when you feel ahead. Practice as if you're behind even when you're winning.

At the height of Amazon's e-commerce dominance, Jeff Bezos insisted the company operate with what he termed a "Day One" mentality – the hunger and paranoia of a startup still fighting for survival.

While competitors celebrated market position, Amazon kept acting like an underdog.

The emotional state that creates victory is different from the emotional state that victory creates. Don't let the scent of success dull your senses.

Victory creates satisfaction, relaxation, room for overconfidence. Defeat, for those with ambition, forces hunger, focus, and humility.

The best time to lose is when you can control it – when the stakes are manageable and the lessons are valuable. Take calculated risks when you're ahead. Seek out challenges that stretch your capabilities. Put yourself in situations where failure is possible but not catastrophic.

If you don't manufacture your own defeats—small losses you can learn and recover from rapidly—the world will manufacture them for you. And its timing is rarely convenient.

Overconfidence is a curse. Stay hungry when fed. Stay vigilant when safe. Stay humble when celebrated. The moment you think you've won is often the moment you start losing.

Competence

Knowledge is potential, but skill is power. The world often seems to elevate style above substance, but competence is the bedrock of lasting success.

Competence lies in mastering the essential and continuously expanding your capabilities. It's the difference between talking a good game and delivering results consistently.

True competence is built through deliberate practice, relentless curiosity, and the willingness to fail repeatedly in pursuit of mastery. You don't need to chase perfection – that's a useless mirage. Focus instead on consistent improvement. Competence compounds. Each mistake, setback, or challenge overcome adds another layer to your skillset.

While others celebrate shortcuts and quick fixes, competence chases the long game. It craves the enduring pursuit of mastery. The accumulation of thousands of hours of focused effort. The result of pushing beyond your comfort zone, of acknowledging and persisting through ignorance, of becoming a novice again and again.

Confidence feeds competence; competence breeds confidence. It sets in motion a spiral of growth. It builds the quiet assurance of knowing you can handle what comes your way.

The path to competence is never-ending. There's always more to learn; always room for improvement. But it's on this path that we discover our real potential; that we become capable of achievements we had once thought impossible.

17

FIND SOMETHING

> *"The ultimate goal of farming is not the growing of crops, but the cultivation and perfection of human beings."*
>
> — Masanobu Fukuoka

Prove to yourself, as quickly as possible, that you can do something well. And then learn to do it better. Competence is a muscle that replicates itself. The first reps are the hardest, but replicating units of skill becomes easier with practice.

The world doesn't reward those who wait on the sidelines for the perfect moment. The perfect moment reveals itself to those who act, and set the world in motion.

If you are yet to develop firm conviction in your competence in any area, choose a task, a skill, a project—something you can master quickly. You need a win under your belt. It doesn't need to be groundbreaking or even related to your ultimate goals. What matters is that you can excel at something swiftly, with focused practice. Learn to code, to bake, or to take photos. These things may seem like trivial minutiae, but they will get you out of your own head.

It's incredible how many people are willing to wait patiently for genius to strike, having made peace with the termites of doubt burrowing through their brains which render them incapable of trying anything.

You don't need to find your life's purpose. You just need to prove to yourself that you're capable of excellence. And excellence can begin anywhere.

Once you know, deep in your bones, that you're capable of something, no one can disabuse you of your potential. You'll have an unshakeable truth you can build on. You can do something well. And if you can do something well, you can learn to do it better. You can refine a craft until you become great.

Your first taste of competence will give you momentum, and begin a chain reaction of confidence in your capabilities. When you succeed, you prove to yourself that you're capable of doing it again. When you fail, you can learn, adapt, and do it better the next time. The key is iteration. Never rest on an initial success; challenge yourself to improve, refine, and expand on what you've done. Keep your eyes inward, not on others. You don't need to be better than anyone. Play the infinite game against yourself to see how far you can go and how good you can be.

To compound your efforts, move quickly. If you spend months in training without a test, you'll lose valuable time and energy that could have been spent improving. Don't syphon away from your own momentum. Don't steal from your future inertia with inaction. The worst that can happen when you try something is failure, and failure is just feedback for your next attempt.

In every task, jump the hurdle of mediocrity where most people happily settle. Improvement is the path to mastery, and mastery is built on continual iteration.

Get good at one thing, then apply what you've learned to another domain. Find more hills you can conquer, however small; more land you can dominate, however seemingly insignificant. Then defend your territory. Don't let new knowledge diminish. Don't forget things you once proved you were capable of. When you forget, it creates a gap that your brain immediately fills with doubt. That seed of doubt will put a crack in your armour. This is how great empires fall.

Do Something on Purpose

As you turn your eye to your ultimate purpose, start by realising a secret that anyone great must eventually learn: you don't get paid to work; you get paid to solve problems. You get paid to add value. It's easy to keep yourself busy while contributing nothing of worth. You might fly under the radar that way and collect a few easy paycheques, but you can't build a mountain when you're hiding under a molehill. Eventually, you'll need to step into the arena. And then your mettle will be tested. You need something you can bring to the table.

If you want to be paid well, know that nobody parts with money voluntarily. They have to be compelled, and that compelling force usually stems from pain. We use money to alleviate our hunger, our tiredness and our lack of time. Money can also solve the pain of boredom, our need to communicate, and our desire to be entertained.

In the professional world, there are people who solve the pain of uncertainty by drafting ironclad contracts. There are people who solve the pain of poor design, branding and corporate strategy. That's just the tip of the iceberg. As our world grows more complex, fresh pains emerge – fresh fields to conquer and new ways to get paid.

In the span of 10 years, we went from social media not existing to it being a fundamental part of every company's marketing strategy. Brands were hobbled overnight because they failed to hire a competent social media manager, even though that job had previously never existed. New jobs are created every day, when new problems arise, and those problems become painful.

We part with money when it makes our life better, more convenient, or in the case of charity, to solve pain for someone who doesn't have the money to do it for themselves. Where pain exists, so does an opportunity to solve a problem. If you want to get paid for anything, find a pain and solve it. Don't wait to see the perfect job title or job description. People rarely know what they want – all they know is what hurts.

If you can diagnose a problem and fix it, nobody will care what was written on a piece of paper; your grades, your degree, your employment contract – these things don't define the value you can contribute. As long as you can keep pain at bay, you'll keep getting paid.

It doesn't matter what kind of pain you learn to solve – just start somewhere. The better you get, the more leeway you'll have to manoeuvre later, and get closer to what you want. There's no shame in good work. It's easy to become so preoccupied with 'finding your passion' that you believe every moment not spent in a state of transcendent self-alignment is a moment wasted.

Regardless of what immigrant parents may tell you, there's nothing wrong with making drinks for thirsty people. Even if it's at a local bar. Nor with making food for the hungry, even if it's at McDonald's. There's nothing wrong with caring for the sick – even if the particular nursing job you have now isn't everything you once dreamed of. All work is meaningful, so long as you solve problems, add value, and build skills.

The best part is knowing that your journey doesn't need to end there.

Find Problems Worth Solving

Once you know that you can solve some problems, you can think of what other problems you might turn your hand to. You can dream of solving bigger problems. More complex ones. More painful ones.

Some of those problems may require more knowledge than you currently have. That's okay. Just remember that the goal isn't to get some arbitrary qualification. The goal is to obtain the knowledge you need to solve a particular problem. Just enough to add more value and provide better answers. As long as you can do that, you'll get paid.

Sometimes you'll find that, despite common beliefs, you can amass enough knowledge to solve particular problems without a pricey associated degree, and also without first devoting years to a craft. You may find ways to leverage skills you already have, from problems you've already solved, and find new, creative answers.

Your unique lens becomes extremely valuable when you can solve problems in a way others can't. Now, you are adding unique value and can solve expensive problems. And you'll be compensated well for it.

That doesn't mean everyone will be transfixed by your problem-solving ability. Some may decide that you're not the right person to solve their particular problem. That's okay. Keep seeking tools to add to your kit. Find mental models, frameworks and ideas to navigate chaos with clarity. Improve your ability to learn and process new information. Make more robust decisions. Begin to recognise patterns across domains.

Add all of these things to your problem-solving toolbox, and become familiar enough with your tools to become versatile in deploying them. Learn the kind of problems you could solve with your electric screwdriver for people who think they're in need of a hammer.

Somewhere in your journey of solving problems, you'll find the ones that you're uniquely adapted to solving. The type of resolution that brings you joy. And you won't just fall in love with it because you went to the right school, or have reached a certain age, or seniority, or whatever magic boundary you think is prerequisite for a dream job. You'll love solving these problems because you're good at it - when there's just something special about the experiences you've gathered along the way and the tools you've acquired that makes you really really good at doing things like this.

Love What You Do

You've likely heard the saying "Do what you love and you'll never work a day in your life". It's a nice sentiment, but it's not necessarily true. The key to finding fulfilment in your work may be less to do with the specific type of work you do, and more to do with your attitude towards it.

Who loves chopping wood in the dead of winter? Who loves carrying water under blistering heat? If it was about love, no one would do it. The labour itself isn't intrinsically fulfilling, yet plenty find fulfilment in it. Work has the meaning you bring to it.

Take Paul Erdős, for example. He was a Hungarian mathematician known for his prolific output and his unconventional lifestyle. He spent much of his life travelling and collaborating with other mathematicians, often sleeping on their couches and subsisting on a diet of caffeine and amphetamines. Few people would volunteer to live like this. That lifestyle isn't fulfilling unless the work means enough to you.

Vincent Van Gogh, in the same vein, only sold one painting in his lifetime. Many aspiring artists wouldn't persist under such circumstances. Nobody loves being broke. But it's easy to keep going when you love the action more than the outcome. The way you feel about the work you do matters more than the work itself.

In a 1990 study at the University of Wisconsin-Madison, researchers set up two groups of rats on running wheels. One group could exercise voluntarily while the other group were forced to exercise for the exact same amount of time, because their running wheels were connected. The rats who exercised voluntarily got more health benefits from it and had fewer signs of anxiety and depression. The rats who felt forced to exercise showed the opposite. They were doing the exact same work, but with drastically different outcomes. The only thing that changed was motivation and meaning.

> Even when you don't start out with a passion for something, if you find meaning in it, you'll put more effort into it and get more satisfaction out of it. As a result, you'll be happier, healthier, and more fulfilled.

Chop wood and carry water. Do the work. Find the purpose.

Choose Passion

The word "passion" comes from the Latin *pati*, meaning 'to suffer'. It's ironic, given how we tend to view passion today only as a source of joy or fulfilment. The word's etymology reveals a deeper truth: passion isn't something you find effortlessly; it's something you endure. Passion is the trial that tests your commitment. Passion is what you sacrifice for. It's what makes you forge forward in the dark, through the cold, down the road full of thorns.

When storms of life come, and waves of weariness overwhelm you, passion is what remains. Passion is that which survives hardship.

We like to imagine passion as a lightning bolt of love which strikes from the heavens, its energising vigour setting our heart aflame. But passion isn't the lightning bolt, it's the bedrock. Passion is what keeps you standing when the earth seems to give way.

You won't discover what you're truly passionate about until you're tested. It's not passion if you only love it when it's easy. But hard things can feel easy when you chip away at them through competence. The better you become at something, the more you understand it. The more you understand it, the more rewarding it becomes. Competence builds confidence, and confidence comes from control of your craft. That sense of control, that feeling of mastery, often solidifies into passion.

The Irish poet and dramatist William Butler Yeats, echoing the words of Benjamin Franklin, said:

> *"Do not wait to strike till the iron is hot; but make it hot by striking."*
>
> — William Butler Yeats

Commitment to a craft, a field, or a discipline will expose a depth of meaning you will never see if you only apply yourself at a surface level. If you coast, you will only ever skim the surface. Your work will feel empty and meaningless because the way you work is vapid and lethargic. You will hate what seems hard, what seems difficult, and never know what value lies beneath.

The deeper you go into any domain, the more appreciation you gain. You begin to understand the nuances, the details, the subtle challenges that make mastery worthwhile. Over time, wearing away at the stone of life's work through intentional effort will eventually give way to genuine satisfaction, and beyond that, passion.

Of course, you shouldn't go digging a field of wanton holes. There's no need to spend your whole life doing work you hate or that you know isn't aligned with your ultimate ambitions. You can be discerning about where you dig. But you can't merely stare at the earth and determine where you might strike oil. You're going to have to pick a spot and start digging until you see what lies below the surface. And in the composition of that soil, you will find clues of where to dig next. The more you dig, the more you'll learn, and the faster you'll find the fertile ground that you can build a future on.

Passion doesn't come from the sky, it comes from the ground. **You don't have to love something to start it – you have to start something to love it.** You simply have to commit, to persevere through the challenges, and see where the process takes you. Passion is a choice. Stop waiting for it to strike you. Choose something worth doing and give yourself the chance to fall in love with it by digging below the surface to see how deep the rabbit hole goes.

If passion comes from suffering, apply yourself until you find something worth suffering for.

Play Pinball, Not Golf

In both golf and pinball, the game ends once the ball goes in the hole. But in golf, you must become singularly obsessed with the hole. Everything else is seen as an obstacle.

Too many people have a golf mindset – their aim is to get from their starting point to an end product or outcome in as few moves as possible, with each move being the product of deep intention and focus.

The problem is, that's really hard. Most people have bad swings, or bad luck, and so it takes years of focused practice to hone their craft. You have to get really good at swinging, and arm yourself with a variety of high-quality tools, to finally get the ball in the hole. And along the way, you have to avoid large stretches of water and sand and swamps and hills of tall grass – any one of which could ensnare you and massively hamper your progress.

I'd advocate you trade the golf mindset for a pinball mindset. Don't go for a hole-in-one – instead, strategically fill your life with lots of things you can bounce off, and collect as many bonus points as possible en route to your destination.

In pinball, you don't need to worry about getting the ball into the hole – it's going to happen, eventually. You accept that as a natural consequence. The ball going into the hole is such an inevitability that it's the one thing you *don't* need to focus on. It becomes inevitable not because you've removed all the obstacles, but because you've multiplied them. And instead of seeing them as obstacles, you see them as waypoints—opportunities to encounter something interesting and be rewarded.

Worrying about living a perfectly streamlined life is the same as worrying about how the ball gets in the hole. Play a different game – focus on trying to collect as many bonus points as possible on your journey. Where you were previously hellbent on driving towards a single outcome through sheer force of will, put your focus only on generating inertia and momentum, and throw yourself into interesting things that you can quickly learn from. Once you have enough velocity, serendipity and gentle guidance will do the rest of the work for you.

You'll ricochet to and fro, encountering numerous people and ideas, taking something from each of them in turn. The faster you go, the more likely you are to encounter those interesting things, and the more likely it becomes that any of those things will nudge you towards a greater outcome. And by the time you reach the hole, you'll be a few dozen wild experiences richer. Every game of pinball ends the same way. The ball goes in the hole. But what makes each game of pinball unique is how interesting you can make the journey.

18

LEARN FASTER

"I have never let my schooling interfere with my education."

— Grant Allen

It's hard to believe that James Baldwin never went to university – but only if you presume that the standard, formalised path is the best way to learn. Baldwin didn't attend workshops or study under famous professors. He wasn't groomed for the literary canon. He worked in diners. He read in Harlem libraries. He taught himself to write by studying the prose he admired, line by line, until the rhythms and cadences and words were part of him. He crafted his style from scratch.

Baldwin's education was rebellion by other means—sovereignty, carved out in paragraphs. By the time *Notes of a Native Son* was published, Baldwin had cemented himself as more than a writer, but a cultural voice sharp enough to cut through a century of noise. He wasn't invited in. He made himself unavoidable. No institution can prepare you for that.

"You write in order to change the world [...] The world changes according to the way people see it, and if you

alter, even by a millimeter, the way people look at reality, then you can change it."

— James Baldwin

This chapter isn't about genius. 'Genius' is convenient shorthand, usually applied in hindsight to people who had no other choice but to do what they were great at. Baldwin didn't follow a convenient path. He made his own. That's the lesson here – that competence isn't limited to formal education or fixed careers. You only need the agency to learn what you need, when you need it, so that no gatekeeper can stop you.

The Learning Lie

We're easily conditioned to believe that learning is something granted. That self-teaching isn't real teaching, and if no one gives you a certificate, then it doesn't count. The idea runs so deep that most people never think to challenge it. They feel unqualified before they've even begun.

The truth is simpler. Most of the time, credentials are a proxy for trust. A shortcut to prove that someone else once thought you were competent. Credentials confer credibility, but rarely reflect ability. And they almost never reflect possibility.

Tara Westover's story makes that clear. She grew up in rural Idaho with no formal education. It wasn't a case of neglect; it was a deliberate exclusion. Her first contact with structured learning wasn't until age seventeen, and even then, she had to teach herself just to qualify for standard education. She studied algebra from a borrowed textbook. Learned grammar from library books. Sat the ACT with barely a safety net. Then crossed the ocean on a scholarship, and earned a doctorate from Cambridge.

It would be easy to frame her journey as exceptional. It is. But that's not the point. The institutions opened their doors only after she'd already proved herself. The permission came after the performance – once she'd already proved some competence.

There's a similar story buried in the life of Mary Somerville. In nineteenth-century Scotland, her family tried to block her from studying maths. So she waited until everyone else went to sleep and read algebra by candlelight. An old, borrowed Euclid textbook was all it took to start. From there, she taught herself celestial mechanics, eventually translating and expanding Laplace's work in a way that brought her into the orbit of the Royal Society.

One route into any career is to qualify for it. The second is by making yourself impossible to ignore. Sometimes those paths will overlap—Westover still ended up at Cambridge—but at other times you'll need to make your own way. Somerville couldn't officially join the Royal Society because women couldn't become fellows, but she was honoured with a pension, and her work was read aloud in her stead by friends like Sir John Herschel. Proof that the sovereign path can take you far further than a conventional path might allow.

In fact, Somerville's 1831 book, *The Mechanism of the Heavens*, was adopted as the standard astronomy text at the University of Cambridge—an institution that wouldn't admit women for another century. None of this success was automatic. Even after taking on the book project, Somerville privately journalled her reluctance, stating: "I am afraid I am incapable of such a task, but ... I shall do my very best upon condition of secrecy, and that if I fail the manuscript shall be put into the fire."

Despite popular opinion, you learn outside the classroom is not a lesser version of what happens inside it. It's often both more honest and more robust because it's self-inflicted. You choose it. You have to stick with it. You have to learn without a deadline, and without a grade to chase. This makes it harder, but creates vastly more optionality. Self-learning isn't strictly a shortcut; it's often also a better route.

Stacks Over Status

The job market still has a fancy for labels. Titles. Degrees. Bullet-point hierarchies that suggest your worth is a function of what someone else once paid you to do. But the people who make real leaps—who change industries, rewrite playbooks, create asymmetric value—rarely do it by 'climbing the ladder'. They do it by shifting sideways, combining skills no one thought to pair.

The real advantage of self-directed learning is that it frees you from your job description. It lets you operate beyond the boundaries of any one role.

I've made several of these jumps myself. From marketing to consulting. Consulting to law. Law to tech. And the truth is, I was rarely the most qualified person on paper. But I had combinations that worked. I could speak well to clients. I could write persuasively. I could condense complexity and build narrative. None of those are job titles. They're multipliers.

The people who rise fastest often aren't the most specialised. They're the ones who learn just enough across disciplines to see what others can't. A software engineer who understands storytelling becomes a founder. A doctor with an eye for design invents better tools. A journalist who understands incentives becomes a world-class investigator.

And then there are people like Josh Waitzkin. As a child, he was a chess prodigy. But instead of doubling down forever, he walked away. Studied martial arts. Became a world champion in Tai Chi push hands. Then turned again—this time into performance coaching and meta-learning. His book, *The Art of Learning*, isn't about chess or fighting. It's about the transferability of skills. How principles migrate. How the mind, properly trained, can shift domains without starting over.

That's the real secret. Not mastery in a single field, but the ability to cross-pollinate. To take what you know and apply it elsewhere—quickly, precisely, and in ways no one's expecting. Career agility comes from your combinations. Long term flexibility is only unlocked when you build a portfolio of strengths that sharpen each other. That's what allows a person to switch industries without switching identity.

Enough to Be Dangerous

There's a point in almost any discipline where you know enough to be useful, but not enough to be orthodox. That's the sweet spot. You're not trying to become an expert, you're trying to become dangerous. Dangerous enough to make things. Dangerous enough to ask good questions. Dangerous enough to operate inside a system without being limited by it.

Every field has a kind of gravity well—a dense pull of jargon, rituals, and received wisdom. Some of it matters. Most of it doesn't. The trouble is, people absorb it all indiscriminately, either by osmosis or rite of passage. When you're learning through institutions, you're rarely taught to filter. But when you're learning on your own, you have no choice. You don't have time to learn things that won't move the needle.

This is where the Pareto Principle comes in. In the early 1900s, Vilfredo Pareto, an Italian economist, noticed that 80% of Italy's land was owned by 20% of the population. He saw the same pattern in gardens – 20% of the pea pods produced 80% of the peas. It wasn't a fluke. The idea became a rule of thumb across systems: a small number of causes often produce the majority of results.

In learning, this principle is critical. Most fields are built on a narrow foundation. A few concepts, techniques, or mental models do the heavy lifting. Learn those, and you'll find you can navigate far more than your experience would suggest. Skip them, and no amount of surface detail will cohere into understanding.

But that's exactly where most people begin—on the surface. They start with detail instead of structure. They collect vocabulary from a single branch of the tree without ever understanding the trunk. It feels productive, but it's cosmetic. Fancy lingo with no load-bearing logic behind it.

Real learning works the other way. You start at the trunk. You build from the centre. At first, it's slower. You won't see the breadth. You'll feel behind. But once the centre holds, everything else radiates outward. You'll be able to move into unfamiliar branches with speed and precision. You won't need to memorise every leaf, because you'll understand how the tree works.

That's the aim: to learn the architecture of a field, not just its vocabulary.

So where do you begin? With the books that show you the roots.

The Textbook Rule

If you want to learn a field fast—and well—start with five books. Not articles. Not blog posts. Not whatever a newsletter tells you is trending this month. Start with the kind of book that doesn't care if you finish it. The kind that assumes you're serious.

Suggesting you read textbooks in the age of AI may sound anachronistic, but it's intentional. AI chatbots will happily let you tinker around the edges of a system. They'll answer whatever you ask, but they'll never tell you what to ask, or where to poke. This means there are unknown areas of knowledge that you may not even be aware of. You don't know what you don't know. So either get a smart friend that knows the field like the back of their hand, or grab a textbook.

Textbooks work differently to popular non-fiction. They have no lifestyle to sell you. They're solely concerned with building your fluency. That means repetition, diagrams, footnotes, and occasionally long-winded chapters that feel like overkill—until you realise they're the only reason you understand the following chapter.

You don't need the newest edition, either. In fact, older is often better. It strips out fads. It shows you what's persisted. If you can follow a textbook from twenty years ago and still arrive at the same insights, it's a sign that you've reached the structural layer of the subject.

I've used this rule repeatedly. Whenever I've switched industries, the instinct is always the same: go upstream. Don't look at what beginners are doing; look at what practitioners rely on. The tools they reference. The explanations they respect. The books they never put away.

The first two books might feel slow—they're almost guaranteed to. You'll be fighting uphill. You won't know the terms, and you won't yet have the mental hooks to hang ideas on. You don't need to read every word – just start by looking at the table of contents, and the introductions and conclusions of each chapter to get a sense of the broad architecture. From there you can go deeper. Your third book will feel different. You'll start seeing patterns. Ideas will link up. By the fourth or fifth book, you'll start predicting where the author is going before they get there. And you can actually start having meaningful conversations with the author and their ideas.

This is the same way Mary Somerville started. It's the equivalent of how James Baldwin started. By considering the best books on a topic and peeling back the layers to see what makes them tick. Five books won't make you a master. And in some fields three might be sufficient – or even one. But this approach will make you fluent. And fluent people learn faster, adapt quicker, and start contributing long before anyone expects them to.

Stop reading to feel informed and start reading to become dangerous. Then, take your learning to the next level with projects.

Learn by Building

There's a point where reading stops helping. When levelling up becomes research ad infinitum. This is where a subtle gap opens up between what you know, and what you can do with your knowledge. You may understand the terms, follow the arguments, and even sound fluent in conversation. But you haven't internalised the knowledge until you've done something with it.

Head-knowledge only creates the illusion of competence. This is where many self-learners stall. They confuse familiarity with fidelity. They become tourists in a subject—well-read, well-informed, but still fundamentally powerless.

Reading gives you fluency. Building gives you force.

Until you apply what you've learned in the wild—under pressure, with consequences—you haven't really tested it. You're still simulating. That's fine in the early stages, but knowledge without contact degrades quickly. You need friction to start a fire. You need the feedback loop that only comes from making something real, seeing where it breaks, and fixing it.

It doesn't need to be grand. A short article, a half-functioning prototype, a presentation for an imaginary client. It just needs to exist in the world, where your understanding meets its limits. You don't need to have read a full textbook before you design your first project. In fact, the earlier you start, the better. That's where the learning compounds and accelerates.

Award-winning film director Guillermo del Toro didn't go to film school. He went to the school of obsession. As a kid in Guadalajara, Mexico, del Toro devoured movies like they were air. Watching and rewatching films, breaking down frames and special effects, his bedroom became a makeshift film studio-come-library, crammed with notebooks full of ideas and homemade creature designs.

Armed with his father's Super 8 camera, he started making short films at 8 years old. By his teens, he was experimenting with make-up effects, turning his friends into monsters for homemade horror flicks. When he finally got his break in the industry, del Toro was a fully-formed visionary with a unique style and a head full of stories. His self-directed education and bank of self-made short films helped him develop a voice that no film school could have taught.

Most people don't need twenty years of secret projects. They just need to build sooner. If you're learning to code, build a tool that solves your own problem. If you're learning marketing, write an ad for a product you love and test it. If you're learning design, redesign a product you hate and explain your thinking.

The point isn't to impress anyone. It's to clarify what you've absorbed, what you've misunderstood, and what you still don't know how to do. But along the way, you'll end up with something crucially concrete. A signal; proof-of-work. What you need isn't a better resumé, it's better receipts. Because once you have proof of your knowledge, you can start building an unconventional career.

Bishop Takes Pawn

Traditional careers are built like ladders: one rung, one title, one promotion at a time. You're expected to prove yourself in place before you're allowed to move up. But the most interesting careers aren't built that way. Follow the rules and you'll move like a pawn. One step at a time. Two at the start, if you're lucky. But the people with real career velocity aren't always the ones with the longest tenure. They don't wait to reach the end of the board before they level up. They start the game as bishops. They move diagonally across roles, disciplines and industries. They combine things most people don't think to connect.

It's not always obvious from the outside, but the pattern repeats. You can progress much faster if you're willing to stack skills in unique ways. Like the chef who leverages her understanding of flavours to become a top perfumer. Or the journalist who uses his investigative background to excel in corporate intelligence. The key is to start learning before you make the jump. Don't wait until you land a new job to start acquiring relevant skills. Instead, use self-learning to position yourself for the move in advance.

I've done versions of this myself. I've worked in branding, law, consulting, and tech—none of which followed a rigid playbook. On the surface I was switching jobs, but in reality I was accumulating leverage. Not because I'd mapped that path from the outset—each transition was a truly random function of opportunity and interest—but because of the way I approached them, forcing seemingly disparate pieces into a coherent skill stack. It was only possible through this approach – learning the next thing while still embedded in the old thing. I didn't always have the right title, but I had enough fluency to contribute, and enough signal to be taken seriously. In every shift the same lesson held: if you can learn fast and prove it, you'll turn gatekeepers into garden gnomes.

Let's return to one core idea—not all skills are made equal. Some compound faster than others. Some unlock more doors. The most powerful ones, like writing, sales, coding, design, and systems thinking, are what you might call multiplier skills. They're rarely job descriptions in themselves, but they amplify every role you touch. A product manager who can write well gets buy-in quicker. A lawyer who can sell becomes indispensable. A founder who can code doesn't have to wait.

These skills create asymmetry. They let you do more with less. They make your other strengths more valuable. And when paired in unexpected combinations, they create emergent value:

- Coding + Design = Indie developer or product founder

- Writing + Psychology = Top-tier marketer

- Law + Sales = Rainmaker

You don't need permission to learn any of these, and there's likely no program for them at your job. You can acquire them long before anyone gives you a job that requires them. Commit to developing them, and you can start building your own asymmetry today.

19

Fail Better

"Ever tried. Ever failed. No matter. Try again. Fail again. Fail better."

— Samuel Beckett

Failure porn is everywhere. In an era of fortune cookie philosophers and LinkedIn influencers, Harvard sweatshirt rags-to-riches stories are in vogue. Founders live to share their story of raising a few million bucks. Everyone else wants the few moments of vicarious bliss they get from indulging in success stories. It keeps the dream alive. It makes the hustle feel worth it – because one day, that could be you!

And it's *been* me. I've been that (co)-founder, with my face in the TechCrunch article, celebrating the million-dollar raise for my startup. You may have read that article and felt the very same way—I know many did. But there was no follow-up article when the shine started to dull, the cracks started to show, and the business began to crumble.

The rags-to-riches formula only works if you get the riches. Somehow, you don't earn the right to tell your story of failure unless you can prove substantial subsequent success by the metrics others think are valuable. Nobody opens Forbes to read the headline: 'Rags to rags, but I learned a lot along the way.'

On the other side of the coin, tales of near-death failures are rarely accompanied by actionable advice on how you can avoid falling into familiar pits. When they do, the stories go through such an extreme funnel of survivorship bias > selection bias > confirmation bias before they reach your ears that the learnings only represent a subset of possible outcomes.

My grumblings aside, there's a tremendous amount you can learn from failure, and particularly from the failures of others—whether or not it leads to tremendous success. Failure is an important element in the cycle of innovation and growth, but it's often overrated. I'm not in the camp that claims all failure is good. Failure only counts as fruitful when you're moving the needle and/or becoming a valuable data point for others. If you're doing neither, you're wasting your time.

Hold Your Horses

People call wins and losses too early. At the edge of the grey area in-between lie unrealised gains and unrealised losses.

In investing parlance, an unrealised loss is when the value of an investment drops below the purchase value. It is not the same as a final, material loss. It simply represents the potential negative return if you were to cash out. If you've still got enough money in the bank to cover the potential loss, there's no need to panic. You're still in the game. There is still time for the tide to turn. The failure is only real once you sell, or once the market deems your position irrecoverable.

Most mistakes, fumbles and slip-ups in life are nothing more than that, but we have a propensity to overreact to negative feedback. We chalk up the loss too early. The cards look unfavourable, and we throw up our hands. We reaffirm this negativity with an internal narrative. 'I should have played it safe.' 'This isn't for me.' 'It's just not possible.' Giving up and turning your back on an attempt is what crystallises the failure. You've turned a paper loss into a definite defeat.

If you don't get a margin call and your position isn't completely wiped out, the game is still on. That was a setback. You can

learn from those too, and the position isn't permanent. Setbacks happen all the time.

Even the most agile and confident rock climbers won't get their hand and foot placement right 100% of the time. What separates a slip or fumble from becoming a near-death experience is their ability to recover while falling. An experienced rock climber will shift their weight and find better leverage before gravity gets the better of them. In the same way, a pro skier on a tough slope can feel the nuances of poor movement through their boots. They actively seek and interpret feedback faster than a novice. A careless slip that would have pancaked a beginner can be avoided with a deft recovery.

Mistake number one is assuming and accepting failure prematurely.

You Can Fail Better

Some failures are better than others. Not all losses are equal. This is another common misconception. A failure that cannot become a data point for future experimentation, by you or by others, is useless. I'd go as far as to say that making easily avoided mistakes is a waste of time. Many failures are the result of common errors.

As humans, we exist on this earth to learn from each other. Despite status and celebrity, we are all born contributors to the project of our collective progress. Haste, pride, fear and ignorance often stop us from seeking available sources of wisdom. Asking friends, neighbours, and fellow online citizens about their experiences, advice, and recommendations might make us feel vulnerable in the short term, but it's a small price to pay to avoid the pain of an avoidable error.

Put aside any traumatic experiences you may have had in middle school with teachers who forced you to read old classics, and the kids that may have mocked or diminished your reading ability. Books allow us to communicate with people who lived long before us and dance with ideas that will outlast us. The 'Medium blogs of yore' are a great place to encounter the best discoveries humans have made in every field. There's a wealth of information out there.

> Do your best to arm yourself before undertaking new challenges. Even in the midst of a challenge, it's not too late to seek advice. Directly—in person, or indirectly—through books, blogs and other mediums. Crystallising losses in private can seem like a lesser evil than acknowledging publicly that you don't have all the answers. But don't force your own fumble.

Mistakes are a natural part of life—get comfortable with that. You'll learn more by iterating towards perfection than by being perfect ab initio.

Make Failure Cheap

No failure is pretty in the moment. Innovating is an ugly business. The first key to a beautiful failure is surviving. It takes grit and resilience to take a pounding and get back up, ready to fight again. Remember that staying on the ground makes defeat certain. Staying on your feet gives you a shot at changing the narrative.

The secret to ensuring you can survive long enough to find success is making failure as cheap as possible.

When British industrialist Henry Kremer offered a £50,000 prize fund to accelerate innovation in human-powered flight, many inventors, engineers and entrepreneurs threw their hat in the ring. It was 1959. Fifty years had already passed since the historic Wright brothers flight.

Kremer's challenge was to fly a figure eight around two markers a half-mile apart. Incredibly, despite the princely reward on offer (over $1m today), the next 17 years were marked with failure.

People were spending years at a time in large teams, backed by serious funding, building beautiful aircraft with polished wood and fine materials. When each machine inevitably failed they would need another year to gather the funding and manpower for the next attempt.

After almost two decades, an engineer and aviation enthusiast, Paul MacCready, decided to try his hand at the challenge. He was broke and had no team behind him but was convinced he could overcome these obstacles. In his mind, everyone was trying to solve the wrong problem. Everyone was trying to build a machine capable of completing the challenge immediately – the perfect aircraft. Instead, MacCready's north star was asking, 'Can you build a machine that can crash cheaply? A machine that can be crashed, mended and relaunched in a few hours?'

So instead of building sophisticated machines, he built scrappy planes out of Mylar, aluminium tubing and wire. These were craft that just about met the spec of what he theorised would be needed, but nothing more. He wasn't optimising for the victory photograph accompanying a grand launch. He was just trying to test as many ideas as possible, in minimal time, with little incremental outlay.

MacCready crashed his planes four or five times a day. His closest competitors would spend 6 months building what they thought was the complete flying vehicle – until it crashed. He was able to crash and learn 222 times before being successful. MacCready won the prize just 2 years later and went on to cross the English Channel for a prize of £100,000 using the same method.

Change the Variables

Understand and adapt the variables behind every failure. When you read stories of successful people doing great things, don't just look to imitate what they've done – look to iterate on the lessons they've uncovered.

No two attempts will be identical. If you follow the same playbook as someone else, line by line, in your own unique circumstances, it's still likely the results will be different. So be intentional about it. Make note of the variables at play, and only make a fresh attempt once you're sure enough variables will be different that you learn something new.

You may still fail. But perfection isn't the objective – new knowledge is the objective. There's a quote that legends from Michael Jordan to Thomas Edison have uttered some version of: "You're not failing 100 times, you're learning 100 ways that don't work". Just make sure it's actually 100 unique failures and you're not just rolling the same dice 'one more time' 100 times like a divorcee at a Vegas casino thinking, *'This time will be different'*.

Utilising the same knowledge in a different context could be the key to unlocking success. Here are a few startups that pivoted from dead ends, often using the expertise they'd developed or acquired to change the narrative:

Pinterest started out as an app called Tote that tried to build a mobile clothing retail outlet. Payment processing infrastructure wasn't great at the time and the app was failing. They pivoted as a way to display any collection.

Instagram was once an app called Burbn that let people check in to locations and share photos of their meet-ups. The app was so complex that people didn't know how to use it. The one thing that resonated with users was the photo-sharing feature. It stuck.

YouTube was originally a video dating site. The idea was for people to upload videos of themselves talking about the partner of their dreams. The founders were on Craigslist paying people to create dating videos. It didn't work. They started uploading their own videos instead.

The Nintendo Power Glove was a famous flop and one of Nintendo's first forays into VR tech. It sold 600k units in the first 6 weeks and eventually faded into obscurity. The same hand-motion tech would later develop into the **Nintendo Wii** controller, which became one of the best-selling video game consoles in history.

As you try, and as you fail, keep gathering data. Seek out the mistakes and learnings of others. Note their successes, but also note their failures. Is there further ground to be broken by adjusting the variables? Can you move the existing knowledge gained into new contexts? Identify which mistakes are not worth replicating. The best mistakes to learn from are ones you didn't have to make yourself. Always consider the factors at stake to ensure any attempt that risks possible failure will yield a valuable lesson.

Make mistakes. Just not the cheap and dirty ones. Make high-quality mistakes. The very best, most exquisite failures possible.

How to Fail Strategically

Before you start: Design for cheap iteration from day one. Ask yourself, "What's the fastest, cheapest way I can test this idea?" Don't optimise for the perfect launch—optimise for rapid learning cycles.

When things go wrong: Distinguish between setbacks and actual failures. If you still have resources (time, money, energy) and haven't been completely eliminated from the game, you're dealing with an unrealised loss. Stay in position and adjust your approach.

After each attempt: Conduct a brief post-mortem. What variables contributed to this outcome? Which can you change for the next iteration? Document your experiments so you're not unconsciously repeating the same approach with different packaging.

Learn from others first: Before making any significant move, seek out people who've attempted similar things. What worked? What didn't? Which mistakes are worth avoiding entirely? The best failures to learn from are ones you didn't have to experience yourself.

Change meaningful variables: Don't just try again—try differently. Adjust timing, approach, audience, scale, or context. Make sure each attempt teaches you something new rather than just rolling the same dice repeatedly.

Build a failure budget: Decide in advance how much you're willing to lose (time, money, reputation) in pursuit of a goal. This prevents emotional decision-making when things get difficult and ensures you can survive long enough to find what works.

20

TRENDS OVER STREAKS

"The strongest of all warriors are these two — time and patience."

— Leo Tolstoy

In 2012, an undrafted player from Harvard set the NBA on fire. Nobody expected Jeremy Lin to break into the league, and once there, nobody expected him to amount to anything. Harvard isn't famous for its basketball program. It doesn't have a history of prodigious talents. Only three of its former students ever made it to the NBA, and their photos are black and white. What Harvard does have, is plenty of Asian students like Jeremy Lin – and Asians, apart from extreme biological outliers like Yao Ming, were a rarity at the pinnacle of basketball.

Lin was a maths wiz with an economics degree. No team thought it worth the punt to waste a draft pick on him, but his hometown Warriors picked him up. He was waived mid-season, picked up by the Rockets, waived again on Christmas Day. The next year he was picked up by the Knicks to keep the end of the bench warm. This is the story of dozens of nameless talents who phase in and out of basketball's periphery.

And then, out of nowhere, as though touched by gods, Lin's star rose. He started putting up numbers that rivalled NBA superstars. Reporters were asking Kobe Bryant if he was ready to guard him. Kobe said, "What the [expletive] is going on? Who is this kid? ... Is he getting, like, triple-doubles or something?" Jeremy Lin subsequently dropped 38 points on Kobe's head, stealing a Knicks win. "Linsanity" gripped New York City and much of the basketball world.

For a few glorious weeks, Jeremy Lin was unstoppable. Fast forward a few years, however, and Lin was bouncing between teams, never quite recapturing that magic. Despite becoming the first Asian NBA Champion in league history as a bench player on the Raptors, by 2019 he was out of the NBA entirely, finding himself halfway around the world on a contract with the Beijing Ducks.

We love a good streak. We're captivated by the athlete who scores in twenty consecutive games, the stock that skyrockets 500% in a month, and the breakout writer who becomes a bestseller with their debut novel. These streaks dominate headlines, inspire awe, and fuel our dreams of overnight success.

But streaks are fickle lovers. They're as likely to break your heart as they are to make your fortune. Lin's story shows their dark side well. Streaks are intoxicating while they last, but they rarely do. Worse, they can trick us into thinking we've "made it," leading us to neglect the foundational work that sustains long-term success. Luckily, they're not the only option. There is a more powerful and enduring model of success – we could focus on trends instead.

The Power of Trends

Jeremy Lin's run was thrilling precisely because it was fleeting. Trends are the opposite – they forego intensity for consistency. A trend doesn't need the wind at its back. A trend survives a few bad days. A trend is a quiet force that carves canyons out of mountains. It has durability. Predictability. What matters is not how big it gets in a day, but whether it continues the next day—and the next.

The longer a trend lasts, the more likely it is to continue. This is the inverse of streaks, which get harder to sustain with every passing day. Trends are like rivers. Their force may vary, but they continue to flow. And the deeper they carve, the more inevitable they seem.

A streak is a spike, a trend is a slope. One fades. The other builds. When something persists—not for days or weeks, but for years—it acquires a different kind of strength. This is where we enter Lindy territory.

The Lindy Effect, popularised by Nassim Taleb, suggests that the future life expectancy of a non-perishable thing (like a book, an idea, or technology) is proportional to its current age. In other words, if a book has been read for 50 years, it's likely to be read for another 50. If a philosophy has survived for a century, expect another century. Time becomes a filter. Each day something survives makes it stronger, not weaker.

> *"If a book has been in print for forty years, I can expect it to be in print for another forty years. But, and that is the main difference, if it survives another decade, then it will be expected to be in print another fifty years. This, simply, as a rule, tells you why things that have been around for a long time are not "aging" like persons, but "aging" in reverse. Every year that passes without extinction doubles the additional life expectancy. This is an indicator of some robustness. The robustness of an item is proportional to its life!"*
>
> — Nassim Nicholas Taleb

Trends of consistent output are what build empires, shape cultures, and change the world. A trend is Amazon's relentless focus on customer experience, year after year. It's The Beatles playing eight-hour sets in Hamburg clubs, honing their craft night after night. It's Kobe Bryant showing up early for practice after practice until his skill and proficiency became undeniable.

The power of trends lies in their resilience. They're not derailed by a bad day, a market downturn, or a temporary setback. They adapt, they persist, and they prevail.

One of my favourite personal maxims is *'trends > streaks'*, meaning it's more important to be the kind of person who will do the right thing 9/10 times on average, than someone who just happens to have done the right thing on the last 9/10 occasions.

> Basing your identity on what you do 'more often than not' is more powerful (and healthy) than trapping yourself with 'what I did yesterday'.

On two occasions I've had a streak on the Duolingo language learning app of over 300 days. On both occasions, as soon as the day finally came where I hadn't logged a lesson before midnight, breaking my streak, I quit the app entirely. Not out of anger, shame or frustration – I just didn't care enough. I'd built a habit of keeping score instead of a habit of doing the work, and once there was no score to keep, there was no work to do.

The problem with streaks is that they only work in retrospect. Every time you miss, you're back to zero. Many such streaks are eventually maintained only by fear of losing the streak, and that desperation is more likely to lead to a streak-ending mistake than a more stable motivation.

When you focus on trends instead of streaks, time is always on your side. While streaks can only be lost, trends can always be built. Every swing you take gives you the opportunity to improve your batting average. A streak is your behaviour. A trend is your identity.

A Tale of Three Investors

In the 1960s, three great investors joined forces. Warren Buffett, Charlie Munger, and Rick Guerin made waves in the investment world. All three were partners. All three saw tremendous success. But they weren't all aligned on their investment strategy, and if you fast forward to the end of their careers, the contrast in outcomes is stark.

Berkshire Hathaway, the brainchild of Buffett and Munger, was eventually valued at around $700 billion (and counting). Guerin's net worth was a respectable $100 million. The difference is a small matter of $699.9 billion.

So what happened? How could three partners have such drastically divergent outcomes? The mystery is simple below the surface. Buffett and Munger treated investing like a marathon, and not a sprint. They focused on value, on companies with strong fundamentals, on patient dealmaking, on investments that would compound over decades. They built a trend, year after year, brick by consistent brick.

Buffett and Munger preached and practised patience. They had a well-recognised mantra that they recited like a religious text: "Be fearful when others are greedy, and greedy when others are fearful."

Guerin, while also brilliant, opted for a different strategy. He used leverage to amplify his gains, chasing the exhilarating highs of investment streaks. For a while, Guerin's star shone the brightest. His aggressive moves yielded spectacular short-term results. For a time, he even outperformed his more conservative partners. While the markets were good, he soared. But markets aren't always good.

In the 1970s market downturn, Guerin's leveraged positions became an anchor. Faced with brutal margin calls, he was forced to liquidate positions to cover his mounting debts. That included selling a prized asset - his share of Berkshire Hathaway. Guerin was forced to sell his Berkshire shares at a fraction of their future value, to none other than Warren Buffet. The very streak that had propelled him to early success now forced him to exit the game just as it was getting interesting.

Buffett and Munger saw the downturn as a sale. They had cash reserves ready and waiting to scoop up solid companies at discount prices. Their trend-focused approach turned a crisis into an opportunity. In life, it's never about who's ahead at the quarter-mile mark. It's about who's still running at pace come the finish line.

Polar Opposites

History has a peculiar way of remembering people. It often favours the dramatic failures over the quiet successes. Nowhere is this more evident than in the tale of two polar explorers: Ernest Shackleton and Roald Amundsen.

Shackleton was the poster boy for heroic leadership. His fame comes largely from the epic failure of the Endurance expedition, where his ship was crushed by pack ice before reaching Antarctica. What followed was a tale of survival against impossible odds, with Shackleton heroically saving his entire crew.

Shackleton's name is synonymous with leadership and his streak of survival in dire conditions. Management gurus quote him. Leadership books lionise him. It's a gripping story; Hollywood material. And then there's Amundsen. If you're drawing a blank when I mention his name, you're not alone.

While Shackleton was busy surviving his own ambition, Amundsen was quietly rewriting record books. Amundsen's successes lack the dramatic flair of Shackleton's exploits. He was the first to reach the South Pole, the first to navigate the Northwest Passage, and part of the first expedition to undisputedly reach the North Pole. Yet his name doesn't evoke the same romantic imagery as Shackleton's. Why? Because Amundsen was boring. Gloriously, effectively boring.

Where Shackleton relied on charisma and improvisation, Amundsen focused on meticulous planning and a trend of consistent execution. He learned from the Inuit, using their clothing and dog-sledding techniques. He established supply depots at regular intervals. He insisted his team travel the same distance every day, regardless of weather conditions.

Shackleton's sexy motor sledges broke down. His ponies couldn't handle the cold. When crisis struck, he rose to the occasion magnificently – but he was always rising to crises of his own making.

Amundsen's dog sledges worked perfectly. His team, dressed in practical furs rather than wool, stayed warm. They trudged onward, day after monotonous day, setting records in the process.

The results? Amundsen reached the South Pole first and did so without losing a single man. For all his heroism, Shackleton never reached the South Pole. He lost men on his first Antarctic expedition. His final expedition ended with his own death from a heart attack.

Amundsen's approach lacked the excitement of Shackleton's. He had no hot streak of heroism, just a trend of consistent progress. There were no dramatic stories of him in the newspaper because there didn't need to be. You won't find many movies about a guy who plans really well and avoids catastrophe. But in the end, Amundsen achieved more, lost fewer men, and left a legacy of success rather than heroic failure.

The Results Take Care of Themselves

You get to decide whether you'd rather be remembered for being spectacular in short bursts and niche circumstances, or for being consistently successful come hell or high water.

An interesting quirk of the '*trends* > *streaks*' mindset appears when you make the distinction between your inputs and your outputs—your actions vs your outcomes. One of the reasons success can feel fleeting is that it's an output metric. It's easier to focus on success rather than progress. But if you want to plot a reliable path, do the opposite. Focus on the trend of your actions rather than the streak of your outcomes.

More often than not, I write every day. I break the input streak all the time. Some days I'm busy, tired, lazy or distracted. But the general trend remains, and suddenly a streak of output emerges: there hasn't been a single day in over five years that someone, somewhere in the world, wasn't reading my work online. Now, even on the days I don't write a word, hundreds of people still see the record of my work. I will continually reap the benefit of the trend that I've built, as long as, more often than not, I keep contributing to it.

Make consistent progress and success will flow naturally. Your actions create a gravitational field, attracting the outcomes they align with, slowly and then quickly as your track record reaches critical mass. As your actions compound, that magnetic force grows stronger, until success becomes inevitable.

Push through resistance

Switching from a streak mindset to a trend mindset is going to be hard. I won't lie to you about that. Especially if you find yourself easily addicted to maintaining streaks, or searching for shiny outcomes, as I often have. There are a few reasons why people struggle to make the transition:

1. We're hardwired for quick wins. Trends don't scratch that itch. There's no kick of instant gratification. Trends are the investment account that grows slowly, not the lottery ticket that promises instant riches.

2. It's easier to motivate yourself for a sprint than a marathon. Trends require a different kind of fuel—one that burns slower but lasts longer.

3. When you're focused on trends, progress can feel painfully slow. It's like trying to watch yourself lose weight. Day to day, you see no change. But give it a year, and suddenly your pants don't fit.

4. While you're steadily building your trend, you'll see others having their "moment" with impressive streaks. It's hard not to feel like you're falling behind. Don't get sucked in. Keep putting one foot ahead of the other.

5. Trends require showing up day after day (more often than not), even when you don't feel like it. It's much easier to muster enthusiasm for occasional bursts of activity. Don't lose the fire.

Trend-Setting 101

Here are seven things you can do to start developing a trends mindset:
1. **Redefine success:** Stop thinking in terms of endpoints. Start thinking in terms of direction. Success isn't a destination; it's a heading on your compass.

2. **Embrace boring:** Learn to love the mundane. The unsexy, day-to-day grind is where real progress happens. Find beauty in consistency.

3. **Shrink the change:** Make your daily actions so small that they're almost laughable. Want to read more? Start with one page a day. The key is to make it impossible to fail.

4. **Give yourself grace:** The beauty of trends is that it never matters if you miss a day. Every day you show up, you contribute to building the trend. To build a critical mass of inertia behind the action you want to trend, just show up as often as possible.

5. **Measure differently:** Instead of measuring outcomes, measure inputs. Don't focus on pounds lost; focus on workouts completed. Don't count dollars earned; count hours invested.

6. **Visualise compounding:** Remind yourself of the power of compound interest. Small, consistent efforts multiply over time. That 1% daily improvement becomes a 37x increase over a year.

7. **Plan for plateaus:** Progress isn't linear. Expect times when you'll feel stuck. These plateaus are where most people quit. Plan for them, and you'll push through.

8. **Create systems, Not goals:** Don't aim to write a book; create a system where writing happens automatically. The goal takes care of itself when the system is solid.

Remember, becoming trend-focused is itself a trend, not a streak. This won't happen overnight. Come back and regularly review this chapter over the next few weeks if you need to, and slowly rewire your brain to value consistency over intensity. Start small, stay steady, and transform your life one trend at a time.

21

THE ADVICE TRAP

> "The edge... there is no honest way to explain it because the only people who really know where it is are the ones who have gone over."
>
> — Hunter S. Thompson

It's easy to find yourself drowning in a sea of guidance. This feeling will proliferate as you progress along the path. From self-help books and TED talks. From mentors and Instagram gurus, and random strangers on the internet who think they know everything. Everyone's got an opinion on how you should live your life. It's seductive, isn't it? The idea that someone out there has cracked the code, and if you just listen carefully enough, you too can unlock the secrets of success, happiness, or making a perfect soufflé.

The problem is that advice is a double-edged sword. It can be the lighthouse guiding you safely to shore, or the siren luring you onto the rocks. You need to learn the difference between wisdom and waffle, because every day I see people fall in love with meaningless platitudes and throw themselves into the ocean following the siren's song.

Chew Your Food

Not all advice is good advice. Daphne E. Jones, the ex-SVP and Chief Information Officer of GE Healthcare, once framed this perfectly:

> "When you're offered advice, take the meat but not the bones."
>
> — Daphne E. Jones

Advice is incredibly useful, but it's a mistake to think you can swallow it whole. Anytime someone offers you a piece of advice, imagine you're being offered a delicious piece of chicken.

"Thank you very much," you might say—"that's fantastic." The problem is, sometimes what they're offering you is a lean chicken breast, and at other times it's a few scraps of gristly meat around a gnarly bone.

Sometimes you see the bone sticking out and quickly assume there's no meat. So you discard the advice, assuming it doesn't apply to you—that it's not useful and there's no value you can extract. On many occasions, discarding the advice would be a mistake. It can still be worth giving it a chew and making sure you get everything you can out of it.

But the more common situation is the opposite. You're offered a plate of advice that appears succulent and well-seasoned. It's coming from someone you respect and admire, and you can see how much they've achieved. The problem is, if you swallow it whole without processing it thoroughly, a small bone could get lodged in your neck. Then you're dead, and upset, and your belly's still empty.

The lesson? Chew your food.

Advice is Abstract

It's common to mistake 'advice' for 'truth'. It's not. Advice is an abstraction – a cliff notes version of someone else's truth, filtered through their perceptions, moulded by their biases, and inevitably simplified in their retelling.

Advice is inherently subjective. Even if the advice-giver tries their best, what you hear will never be the full story. The closest you could get to the truth would be to live through the advice-giver's memories using a VR simulacrum, or Dumbledore's pensieve.

This doesn't mean advice is useless. Far from it. But understanding its nature—its inherent limitations and distortions—is crucial to using it effectively. After all, you wouldn't try to navigate New York City with a map of London, would you?

The Anatomy of Advice

For any experience to be passed on and shared, it has to be boiled down into an abstraction.

This means that whenever someone gives you their advice, they're either boiling down an experience they've had, or a series of experiences they've gathered from themselves and others, and condensing it into a single takeaway. But how do you know whether the advice is useful?

There are four barriers you'll have to be careful of, which determine how useful abstracted advice can be. Imagine each of these like four levels of a funnel. At each level, the advice has the potential to become diluted, less potent and less useful:

1. **Legibility** – *how accurate is the person's recollection of the situation their advice is based on?* The accounts of first-hand witnesses are famously flawed. Sometimes what we remember isn't exactly what happened.

2. **Fidelity** – how much information is missing from the recording? The facts they recall may be accurate, but are they complete? *Are they fully aware of all the variables that resulted in the outcome they're referencing?*

3. **Synthesis** – how well can the person translate the information they have into a generalisable takeaway? i.e. *did they learn the right lesson(s)?* Are they biased to interpret the objective facts in a particular subjective way?

4. **Pattern-matching** – assuming the information you get is accurate, complete, and faithfully interpreted, *how easily can you map the advice you're getting to your own situation?*

It's worth noting, regarding the last point, that applicability isn't the same as pattern-matching. The ease with which a pattern can be fit to match your situation is different to your ability to find and match patterns in the first place. Applicability is a state. Pattern-matching is a skill. Your ability to pattern-match effectively will ultimately be the larger bottleneck to your ability to get the most out of advice you are given.

> Take the time to process any advice you get thoroughly. All advice is useful information, but not all of it is worth applying. Take the meat, but not the bones.

Learning to Pattern-match

As we've discussed, any advice you get is an abstraction of someone else's experience. It's a distillation of what they have (1) lived through, (2) reflected upon, and (3) learned. Advice will never have the same fidelity as living through what they did. And it might not be useful for you if they didn't do the work to make the abstraction accurate at each of those stages.

To make advice useful, you should abstract it even more, and then compare the 'zoomed out' image to other abstractions (advice from others) to see where you can notice overlapping patterns.

Treat the bits of advice you encounter as pieces of a jigsaw puzzle. Each piece might look like a complete picture on its own. And in fact, it might reveal enough for you to immediately know where to place it. But as you collect more pieces and start fitting them together, a bigger picture often emerges – both more complex and more useful than the original piece in isolation.

Sometimes you will realise that the first piece wasn't what you thought it was. It could have been upside down, the wrong way around, or from a different part of the picture entirely. Either way, the additional context will make it far more instructive. This is the power of pattern matching.

Instead of treating each piece of advice you get as a self-contained picture or an isolated commandment, look for connections. Try to abstract things further, like when you squint to make your vision fuzzy. Don't focus on the details. Focus on the shapes and the negative space those shapes create. Pattern matching is about noticing broad commonalities, not minutiae.

This is the crucial difference between knowing what successful people do and understanding why they do it. The 'what' is seductive in its simplicity—it promises a clear path to follow. But without the 'why', you're navigating in the dark.

The 'Why' and 'Who' Matter

When Jeff Bezos makes a business decision you might learn from, what matters isn't simply the action itself. It's his underlying philosophy, the market conditions, and his long-term strategy. Understanding these 'whys' allows you to adapt the principle to your own unique circumstances, rather than copying a move that might be irrelevant or even harmful in your context, if any one of those variables is different for you.

If one person tells you that the secret to morning productivity is to get up at 5am and another one tells you that the secret is journalling, it could be easy to get confused. Which way is right? Which routine is best? Squint—blur out the details and ask what they're really saying.

When someone says you should wake up at 5, what they're really advocating for is some uninterrupted time where you can clarify your thoughts, take care of rote tasks that may have messed up your schedule later in the day, and perhaps do some deep work.

The person who advocates for journalling is really advocating for some uninterrupted time where you can clarify your thoughts and empty your head, sifting through unprocessed feelings and ideas for anything useful.

These two things sound different but they're rather similar when you squint. There's a pattern that might be useful, beyond the details of prescriptive advice. You might find a completely different way to accomplish the same underlying objectives that are more suitable for your lifestyle.

You should also look to pattern match across domains. It's easy to develop a particular worldview when you're embedded in a certain context. Childless tech founders in their forties may not have all the answers. But if you hear similar advice from a tech entrepreneur, a sports coach, and a relationship expert, sit up and take notice. These cross-disciplinary patterns often point to fundamental truths that transcend specific fields.

This is largely why I host a podcast with such a wide range of guests. It's suboptimal for growing an audience quickly, but it's ideal for learning quickly and multiplying ideas across domains. In a week I could speak with a physicist, a venture capitalist, and a science journalist, and surprisingly often there are patterns you can draw which reveal deep truths about human systems and other fundamental axioms.

Pattern matching isn't about finding a one-size-fits-all solution. Its power comes from developing a keen eye for underlying principles. This makes the difference between copying someone's answers and understanding the method to solve the problem yourself.

Questions to Ask

Here are a few questions I commonly ask myself whenever I hear some advice, before deciding whether to act on it. The questions follow a logical progression:

1. What's the context behind this advice?
2. What assumptions is it based on, and what changes if each of the assumptions change?
3. What are the underlying concepts which may transfer regard-

less of personal context?

4. How might this need to be adapted for my situation?

5. Is this person incentivised to ignore, overlook, or mask potential downsides or risks (survivorship bias, resulting bias, confirmation bias)?

6. Am I incentivised to ignore, overlook, or reject this advice because I don't like the message or the messenger (value alignment, power or lack of it, pride, cowardice)?

7. Am I incentivised to listen to this (authority bias, halo effect, confirmation bias)?

8. If this is wrong, or if I'm wrong, why might that be, and how can I hedge against that?

Charisma

Charisma is often misunderstood. From afar, it may seem to be a function of becoming the loudest person in the room, being the prettiest or most rakish, or having the most magnetic personality. But up close, charisma is the ability to inspire, influence, and lead others through the force of your character and ideas.

The biggest misconception, however, is that charisma is innate. That it's a gift from the gods rather than a trainable skill. That you either have it or you don't. But in truth, anyone can learn to wield it, though some are naturally more adept than others.

Those who have internalised the power of charisma are able to communicate uniquely, conveying a depth of ideas that transfer energy and vibrancy directly to the people they interact with. They're able to listen, both absorbing data and making people feel listened to. They have the ability to make others feel seen, heard, and valued. They can articulate a vision so compelling that others are drawn to it, eager to be part of something greater than themselves.

The dark side of charisma is often highlighted in its capacity for manipulation or deceit, but its purest form is the direct opposite: authenticity, aligning your words and actions with your deepest values. Charisma is the courage to stand for something, to challenge the status quo, to inspire others to reach for their highest potential.

Used well, charisma is a force multiplier, amplifying the impact of your competence and confidence. Unlike the charlatans who employ puffery and pretence to get what they want, those with real charisma don't seek to dominate or control. Theirs is a force that empowers others, bringing out the best in those around them.

22

The Levels of Charisma

> *"Power is the ability to define reality and to convince other people that it's their definition too."*
>
> — Dr. Wade Nobles

You're at a party, nursing a drink in the corner, when suddenly the room shifts. There's electricity in the air. A newcomer has arrived and, without saying a word, has captured everyone's attention. People gravitate towards them like moths to a flame. With a glance, they can charm anyone. With a touch, they can stoke passion in the weakest soul, rousing them to action. This is what most people think of when they imagine charisma. It's certainly the spirit of gravitas depicted in popular media. But I think the reality is both more subtle and more powerful.

I'll be honest. I have anxiety. I don't want to be the centre of attention. I don't need everyone's eyes to be on me. What I want is to be able to make friends quickly, garner goodwill, and get what I want.

Fortunately, it turns out that the magnetic pull of charisma isn't a special magic reserved for a chosen few; those people born to be masters of the universe. Beneath the curtain is a diverse set of skills that can be learned, honed, and mastered; a toolkit, rather than a single ability.

Whether you're aiming to climb the corporate ladder, expand your social circle, or simply feel more confident in your skin, understanding the nuances of charisma will allow you to harness this precious power and transform your life.

We can start by dissecting it. I say there are three types of charisma. I frame them as levels to denote rareness and difficulty, but they're actually completely separate abilities that can be cultivated individually or compounded:

Level one – Social Competence: This is the most common and learnable form of charisma. It's based on social skills, empathy, and the ability to make genuine connections with others. At maximum proficiency, these are your 'champions of the people'.

Level two – Manifest Will: This type of charisma stems from an unwavering focus and determination. People with this quality draw others in through the weight of their conviction and the intensity of their purpose. We often refer to people like this as 'gravitational forces'.

Level three – Mandate of Heaven: This is the rarest and most powerful form of charisma. Those who possess it seem to bend the world to their will, making wild goals seem not just possible, but painfully obvious. We call people like this 'reality distorters'.

We'll explore each in turn and go deeper in the following chapters.

The Art of Being Liked

We've all encountered them—people who seem to glide through life collecting allies without effort. Opportunities find them. Doors open. Strangers become friends, then advocates, then partners in whatever vision they're pursuing.

What sets these people apart isn't superior talent or devastating wit. They've mastered the art of making others feel genuinely valued in their presence. This is Social Competence: the ability to create authentic connection that transforms casual encounters into lasting goodwill.

Social Competence operates on three principles: emotional awareness (reading the room and managing your own reactions), authenticity (dropping pretense for genuine engagement), and positive energy (bringing enthusiasm rather than extracting it). Master these, and you become a person others remember fondly, and want to help succeed.

The Frequent Flyer

Richard Branson became a billionaire by discovering something that business schools rarely teach – the shortest distance between two strangers is a smile.

In 1978, the twenty-eight-year-old record company owner found himself stranded in Puerto Rico. He'd been waiting for a connecting flight to reach a beautiful woman called Joan in the British Virgin Islands, who would later become his wife. But when he looked up at the information board, one word turned his blood cold: CANCELLED. Most passengers would have grumbled, found a bar, and soaked their sorrows in negronis until the next departure came around. Branson, a Sovereign soul if ever there was one, saw things differently.

He was desperate to see Joan that night, and knew there was an opportunity fermenting in the collective frustration of his fellow passengers. He wandered to the back of the airport, found a charter pilot, and haggled his way into renting a small plane for $2,000. In the back of his mind there was a worry that his credit card might bounce, but he had a plan. Walking back to the gate, he borrowed a blackboard from airport staff and wrote in bold letters: "Virgin Airlines: $39 to British Virgin Islands."

"I went out to round up all the passengers who had been bumped, and I filled up my first plane," Branson later recalled. Within minutes he'd turned a room of angry strangers into trusting collaborators. As they boarded, a fellow traveller offered a suggestion that would change everything: "Sharpen up your service a bit and you could be in the airline business."

The comment stuck. Back in London, Branson picked up the phone to Boeing. He had no connections to their executives there, and had to weasel his way up the chain from the receptionist's switchboard. "I got on the phone to Boeing, and they were amused to hear an Englishman from the music business asking what kinds of deals were available on a jumbo jet," he remembered. After spending an entire afternoon and evening negotiating, Boeing agreed to lease him a secondhand 747 with an unprecedented safety net – if Virgin Atlantic failed, he could return the plane after one year.

It was this same gift for human connection that would prove crucial years later when British Airways launched what became known as their "dirty tricks" campaign. While Virgin had only four planes compared to BA's hundreds, Branson's airline was winning customers through superior service and his own magnetic accessibility. BA's response was systematic sabotage: illegally accessing Virgin's computer systems, calling Virgin passengers while pretending to be Virgin staff to switch them to BA flights, and spreading false stories about Virgin's financial troubles.

Branson didn't retreat behind corporate walls. Instead, he did what came naturally – he connected. During the ensuing legal battle, while BA executives maintained aloof corporate distance, Branson was everywhere: talking to journalists, engaging with the public, making Virgin's case through personal relationships rather than press releases. In the public's eyes, he was the folk hero shaking hands and kissing babies, while BA was the corporate brass trying to strangle a newcomer and maintain their cold grip on the industry.

When Virgin won the case in 1993—£610,000 in damages plus £3 million in legal costs, the largest libel settlement in British legal history at the time—Branson made a characteristically personal decision. "It was Christmas time," he said. "It became known as the BA Christmas bonus – we distributed it to all our staff equally."

Branson didn't have superior strategy or deeper pockets. But despite being the underdog, he could craft wins and slice market share from thin air through an instinctive philosophy that business happens between people, not corporations. This ability to make genuine human connections—to see opportunity in shared frustration, to transform strangers into allies, to remain approachable under pressure—is the essence of Social Competence. From passengers in Puerto Rico to Boeing executives to his own employees, Branson consistently chose connection over formality, and accessibility over authority. It made him universally loved, a magnet for goodwill, and a very rich man in the process.

The Gravity of Purpose

Some leaders don't win hearts with charm – they capture minds with conviction. Where Social Competence relies on connection and likability, Manifest Will operates through sheer force of determination. People adept at leveraging this level of charisma possess a focus so intense it becomes magnetic, drawing others into their orbit through the gravitational pull of their certainty.

Manifest Will doesn't require that you become the most beloved figure in the room, only the most focused. What it requires is a vision so clear that others begin to see through your eyes. When others waver, you stand firm. Where convention retreats, you advance. This type of charisma turns the dance of nervous shilly-shallying into a thrust of urgent resolve – an energy that reverberates outward, impacting everyone around you.

The power of Manifest Will comes from its authenticity. You can't fake real conviction. You can't fake being serious. Either you believe deeply enough to risk everything for your principles, or you don't. When you do, that commitment becomes contagious, inspiring others to rise to a level of courage they didn't know they possessed.

The Persistent Publisher

When Katherine Graham walked into her Georgetown living room on the evening of June 17, 1971, she carried the weight of an impossible decision. Hours earlier, a federal judge had silenced The New York Times with an injunction, halting their publication of the Pentagon Papers—a secret government study that revealed decades of lies about America's presence in Vietnam. Now, The Washington Post had its own copy, and Graham faced a choice that could destroy everything her family had built.

The scene in her living room was tense. Ben Bradlee, her executive editor, paced near the fireplace, arguing passionately for publication. The lawyers sat rigid in their chairs, warning of criminal prosecution and financial ruin. Board members threatened resignation. The company's stock was about to go public—a decades-long dream that could evaporate overnight if the government came after them.

Graham had inherited The Post eight years earlier when her husband Phil took his own life, ending a long battle with manic depression that had tormented their family for years. She'd found herself, a 46-year-old widow with four children, thrust overnight into the world of hard-boiled journalism. She had previously carved out a small life as a homemaker and socialite, running dinner parties rather than newspapers. Now she was up late, casting the final vote on decisions that could topple governments. "I was never supposed to be in this job," she often said. That night, surrounded by men telling her what she couldn't risk, she felt the familiar weight of self-doubt.

Graham had been bullied into silence during her marriage, as Phil, between bouts of mania, would berate her in front of their children and her friends, mocking her weight, clothes, intelligence, and Jewish heritage. A childhood friend described his presence on her as being "like a dentist's drill [knowing] just where to hit the nerve", continuing, "she became like the abused child who lurks in the shadows for fear of getting hit."

But in the eight years since his passing, something had changed in Graham. The hesitant widow who once apologised for her opinions had discovered an unshakeable core. As the room fell silent, waiting for her decision, she thought about what The Post stood for. What her father had built. What Phil had believed in before his illness consumed him.

"Go ahead, go ahead, go ahead," she said quietly. "Let's go. Let's publish."

The words hung in the air for a moment. Bradlee broke into a grin. The lawyers shook their heads. And Graham picked up the phone to call the printer, knowing she'd just bet her company's future on the belief that Americans deserved the truth.

The next morning, Post delivery trucks rolled through Washington with the Pentagon Papers splashed across the front page. The stock offering proceeded as planned. The government sued, as promised. But something else happened too – journalists across the country, watching a widow stand up to the most powerful administration in the world, found their own courage.

Graham's decision that night was a bold signal that journalism's highest calling wasn't to comfort the powerful, but to afflict them with truth. This willingness to risk everything for principle—not once, but repeatedly over the coming years—transformed The Post from a regional newspaper into America's conscience.

Her unwavering will was on display again during the Watergate scandal. For months, The Post was virtually alone in pursuing the story, facing intense pressure from the White House and scepticism from other news outlets. But Graham stood firm, backing her young reporters, Woodward and Bernstein, even when the stakes seemed impossibly high.

Other newspapers, inspired by The Post's courage, began to pursue more investigative reporting. Young journalists, drawn by Graham's commitment to truth and accountability, flocked to work at The Post.

Graham became a titan of journalism through Manifest Will, not speeches or showmanship. Her single-minded focus on quality journalism and her commitment to the truth became a force that others couldn't help but be drawn to.

Years later, Bradlee would remember that night in Georgetown: "She had guts and she had strength and she had courage."

The King of Not-so-Real-Estate

The rarest form of charisma transcends influence entirely. Beyond connection and conviction lies something both more potent and more dangerous: the power to reshape reality itself. Many refer to this power as a "reality distortion field." Others have termed it pure charisma. I call it the Mandate of Heaven.

Its most skilled practitioners aren't just capable of convincing people that they're right – they make their vision feel like destiny unfolding. They present ideas with a force that makes skepticism feel like failure of imagination. In their presence the impossible becomes inevitable, and hardened rationalists find themselves believing in miracles.

Nowhere is this clearer than in the journey of Adam Neumann.

In 2010, Adam Neumann was a struggling entrepreneur with a handful of failed startups under his belt. By 2019, he had built WeWork into a $47 billion company, convinced some of the world's savviest investors to pour billions into his vision, and become a near-mythical figure in the startup world. His charisma was legendary. He trafficked in dreams, not ideas or detailed strategy. In meetings he was known to pace, often barefoot, gesticulating wildly, animated intensely. He was bombastic in every sense of the word.

A key event in Neumann's canon was a cold morning in January 2017, when one of the richest men in the world paid a visit to his office. Masayoshi Son, the billionaire founder of SoftBank, walked into WeWork's headquarters in Chelsea expecting a routine property tour. Yet somehow, in a matter of minutes, he was ready to part with over $4 billion, entrusting it to Neumann's master plan.

Legend has it Neumann bounded toward Son barefoot, his eyes bright with messianic fervour. What was supposed to be a brief walkthrough became something closer to a religious conversion. Neumann didn't show Son office spaces; he painted visions in the skyline. He spoke of reshaping cities, curing loneliness, and elevating human consciousness. At one point he even mentioned WeWork's potential to house orphaned children.

"We're not in the real estate business," Neumann declared, voice rising with conviction. "We're in the business of changing how humanity works, lives, and thinks."

By the time Son left the building, he'd committed to invest $4.4 billion—at the time, one of the largest startup investments in history. Not based on spreadsheets, data, forecasts or business models, but because for those crucial minutes, Neumann had made the impossible feel inevitable.

This was Adam Neumann's singular gift: the ability to bend the world around his vision through sheer force of personality. Employees spoke of him with reverence. "When you're in the room with Adam," one executive recalled, "you believe that anything is possible." Another once told me personally, "He could convince you the sky was green."

Neumann's reality distortion field operated at a level that defied conventional business logic. He convinced his board to let him buy buildings in his own name, then lease them back to WeWork at a profit. He trademarked the word "We" and sold it to his own company for $5.9 million. When pressed about WeWork's mounting losses, he offered explanations that sounded more mystical than financial: the company's value, he insisted, was based on "energy and spirituality" rather than traditional metrics. By 2019, WeWork was valued at $47 billion—more than Ford or Delta Airlines. Neumann had transformed simple office leasing into a world-changing movement, at least in the minds of investors who should have known better.

Of course, reality has a way of reasserting itself eventually. That year, as WeWork prepared for its IPO, the spell began to break. Investors and journalists started questioning the company's business model, governance, and Neumann's behaviour. The IPO was postponed, and Neumann was ousted as CEO.

Yet even in defeat, Neumann's Mandate of Heaven remained intact in one crucial way: while WeWork's shareholders lost billions, Neumann himself walked away with a golden parachute worth hundreds of millions. He had convinced the world to fund his vision, and when that vision failed, he convinced them to pay him handsomely to leave. In a wicked twist of irony, even as WeWork's stock imploded, Neumann's personal wealth grew, eventually surpassing that of the company's.

Neumann's story shows how a single individual can reshape perceptions, influence decisions, and even, for a time, alter the fabric of reality as others perceive it. It's equally a reminder of the awesome potential—and potential dangers—of charisma at its most potent.

Each level of charisma operates differently, but all share one quality: they transform how others see the world. Social Competence makes people want to help you. Manifest Will makes them want to follow you. The Mandate of Heaven makes them believe in futures they couldn't previously imagine. Understanding these distinctions determines which type of influence you'll cultivate and how you'll wield it.

This final section of our exploration of agency will show you that it goes beyond your personal confidence and competence. Eventually, you must develop the ability to bring others along on your journey. Charisma is the last key. The chapters ahead will show you how to develop it, starting with the foundation that makes all others possible.

23

MAKE FRIENDS IN THE LINE

> *"The art of conversation is to be prompt without being stubborn, to refute without argument, and to clothe great matters in a motley garb."*
>
> — Benjamin Disraeli

I've been in two Adidas commercials. It's a fun fact that comes out now and then, and it usually doesn't raise eyebrows if you already know that I played basketball as a teenager. But there's a part of the story that I often neglect to mention: I wasn't actually supposed to be there. I'd walked onto the set of a global sports brand's commercial and talked my way into a decent payday. It was surprisingly simple, and also the first time I realised that Social Competence could be a superpower. I'll tell you the story, and in the next chapter, I'll show you how to mimic this magic in your own life.

So I'm at the park. It's hot, summer, and a little past noon. These were the early 2010s. For a few years before this point, I'd harboured a secret dream of potentially playing college basketball in the US. I'd even dreamt up a convoluted plan to go to a particular university that had an exchange program with a D3 college in Florida, where I would try out as a walk-on in my sophomore year. But I was 5'10 and hardly a knockdown shooter. It was a pipe dream, but dreams die hard. So I'd still show up at the court most days of the week, drain 200 shots, and play some pick-up ball.

As I approached the courts that day, I saw that they were shut down. The whole area was cordoned off. In this particular neighbourhood, that usually only happened when there was a stabbing nearby. Police would lock off the street from top to bottom, divert buses, and shut down the court. It had happened once or twice in the past while I was playing there—it was annoying. But that day something seemed different. I could see camera crews, lighting rigs, and clusters of people milling about.

My curiosity was piqued—I got closer. Looking at the court, I could see some people wore street clothes like me, and others sported top-tier basketball gear. I got right up to the cordon and recognised a few faces—these were some of the UK's best players.

I scanned the area for any clumps of people who looked approachable, then stepped under the cordon, sidling up to a group of boys who looked my age. They were actually a few years older than me, but they were friendly and filled me in. It was an Adidas commercial. They were one of a few groups of extras just waiting for the crew to finish setting up for the shoot. We chatted for a while and became fast friends. Eventually, I dropped the question. "How do I get involved?"

Armed with directions from my new mates, I approached a crew member. The conversation was awkward and bumbling, although in my head I was imagining the smooth chat of Frank Abagnale in "Catch Me If You Can". That crew member got me to the casting director, who, eager to get me out of his hair, pointed me towards wardrobe.

The wardrobe lady eyed me sceptically, from my shabby, worn t-shirt to my tatty yellow sneakers, which, as fate would have it, were designed by Adidas. I'm sure those shoes were white when they left the factory, but they were already cream by the time I picked them up at the charity shop and were now approaching rusty orange in my custody.

Sensing wardrobe lady's hesitance, I cracked a joke about the shoes. It made her laugh and distracted her from the fact I had clearly just walked in off the street and wasn't supposed to be there. She decided I was already almost perfect for the gritty 'urban' aesthetic. I was hoping for some new shoes but left with a change of shorts and a hoodie, having signed an NDA that I barely read.

Just like that, I was in a commercial for Derrick Rose's new basketball sneakers, part of 'The Return' campaign. Ironically, Rose injured himself again shortly after, so I got called back for another campaign and some Adidas Originals spots.

This story isn't about luck. It's about the power of Social Competence. By being approachable, making connections, and finding common ground with strangers, I turned a chance encounter into an unexpected opportunity. And the best part is it wasn't really intentional or calculated – it was just a natural consequence of having a crumb of charisma. I didn't have the basketball skills of the pros on set, but I had something just as valuable—the ability to connect with people quickly and authentically.

Opportunities are everywhere, often disguised as everyday interactions. By sharpening your social skills and being open to connections, you can carve luck from thin air. Being genuinely interested and easy to talk to is all it often takes to open doors to parallel universes.

The next time you're standing in line, waiting for a coffee, or killing time before an appointment, remember that your next opportunity could be in the world of the person next to you—and you'll never know until you crack a chat. Smile, strike up a conversation, and make a friend, even just for a moment. You never know where it might lead.

Small Talk 101

Literature and film are littered with chemical compounds that make you superhuman: Chemical X, Compound V, NZT. I think the closest real-world analogue is charisma—the power to gain allies, change minds, and drive the outcomes you want, often without lifting a finger.

Social Competence doesn't come to everyone naturally. While I found some aspects easy at a young age, others took a lot of work for me, which I now realise may have been partly due to undiagnosed aspergers. I had to read a lot of books and spend a lot of time practising and pattern-matching to get as good at engaging with people as I am now, and hopefully, this chapter will help anyone with similar struggles.

The key unlock is mastering 'small-talk'. A lot of people have already decided that they hate small talk. They hate the cringe—the bumbling awkwardness of manufactured conversation. I think that perception can change once you stop seeing small talk as small. 'Small talk' is truly an awful misnomer that seems to cover all types of conversations that don't centre around a single topic of interest. But it also happens to be a wicked way to win a deal, make a friend, and get into any room. Treat small talk like a big deal, and it's more likely to lead to big outcomes.

> Small talk becomes effortless when you approach every interaction with genuine curiosity about the other person. Ask yourself what you can learn from them. Remember that everyone has an inner world that is just as rich and complex as yours and full of things you haven't yet noticed or discovered. Your job is to uncover their worldview and unravel it so that you can navigate it with them and find avenues worth exploring.

The rest of this chapter will serve as a short but universal guide to making conversation. If you're already great at this, you can skip it. But a surprising number of people never learn this skill intentionally—it's something you're expected to grok by accident and absorb through trial and error. This approach does everyone a disservice and is at the root of many of our struggles to communicate and feel heard. Small talk is the foundation of Social Competence. I'd recommend reviewing this chapter as a refresher even if you feel sufficiently skilled—we'll go one level deeper in the next one.

Break the ice

The hardest part of a conversation is usually striking one up in the first place. I find it easiest to start with a simple, genuine compliment. "That's a great jacket; where did you get it?" or "I couldn't help but notice your laptop sticker. Are you a fan of [band/show/etc.]?" People generally respond positively to sincere compliments, and it provides an easy segue into further conversation.

Quick tip - avoid any compliment that's physical e.g. their eyes, hair, or physique, unless you're hitting on someone or you enjoy creating awkward situations. I prefer complimenting something that would have been an intentional choice or could connect to a story. Compliment someone's flashy socks and you might hear about the wacky presents their partner buys them. Compliment a leather handbag or ornate earrings, and you might get a story about thrift shopping in Portugal.

Another effective technique is the "assumption and question" approach. Make a friendly assumption about the person or situation, then ask a related question. For instance, at a conference: "This must be an exciting field to work in. What drew you to it initially?" This shows interest and invites the other person to share their story. This works best when the assumption you set up is weak and easy to disconfirm if they disagree, which can lead to an equally interesting conversation.

Remember, the goal is to find common ground or spark the other person's interest. Keep your tone friendly and your body language open to invite further conversation.

Keep Things Flowing

Maintaining momentum is a precious art. One effective technique is the "thread-pulling" method. I get to practice this regularly on my podcast but you can do this in any conversation. Listen carefully to what the other person says and "pull" on interesting threads to expand the conversation.

For example, if someone mentions they just returned from a trip, you could ask:

- "What was your favourite part of the trip?"
- "How does it compare to other places you've visited?"
- "Any recommendations for someone planning a similar trip?"

These questions work especially well when they're more uncommon or require the person to pause a moment and think about the answer. Remember, you can also share your own experiences or thoughts when relevant to create a balanced exchange. This back-and-forth helps build rapport and keeps the conversation flowing naturally. However, be careful to listen fully to what someone has said before jumping in with your own story. Pull on their string before throwing them yours.

Follow up on their responses with genuine interest. Listen deeply. Take them seriously. Share relatable anecdotes when appropriate, but always bring the focus back to them.

Connect the Dots

Make your conversation recursive. Look for opportunities to create callbacks and inside jokes between you, based on things you've connected on, or patterns you've noticed in their stories. Don't think of the conversation as a linear path, but a series of interconnected loops. You go off on a loop and come back to the path, go off on another loop, back to the path. But the path itself is a loop. So every topic can connect or stay separate. The more loops you open up, the more likely they are to connect and intersect.

So as you learn about them, try to figure out where the idea, people, and theme loops from your conversation might connect and where they don't. If you have a gift for humour, this is where you can maximise it to create jokes that only work within the context of your conversation. If you can make someone smile, you can make them laugh. And if you can make them laugh, they'll want to keep talking to you.

If you can identify any open loops, now you have pretext for another conversation. Whether they are applying for a job, looking for a book, or waiting for some good news, if there is anything which comes up that does not yet have a concrete answer, that's an opportunity to follow up with them later and find out if they've closed the loop.

Body Language and Non-verbal Communication

Your body speaks volumes before you even open your mouth. Maintain appropriate eye contact—enough to show interest, but not so much that it becomes uncomfortable. Aim for about 60–70% of the time. It's worth noting that eye contact doesn't necessarily need to be direct. I find it quite difficult to maintain eye contact for long periods, and at other times it might be too intense. Just imagine an upside-down triangle connecting their eyes down to their mouth, and you can bounce your focus loosely between those points.

Keep your posture open and welcoming. Uncross your arms, face the person you're talking to, and lean in slightly to show engagement. Smile genuinely; it's contagious and puts others at ease. Smiling is probably the smallest thing that drives the largest slice of your outcomes. If you're nodding your head, thinking you already know this, think again. It's something far too many people take for granted and don't utilise intentionally. Every time you have a conversation with someone, flash a smile in the moment before anyone says the first word, and it will shift the tone of your entire conversation.

Try mirroring techniques subtly and sparingly. Match the other person's tone of voice, speaking pace, and energy level. This creates a subconscious sense of harmony and makes the other person feel more comfortable with you. It's important not to force this; the point isn't to mimic their movements but to pattern-match their overall tone. If their body, voice, and tone all align with being laid back, you might not want to sit like there's a stick up your bum. Relax where they relax. Button up where they button up. You're not a mime impersonating them; you're just a new 'old friend'.

Use facial expressions to show you're actively listening. This can be difficult for anyone on the autism spectrum, but the basics are easy enough to learn. Nod occasionally, raise your eyebrows to show interest, and smile when appropriate. These cues encourage the other person to continue speaking. I previously mentioned smiling being gold, but there's one caveat: listen carefully to what the other person is saying so you know when to stop smiling. You don't want to be fake laughing when someone mentions a dead uncle. If they mention something bad or sad, try to reflect the appropriate emotion, even if only briefly. This will help them to feel heard and keep them talking.

One of the biggest barriers to overcome for people on the spectrum is the persistent disconnect between what you think is showing on your face and what is actually showing on your face. This is a long-time stumbling block for me, also. The best advice I can give is to practice and try not to be perturbed or withdraw when you get things wrong.

Pay attention to personal space. In most Western cultures, maintaining about an arm's length of distance is comfortable for casual conversations. However, be aware that personal space norms can vary across cultures. Remember, your goal is to appear approachable and engaged. Your body language should say, "I'm interested in what you have to say," even when you're not speaking.

Active Listening

Active listening is the cornerstone of engaging small talk. It's not just about hearing words, but truly understanding and responding to the speaker.

- Paraphrasing and summarising: Occasionally restate what the other person has said in your own words. "So, it sounds like you're saying..." This shows you're paying attention and helps clarify any misunderstandings.

- Ask clarifying questions: If something isn't clear, don't be afraid to ask. "Could you tell me more about that?" or "What do you mean by...?" This demonstrates genuine interest and can lead to deeper conversations.

- Use verbal and non-verbal cues: Nod, maintain eye contact, and use small verbal affirmations like "I see," "Uh-huh," or "Interesting" to show you're engaged.

Remember, the goal is to understand, not to prepare your response. Give the speaker your full attention, and you'll find conversations become more natural and rewarding. It's common to think that charismatic people talk a lot—I actually think the opposite. Charismatic get other people talking, which makes them interested, in turn, to hear everything you have to say.

Handling Awkward Moments

Even the most skilled conversationalists encounter awkward moments. Here's how to navigate them gracefully:

Dealing with silence:
- Embrace brief silences as natural parts of conversation.
- Use the pause to reflect on what's been said and formulate a thoughtful response.
- If silence persists, try a new topic: "That reminds me, I've been meaning to ask..."

Gracefully changing topics:
- Use transitional phrases: "Speaking of which..." or "That's interesting. It makes me think of..."
- Acknowledge the current topic before shifting: "I appreciate you sharing that. I was also wondering..."
- When in doubt, ask an open-ended question about a new subject.

When you've run out of things to say:
- Circle back to an earlier point in the conversation: "Earlier you

mentioned... Could you tell me more about that?"

- Share a relevant personal anecdote to restart the flow.
- Use the environment: Comment on something happening around you.

If you say something inappropriate:
- Apologise sincerely but briefly: "I'm sorry, that came out wrong."
- Redirect the conversation to a safer topic.
- If necessary, excuse yourself politely to reset the interaction.

Politely ending conversations:
- Signal the end: "It's been great chatting, but I should..."
- Express genuine appreciation: "I've really enjoyed our conversation."
- If appropriate, suggest future contact: "Let's connect on LinkedIn / Are you on Instagram?" or "Hope to see you at the next event!"

Remember, awkwardness is often more noticeable to you than to others. Stay calm and confident, and you'll smoothly navigate these moments.

Most 'awkward' moments come from the gap between expectation and reality. Maybe you said something that caught someone off guard. Maybe their last response ended abruptly and you're not sure where to go from there. I think the best tip I can give is to treat every engagement like a shooting star - a brief flash of magic you should cherish in the moment and will likely never see again.

Don't get caught up in expecting some outcome from your conversation. Pour 100% of your energy into making the time someone spends in your presence feel as magical as possible, and that magic comes entirely from getting them to talk, for as long as they're comfortable. The conversation could end at any point and that's okay. If you're not sure, it's okay to end the conversation. I say this specifically for people who haven't mastered Social Competence yet - the more practised you are at linguistic judo, the better you'll get at sensing where there's an opportunity to keep a conversation going, press for an outcome, or retreat.

You'll note regarding following up that I mention non-personal forms of communication compared to phone numbers or email. This can be down to your context and judgement, but I find it's usually better to start the online conversation in a networked space, which gives you the room to exchange numbers or email later, without any immediate pressure on the other person to connect with you.

Practice Exercises and Challenges

Improving your small talk skills requires practice. Try these exercises:
Weekly small talk goals:
- Set a target to initiate conversations with X new people each week.

- Challenge yourself to learn one new thing about a coworker or acquaintance each week.

- Practice active listening in every conversation, no matter how brief.

Conversation starters for different situations:
- Prepare 3-5 open-ended questions for various settings (work, social events, public spaces).

- Create a list of current events or interesting facts to bring up in conversations.

- Practice transitioning between topics smoothly.

The "Five Fact" challenge:
- In each conversation, aim to learn five new facts about the person. This encourages active listening and asking follow-up

questions.

The "Yes, and..." technique:
- Practice building on what others say by using the improv principle "Yes, and...". This helps create a flow in conversation and shows you're engaged.

The "Curiosity Journal":
- Keep a journal of interesting things you've learned from small talk. Use these as conversation starters in future interactions.

Consistency is key. Try to incorporate at least one of these exercises into your daily routine to see significant improvement in your small talk skills. The key to mastering small talk is consistent practice and a willingness to step out of your comfort zone. With time and effort, you'll find that engaging in meaningful conversations becomes second nature.

As I mentioned, there are many books I've read about interacting with people and building relationships. I hope this chapter practically condenses what I've learned to give you a useful starting point. For my full list of recommended books and resources, go to tools.becomesovereign.com/list.

24

ROCK THE BOAT

> *"What you are stands over you the while, and thunders so that I cannot hear what you say to the contrary."*
>
> — Ralph Waldo Emerson

One way to get what you want is to make sure everyone gets along. But sometimes, you need to rock the boat. Going against the grain, putting a fork in the works, and agitating for change without looking like a scumbag requires serious charisma.

Stoking the fire in your belly and learning how to give voice to your righteous indignation is crucial to bridging the gap between Social Competence and Manifest Will. First, you learn to be likeable. Then, by cultivating audacity, you learn how to survive being unlikeable, seeming unreasonable, or doing hard things that won't immediately be met with raucous adulation.

What You're Worth

When I first started in corporate law, I was paid far less than a typical first-year. I'd accepted that for a few reasons. First, I was honestly just happy to be there. When I was at Google, still trying to break into law, I told my mentor that there were only four law firms I was aiming for. I ended up at my first choice – a global firm known for excellent training, which was also highly selective, taking on only 10-15 people per year. Second, I had no law degree. The firm was taking a huge bet by hiring me and had priced that risk into my compensation. But the real problem with my pay emerged later.

According to the original plan, I would spend my first 18 months pottering about in non-fee-earning teams, supporting the lawyers by doing research and running compliance reports. Simultaneously, I'd be completing my law degree on evenings and weekends. Then, I could be smoothly transitioned into billable work. This plan would have worked smoothly for a lot of people. It didn't for me—I was there to work.

After about a month of settling in, I started to patrol the corridors, poking my head into the offices of various partners, asking what I could help on. I was an enchanting menace. I'd do whatever you needed if you let me get close to your deal. If you let me do some photocopying I'd make an extra copy and read up on your deal so I could pop up again seeming more useful because I had more context. I'd arrive at 8:30 before anyone else, read industry journals, and then start doing the rounds as the first partners arrived, hunting down work like fresh meat. If I found a scrap I would latch on ravenously until there wasn't anything left. This was the same method I used to scavenge my way onto the YouTube and Google Play Store teams at Google. It was a well-honed formula by now.

I was on my first deal within two months—a £10 million construction dispute which showed up in the news. The firm quickly changed their plan for my role, as well as my job title. It wouldn't be the last time that happened, and over the next 12-18 months, as I gained experience, the arbitrage opportunity became obvious.

By then, it was clear that I was competent – you could put me on a deal just like any other second-year and expect equal results. But because I didn't have a law degree, you could bill me out to clients for cheaper. In the event that it took me slightly longer to learn something, it would still work out financially for the client. So I got a ton of experience, and I worked a lot of hours.

I kept a second set of all my toiletries in my desk drawer so I could shower at the office, and a pair of comfy evening slippers to pad around the corridors at night. At home, I was sleeping on a second-hand futon that I'd bought for £10 from a bloke in East London, so believe me, I was happy to spend 15 to 20 hours a day in a swanky office with free coffee and biscuits. If I worked late enough every night, I'd also get a free dinner and a taxi ride home on the client's tab.

I saved a lot of my meagre salary just by spending as long as possible in the office on one deal or another. I'd eat dinner at my desk every night. I'd go to the office on Sundays after church. Eventually, the night guard at the front desk would memorise my home address so he didn't need to ask for it when I called down for a cab.

But soon these sweet little luxuries would turn to ashes in my mouth. The cab drivers were starting to recognise me at 2am as I slumped into the back seat in a sleep-ridden haze. HR would call me in because I wasn't taking any holiday. I'd come in to the office to get ahead on a Sunday afternoon and leave early Tuesday morning. A partner shouted my name from down the hall and told me to take my long made-up job title out of my email signature because he wanted to put me on a billion-dollar deal and didn't want the client to think their main point of contact was some underqualified freak.

I wasn't the first person to notice the issue unfolding. It had become a frequent conversation among my cohort and even the senior associates, that I was doing the same work for far less pay. Eventually, confident in my output, I decided something would need to change. I approached two other juniors who I knew were being underpaid for one reason or another—I needed co-conspirators. If we presented a united front, I explained, there's no way the business could turn us down. I showed them the numbers I'd calculated based on our salaries, billable hours, and other contributions. I even drafted the email I wanted to send to management and had everyone check it.

Somehow, between my first suggesting it and the time of pulling the trigger on an official email, my co-conspirators had pulled out. They didn't want to rock the boat. If I wanted to fight for more pay, I would have to do it on my own. Fine, I thought, bitterness still sour on my tongue. I removed their names from the email and hit send.

A few weeks later, I got invited to a nondescript meeting with Human Resources. It was short, tense, and I left with a brown envelope listing my new salary. There was only one string attached—I wasn't allowed to discuss my new compensation with anyone.

I was 23 years old and slowly learning the truth: exceptions can always be made for those who decide to be exceptional, and have the audacity to prove it. But the rules will always apply to those who find their coddling consistency comforting.

In the Presence of Lords

I've been invited to the House of Lords a few times now. The first time was to collect a writing prize for a piece of short fiction. The second was because I forced my law firm to do some work.

I'll make the second story quick - you'll probably notice a similar pattern play out.

I'd been one of the founding members of the firm's diversity network and had won the firm's global CSR award for the pro-bono work I'd been doing alongside my billable hours. I spent a few hours a week giving legal advice to prisoners, and a few hours a month running employability clinics for refugees.

I was also pretty adamant that we could be hiring more minority talent. Before my intake, we hadn't had a Black first-year since the Bush administration, and I knew there were plenty of competent diverse people out there, because our competitors were hiring them. Think what you might about 'DEI' but equality of opportunity is something everyone should be on board with.

Around this time, the firm had received a proposal to consult with the UK government alongside a few other firms, regarding the pay and mobility of ethnic minorities within large companies. The government sent us their report, a deadline for our contribution, and we got to work.

At first, it was exciting. Everyone was engaged conceptually. But the report was over 70 pages and no one actually wanted to read it. The deadline was just after Christmas and most people were mentally checked out heading into December. It felt like no one was taking any action, and the meetings we'd set to discuss it kept getting postponed. Fine, I said. I'd already read the report—I could summarise it. It took a few days, as this was unrelated to my regular client work, but with the help of a fellow junior, I eventually sent a six-page summary to everyone on the ERG team, as well as Human Resources – we'd need their buy-in and sign-off in order to respond.

People sent emails patting me on the back. But still, no one actually did anything. For the next two weeks, it was a slow process of poking key names via email until they agreed to meet, and until HR agreed to sign-off. The week before Christmas, I decided I was tired of waiting. I drafted a three-page response on behalf of the firm and sent it around to everyone, giving them a chance to tweak or object, otherwise I would just send it off. They didn't, so I did.

A few months later, I was sitting at a roundtable in the House of Lords alongside representatives from other large corporations. And it wouldn't be the last time.

The world looks hard. Processes, structures and organisations look large, difficult and opaque. But the world is surprisingly easy to navigate for a focused mind.

Most people like the idea of things they'll never do, and they do things that they hate the idea of. The world is full of such people, running on autopilot, taking what they're given, accepting 'the way things are'. All it takes is someone showing up who is serious about driving a singular outcome, and the waves will part until you feel the bedrock of the ocean beneath your sandals. That doesn't mean making things happen is easy – but it's often easier to reshape the world than it is to change the mind of someone who is relentlessly determined.

If there is something that you want, do your best to make it palatable. Try your hardest to convince others to join your mission, and take the task at hand seriously. But if the gate remains closed, remember that even stone can be split with a hammer and a nail. It just takes precise, focused, consistent effort. Do what needs to be done.

The Mountain-moving Space Man

When Elon Musk founded SpaceX in 2002, the space industry was stagnant. NASA, once the pinnacle of human achievement and innovation, had become mired in miles upon miles of red tape, bureaucracy and risk aversion. The last moon landing was a distant memory, and the dream of interplanetary travel seemed to have faded into science fiction.

Musk had a single audacious goal: to make space travel affordable and eventually colonise Mars. It was a vision that many considered absurd, if not impossible, on any reasonable time horizon. Traditional aerospace companies and experts scoffed. They argued that space was the domain of governments and massive corporations, not upstart entrepreneurs. The technical challenges were too great, the costs too high, the risks too unmanageable.

But Elon was undeterred. He invested his own fortune from his time running PayPal and previous startups. He worked 100-hour weeks and pushed his team to reimagine every aspect of rocket design and manufacturing. Unlike traditional aerospace companies which outsourced to a minefield of contractors, SpaceX began manufacturing most of its components in-house, allowing for faster iteration and dramatic cost reduction.

The early years were brutal. SpaceX's first three launch attempts failed spectacularly, nearly bankrupting the company. Musk revealed that if the fourth launch of their Falcon 1 rocket had failed in 2008, SpaceX would have run out of money and likely shut down. But it succeeded; that final burst of heavy hope hurled high towards the heavens, making SpaceX the first privately funded company to orbit Earth.

This success, along with Musk's unwavering focus and relentless drive—his Manifest Will, began to attract the industry's top talent. Engineers who had grown frustrated with NASA's sluggish pace flocked to SpaceX, drawn by the promise of doing the impossible.

The company's momentum grew. Later that year, SpaceX won a $1.6 billion NASA contract, providing crucial funding and legitimacy. But Musk wasn't content with just reaching orbit. He pushed for what many considered impossible: reusable rockets. It would take until 2015 for SpaceX to successfully land an orbital-class rocket, but the feat has since transformed the economics of space flight.

By 2023, all countries outside the United States combined for 114 orbital launches. China was responsible for 55 of those, and Russia managed 17. NASA only had 8, and the entire European Space Agency contributed 5. But SpaceX, a single company, nearly matched this global effort with 87 launches of its own.

In Q1 of 2023 alone, SpaceX launched roughly 7.5x more spacecraft (763) than the rest of the world combined (106). They've dramatically reduced the cost of reaching orbit, made reusable rockets a reality, and reignited global interest in space exploration.

Musk's singular focus didn't just create a successful company; it fundamentally altered the status quo. He elevated everyone's energy and urgency, forcing both government agencies and private companies to innovate faster and think bigger. Established players like Boeing and Lockheed Martin were compelled to form the United Launch Alliance to compete, driving innovation across the entire industry.

Even projects like Starlink, SpaceX's satellite internet constellation, serve Musk's ultimate vision. It builds toward providing global internet coverage, while functionally being a stepping stone to funding Mars colonisation.

You don't need to like Musk. You don't need to like Mars. You don't have to agree with his politics or share his ambition. But through live-streamed launches and active public engagement, Musk and SpaceX have rekindled public interest in space exploration, making it part of the cultural zeitgeist once again.

Even if Musk never reaches Mars, his actions have already reshaped our collective vision of what's possible in space. One person, armed with conviction and the audacity to act, has changed the trajectory for an entire industry, and perhaps all of humankind.

When faced with entrenched systems and sceptical incumbents, the force of your Manifest Will can indeed move mountains – or in this case, launch them into orbit.

25

USING YOUR BIG VOICE

"The supreme excellence is to subdue the enemy without fighting."

— Sun Tzu

The Mandate of Heaven, in Chinese history, was the right to rule the empire, so long as you proved yourself worthy of maintaining it. It's the equivalent of the Divine Right of Kings in European history—a doctrine of monarchical absolutism which made the King above the law and unquestionable by parliament. The distinction, however, is that the Mandate of Heaven wasn't passed on by birth – it had to be earned and maintained through virtue. You didn't just answer to God. Earning the Mandate of Heaven required earning favour both in the heavens and among the people.

There's a term today that I think has similar resonance: 'reality distortion field', first commonly used to specifically describe the force of charisma channelled by a young Steve Jobs in the 1980's, and its effects on the developers working on the Macintosh project.

The term has since been used to describe the auras surrounding people like Bill Clinton, Bobby Fischer, and Adam Neumann. Even Bill Gates, once the richest man on earth, described himself as 'a minor wizard' because he was the only person seemingly able to resist being enchanted by his contemporary Steve Jobs.

Andy Hertzfeld was one of the first engineers that Jobs recruited to the Macintosh team. He recounted a conversation with teammate Bud Tribble about Steve's charisma:

> *"Bud usually didn't come into work until after lunch, so I met with him for the first time the following Monday afternoon. We started talking about all the work that had to be done, which was pretty overwhelming. He showed me the official schedule for developing the software that had us shipping in about ten months, in early January 1982.*
>
> *"Bud, that's crazy!", I told him. "We've hardly even started yet. There's no way we can get it done by then."*
>
> *"I know," he responded, in a low voice, almost a whisper.*
>
> *"You know? If you know the schedule is off-base, why don't you correct it?"*
>
> *"Well, it's Steve. Steve insists that we're shipping in early 1982, and won't accept answers to the contrary. The best way to describe the situation is a term from Star Trek. Steve has a reality distortion field."*
>
> *"A what?"*
>
> *"A reality distortion field. In his presence, reality is malleable. He can convince anyone of practically anything. It wears off when he's not around, but it makes it hard to have realistic schedules. And there's a couple of other things you should know about working with Steve."*
>
> *"What else?"*

USING YOUR BIG VOICE

> *"Well, just because he tells you that something is awful or great, it doesn't necessarily mean he'll feel that way tomorrow. You have to low-pass filter his input. And then, he's really funny about ideas. If you tell him a new idea, he'll usually tell you that he thinks it's stupid. But then, if he actually likes it, exactly one week later, he'll come back to you and propose your idea to you, as if he thought of it."*
>
> *I thought Bud was surely exaggerating, until I observed Steve in action over the next few weeks. The reality distortion field was a confounding melange of a charismatic rhetorical style, an indomitable will, and an eagerness to bend any fact to fit the purpose at hand."*
>
> — Andy Hertzfeld (The Original Macintosh)

I want to focus on one aspect of this that I think can be utilised by anyone with sufficient practice – I call it 'The Big Voice'. The Big Voice is the thing that bridges Manifest Will and the Mandate of Heaven. While Manifest Will clears obstacles from your path, the Mandate of Heaven turns enemies into allies. Mastering The Big Voice will allow you to bend reality with your words, to charm, persuade, and create desired actions in others. It's more than just speaking – it's about the transmission of energy which communicates a feeling or fact to the other person.

At first glance, this might sound like some kind of Jedi mind trick, but it's actually something far more powerful and, crucially, attainable. What I call your Big Voice is more akin to the 'Voice' technique used by the Bene Gesserit in Frank Herbert's Dune—a skill honed through keen observation, deep understanding of human nature, and precise control over one's communication.

It's important to point out that I'm not actually advocating for any form of mysticism here. I don't think you can change someone's mind by concentrating really hard, or make someone do something with a whisper and a wave of your hand. That's not the point. But... what if you could? How would it change the way you acted, if you genuinely believed that your words had near-magical impact? If you knew that your words could be received as charm or threat, depending on your intent? And that if you really wanted to persuade someone of something, you could? Developing your Big Voice starts with creating and then transmitting this kind of energy.

How to Get Free Coffee

I got a free cup of coffee while writing this chapter. I wasn't trying to prove a point. And I didn't ask for it either. But I wanted it, and so it happened. That happens a lot. I'm writing this in an upscale cafe in South Kensington, a notoriously nice part of London. I needed the toilet, but the bathroom was apparently out of service. I smiled and interacted with the server, and asked if they'd still let me use it, even though it was out of service. They were happy to help – it turns out the only thing wrong with the bathroom was a broken lock on the door handle.

After using the loo, I strike the conversation up again. I ask if it's been a busy day. They tell me about it. I laugh. They tell me more. I engage. They ask if I want anything. I tell them I'll get a coffee. There's a long queue of people behind me by this point, but in that moment, there's only the two of us. They make me the coffee. I reach for my wallet, they wave me off – it's on the house. I thank them and go. Before I leave this cafe, when I'm done writing, I will make eye contact, wave goodbye, and say thank you again.

It sounds like a mundane interaction, but it happens all the time. My friends never understand it. I might go to a restaurant, and dessert is on the house. I go to the cinema, bring my own popcorn, and I ask for a free bottomless drink. I don't even give a reason. They just give it to me. I go to the airport, and they ignore my extra bag. I don't hide it. They'll just ignore it. I know they will, because it happens all the time. And all of this works equally well in a business context – I can haggle to the death and rarely lose a negotiation. I rented my house off-market before the previous tenants had moved out, and later bought it off-market, for close to $150,000 under value.

This type of reality distortion requires three important things:
1. Not overreaching for the thing that you want
2. A willingness to ask and be rejected
3. Caring more about the person you're engaging with than the outcome

I want you to try what I call the free coffee test. Go to a cafe or coffee shop. Flash a smile at the person at the counter before either of you has a chance to say anything, to set the tone for a positive engagement. And then forget about getting a free coffee. For 30-60 seconds, oppress them with earnest and sincere love. You have to mean it—you have to care. You have to ask them how they're doing and want to hear the answer. Three weeks from now you should be able to come back here and ask how their brother is doing, or how their exam went, or if they enjoyed that concert. Have a meaningful interaction, and smile a lot. Make them smile, if you can. And then make a small order.

Maybe you'll pay—maybe you won't. It doesn't matter. But if you do this ten times, in different places, with different people, you'll probably get that free coffee. And hopefully, in the process, you'll realise the coffee isn't the point. What you've taught yourself to do, is connect with someone in a very short space of time, enough that they'll want to do something for you. You won't need to ask. It will come from them. They'll want to help you, or make your day better in some small way. And you'd better seem extremely grateful.

I'll need you to promise that you'll never use this power for evil. I even hesitate to share it, but it's important you understand that everyone from great presidents to great con artists has learned this same trick. Being able to transmit energy through words and body language.

The key to nurturing your 'Big Voice' is learning to transmit energy, and the most powerful way to do so is by practising in person. It will require pulling together everything we've discussed so far. Small talk and Social Competence—your ability to make friends with anyone, and Manifest Will—your ability to drive outcomes through displays of intense focus. The Big Voice technique requires learning to concentrate those two powers in different quantities, and communicate them to others through your voice, body language, and written communication.

Let's start with a deeper look into body language.

Meeting the Big Dog

There are at least 1000 people with a story of how they met Bill Clinton, and most of them are identical. They were at an event, or in a line someplace, and the President was coming. And there was a buzz in the air, and he came towards them. And he looked them in the eyes and he shook their hand and they spent the next 15 years thinking *"Wow, President Clinton shook my hand."* It's an incredible power that man had. Unfortunately, he pushed it a little too far and got a young lady mixed up in a sad state of (very literal) affairs while he held the most powerful seat in the land. And yet, even despite that, people love him.

Clinton's eye contact and knack for remembering faces and names are, in presidential lore, tools as legendary as Zeus' lightning bolts or Poseidon's trident.

There was a particular Forbes article that stood out to me, written by a self-confessed "staunch Republican", a Reagan Republican at that, who was "skeptical of Democratic liberalism and *dismayed* by Mr. Clinton's less than presidential behaviour". Well, this person eventually got a chance to meet Clinton, years after his time in power. Here's how he later characterised that meeting:

> *"The first rumor about Bill Clinton that I wanted to address was, upon meeting him, as every single person I know who has met Bill Clinton says is true (and many of them weren't fans), does he have the "star power" and "aura) that he's famous for?*

Well, that rumor didn't take long to ferret out. Having had the luxury of knowing lots of rich, powerful people, and several of the biggest movie stars in the world, I'm not easily impressed.

But, I was. The man has more than star quality he has genuine "presence."

When someone you don't know, that you'll never meet again, who is just going to shake your hand and sign a book for you and say thank you before turning to the next person in line, actually engages you with a genuineness that is as surprising as it is disarming, you realize that person is different.

[...] His handshake was not quick, it was purposeful. [...]

[...] He looked at me and with as much sincerity as I've ever encountered. [...]

[...] I learned instantly that Bill Clinton doesn't just acknowledge problems he has solutions at the ready. [...]"

— Shah Gilani, Forbes (The Rumors About Bill Clinton Are True)

Clinton's charisma is especially powerful because people know what he's doing—they're just powerless to stop it. The playbook is right there. The problem is most people think they're watching a magic trick and not reading an instruction manual. The trick to getting people to listen to what you have to say, even if they've already decided they don't like you, is first by cementing them in a magic moment. If you're meeting in person, that means eye contact, body language, and a focused but warm intensity (sincere earnestness). These are all things you can practice in your everyday life, creating micro-moments with friends and strangers, until you get quite good at it.

This is actually why I love the free coffee test. The key isn't the free coffee – it could be a phone number, a book recommendation, or just a great conversation. Any of these signs are like the green light at the end of a training simulation, showing that you've passed the test. The better you get at creating magical moments, the more frequently these magical things will happen.

If you've tried at least 20 times to connect with strangers after reading the above, and nothing is working, try asking a friend if something is up with your approach. The most likely offence is that you're trying too hard. If you lean 100% into the moment and put all your focus on the other person rather than yourself, this should eventually become effortless, and then you'll just be remembering to turn intensity knobs up and down rather than spending the entire interaction inside your head, operating your body like a Japanese Gundam robot.

Once you've got the body language down, let's work on your words.

Change the World With Me

In 1983, Apple was on the cusp of launching the Macintosh, a product that would revolutionise personal computing. Steve Jobs, knowing he needed a seasoned executive to help market this groundbreaking device, set his sights on John Sculley, then president of Pepsi-Cola.

Sculley was at the top of his game, having led Pepsi to unprecedented success in its cola wars with Coca-Cola. He had little reason to leave his prestigious position for a young, volatile tech company. Jobs had been courting Sculley for months, but Sculley remained hesitant.

It all came down to a walk in Manhattan. Jobs, sensing this was his final chance to win Sculley over, turned to him and delivered a line that would become legendary in Silicon Valley lore:

> *"Do you want to sell sugar water for the rest of your life,*
> *or do you want to come with me and change the world?"*

— Steve Jobs

In these 25 words, Jobs demonstrates the essence of the Big Voice. Let's break down why this pitch was so powerful:

1. **Reframing**: Jobs reframed the supposed prestige of Sculley's entire career at Pepsi as "selling sugar water", instantly diminishing its importance in the grand scheme of things.

2. **Contrast**: Jobs juxtaposed the mundane ("sugar water") with the extraordinary ("change the world"), creating a stark choice.

3. **Connection**: The phrase "come with me" made it not just about a job, but a personal journey the two of them would embark on together – it instantly evokes camaraderie and brotherhood.

4. **Vision**: "Change the world" appealed to Sculley's deeper aspirations and sense of purpose.

5. **Inevitability**: The question wasn't if Sculley would join Apple, but which path he would choose for his life.

Jobs didn't argue or try to convince Sculley. He didn't list the benefits of working at Apple or the potential financial rewards. Instead, he presented a vision so compelling that it made Sculley's decision seem predestined. If he wanted the opportunity to do more than the mundane, there was only one path worth taking.

The power of Jobs' words was more a function of his delivery than its content. Per Sculley, Jobs spoke with such conviction and charisma that the offer became irresistible. It wasn't just a job opportunity; it was a call to adventure – a chance to be part of something greater. Sculley left Pepsi and joined Apple as CEO, a decision that would shape the future for both Sculley and Apple in ways neither could have predicted.

Jobs had presented a fork in the road of Sculley's life, making the choice seem monumental and transformative. A prime example of how carefully chosen words, delivered with conviction and aligned with a compelling vision, can alter the course of events and inspire others to action.

This doesn't just work in person – it can be equally effective at a distance, in writing.

I Want What You Want

We're going to stick with Steve Jobs for now – you'll notice he's a fount for anecdotes like this, such was the power of his Mandate of Heaven. Take a look at this email exchange between Steve Jobs, then CEO of Apple, and Bruce Chizen, then CEO of Adobe:

> *From: Steve Jobs*
> *Sent: Thursday, May 26, 2005 9:36 AM*
> *To: Bruce Chizen*
> *Subject: Recruiting*
>
> *Bruce,*
>
> *Adobe is recruiting from Apple. hey have hired one person already and are calling lots more. I have a standing policy with our recruiters that we don't recruit from Adobe. It sems you have a different policy. One of us must change our policy. Please let me know who.*
>
> *Steve*
>
> *On May 26, 2005, at 4:15 PM, Bruce Chizen wrote:*
>
> *I thought we agreed not to recruit any senior level employees (at Adobe this is Sr. Director/VP and represents about 2% of the population). I am pretty sure your recruiters have approached more junior ones*

I would propose we keep it this way. Open to discuss. It would be good to agree.

From: Steve Jobs
Sent: Thursday, May 26, 2005 6:27 PM
To: Bruce Chizen
Cc: Steve Jobs
Subject: Re: Recruiting

OK, I'll tell our recruiters that they are free to approach any Adobe employee who is not a Sr. Director or VP. Am I understanding your position correctly?

Steve

Subject: RE: Recruiting
Date: Fri, 27 May 2005 20:53:36 -0700
From: Bruce Chizen
To: Steve Jobs

I'd rather agree NOT to actively solicit any employee from either company. If employee proactively approaches then it's acceptable.

If you are in agreement I will let my folks know.

— [In re: High-Tech Employee Antitrust Litigation (2011).]

What do you notice? There is something Steve Jobs wants. That's obvious. There is an outcome he would prefer, but he doesn't even need to say it. You can feel the energy in his words. He only needed to state unvarnished facts, yet the message was clear: "I believe you are acting unreasonably. I, so far, have been acting reasonably. Would you prefer it if we were both unreasonable?" Or to put it even more simply:

"You are on a path to becoming my enemy. Would you like to change course?"

This usefully illustrates how the same core principles we've discussed can extend beyond just charming people – but to make them take you seriously, and turn potential enemies into allies.

Let's break down the elements of Jobs' "big voice" in this email chain:

1. **Directness**: Jobs immediately states the issue without preamble.

2. **Factual tone**: He presents the situation as objective fact.

3. **Implied reciprocity**: He mentions Apple's policy of not recruiting from Adobe.

4. **Ultimatum framed as a choice**: "One of us must change our policy."

5. **Ball in their court**: "Please let me know who."

It's also worth noting that Jobs didn't wait for this action to become a trend – he wrote to Bruce as soon as a single employee had switched allegiances. Chizen responded by trying to clarify and negotiate, suggesting they maintain their current unspoken agreement of not recruiting senior-level employees.

Jobs' reply here was masterful:

"OK, I'll tell our recruiters that they are free to approach any Adobe employee who is not a Sr. Director or VP. Am I understanding your position correctly?"

This response:

1. Appears to agree while actually escalating the situation.

2. Forces Chizen to clarify his position, rather than hiding behind nebulous status quo.

3. Refrains from jumping straight to vindictive conflict.

4. Puts pressure on Chizen to reconsider his stance, again, with

the ball in his court.

The result? Chizen quickly backpedaled:

"I'd rather agree NOT to actively solicit any employee from either company. If employee proactively approaches then it's acceptable."

Without making threats or explicitly stating his desires, Jobs managed to:

1. Highlight the issue

2. Imply consequences

3. Give Chizen a face-saving way to comply

Jobs gave Chizen a choice to make, but the outcome was inevitable. Many other people might bang their fists on the table if they found out their employees were being poached. They might make threats and hurl accusations. They might puff out their chests and speak dramatically about the consequences of going against them. But with a few simple, choice words Jobs transmitted his Manifest Will—his desire to win at all costs, if provoked.

Instead of threatening, or immediately retaliating, Jobs gave his competitor a chance to back down gracefully. He implicitly said '*I want what you want, but I'll win either way*'. By using carefully chosen words to reshape Chizen's view of reality, Jobs made his preferred outcome seem like the only logical choice.

Finding Your Big Voice

To master the Big Voice in your own life, start by observing and analysing interactions around you. Hone your awareness. Pay attention to how influential people communicate, both in person and in writing. Notice the subtleties in their language, tone, and timing. Make note of how people react to different phrasings and tones, and start to slowly pick up framings you can add to your repertoire.

Practice crafting your messages with intention. Before important conversations or emails, take a moment to consider your desired outcome. Not just your immediate desire in the moment, but the ultimate goal you're driving towards. Think about how you can frame your words to guide the other person towards that outcome without explicitly stating it. Remember, the power of The Big Voice lies in suggestion and implication rather than direct demands.

Develop your ability to state facts objectively and concisely. Don't process everything through the lens of a position you've already decided to take. Think about how you might frame things if the tables were turned. If the other person's position turns out to be more reasonable, be prepared to adopt it at a moment's notice. But in turn, learn to present situations in a way that makes your perspective seem like the natural, logical stance. This requires a deep understanding of the context and the ability to anticipate how others might react.

Work on your timing and patience. The Big Voice isn't about immediate gratification. It requires planting seeds and allowing others to come to the desired conclusion on their own. Sometimes, this means waiting for the right moment to speak or letting silence do the work for you.

Create an air of calm authority. This comes from a combination of self-assurance and a deep understanding of the situation at hand. Always be well-prepared and confident in your position. Remember, the "big voice" isn't about volume or forcefulness, but about the weight and impact of your words.

Cultivate an aura of inevitability around your ideas. Present your vision with such conviction that alternatives seem less appealing or even impossible. This doesn't mean being inflexible, but rather framing your perspective as the most sensible path forward.

Practice active listening. Understanding the other person's position and motivation is crucial for effective persuasion. Use this understanding to frame your responses in a way that addresses their concerns while steering towards your desired outcome.

Practice giving others a way to save face when they concede to your point of view. The goal isn't to win arguments, but to achieve outcomes. By allowing others to feel they've made their own choice, you make it easier for them to align with your position.

Finally, be patient and persistent. Developing your Big Voice is a gradual process. Start with low-stakes situations and gradually apply these techniques to more important interactions as your confidence grows. Remember, the goal is not to manipulate, but to communicate your vision and goals effectively, creating win-win situations whenever possible.

26

KEYS TO THE CITY

> *"You can make more friends in two months by becoming interested in other people than you can in two years by trying to get other people interested in you."*
>
> — Dale Carnegie

History books are replete with tales of singular geniuses who, through force of will and intellect, changed the course of human events. Think of Einstein revolutionising physics in his spare time while working as a patent clerk. Steve Jobs willing the iPhone into existence. Beethoven composing symphonies while deaf. These narratives are compelling, but ultimately misleading.

These individuals were undoubtedly brilliant and driven, but the myth of the lone genius remains merely a myth. The comforting fiction suggests extraordinary individuals single-handedly shape the world through pure talent and determination. It is, in my mind, undeniable that both great and terrible individuals shape history. But the mythology masks the influence of contemporaries, colleagues, enemies, sycophants and teachers who equally play a role in moving the arc of the world's story.

Start with Einstein, that poster child for solitary genius. The image of him scribbling equations in isolation is etched into our collective consciousness. But dig a little deeper, and you'll find a different story.

Einstein's groundbreaking work on relativity was deeply influenced by his discussions with Michele Besso, a close friend and fellow physicist. Einstein actually helped Besso get a job alongside him at the patent office – the two would spend all day chatting and collaborated in shared journals after hours. Einstein called Besso "the best sounding board in Europe" for scientific ideas and later acknowledged Besso's invaluable contributions to his paper on special relativity.

Or consider Marcus Aurelius, the great Stoic philosopher and Roman Emperor. His "Meditations", a cornerstone of Stoic philosophy, might seem like the private musings of a solitary mind. But Aurelius was profoundly shaped by his tutor Fronto and the Stoic philosopher Epictetus. His writing offers more than personal reflections; it represents the culmination of ideas discussed and debated within his intellectual circle.

Biblical David had Jonathan. Tolkien had C.S. Lewis and the rest of "The Inklings". Churchill had his "Secret Circle", a group of trusted advisors including Frederick Lindemann and Brendan Bracken, who provided crucial support and counsel during the darkest days of World War II.

Even Steve Jobs, often portrayed as a singular visionary, relied heavily on a network of collaborators, from Steve Wozniak in Apple's early days to Jony Ive in its resurgence, and eventually Tim Cook, the bean-counting operator who would make Apple one of the world's most profitable companies after Steve Jobs passed away. Jobs' genius wasn't just in his ideas, but in his ability to inspire, cajole, and sometimes strong-arm others into turning those ideas into reality.

For every 'great man of history,' there are dozens of unnamed co-conspirators. Allies, peers, confidants, and competitors who spurred them on, challenged their ideas, and supported them on their path. These supporting players don't always make it into the history books, but their contributions are no less real or important.

This understanding doesn't diminish the achievements of remarkable individuals. Rather, it serves to recognise that even the most brilliant among us don't operate in a vacuum. Innovation and progress are fundamentally collaborative processes, built on a foundation of shared knowledge and mutual support.

So why does this matter? Because buying into the myth of the lone genius can be profoundly disempowering. It suggests that unless you're born with supernatural talents, you're destined to be a bit player in someone else's heroic narrative.

The reality is far more encouraging. Success—whether in business, art, science, or any other field—is less about innate genius and more about your ability to connect, collaborate, and leverage the strengths of those around you. It's about building a network of relationships that can support you, challenge you, and open doors that would be too heavy to pry open alone.

In the coming pages, we'll explore how to do just that. We'll look at how to build and leverage social capital, how to navigate different circles, and how to turn connections into opportunities.

The Power of Connections

When we peel back the curtain on any great achievement, we invariably find a web of connections underpinning it. These connections—friends, peers, mentors, and patrons—are the invisible scaffolding that support and elevate individual talent.

The Renaissance period is heralded as the explosion of creativity and innovation that reshaped Western civilisation. We often think of it through the lens of singular geniuses like Leonardo da Vinci or Michelangelo. But the sparks of individual brilliance cultivated through that period were fuelled by the vibrant intellectual and artistic communities in places like Florence and Venice. It was the Medici family's patronage, the competition between rival city-states, and the cross-pollination of ideas between artists, scientists, and philosophers that created the perfect storm for innovation.

In more recent times, look at the rise of Silicon Valley. The popular narrative focuses on garage startups and young programmers striking it rich. But the real story is one of interconnectedness. The success of companies like Apple, Google, and Facebook doesn't just represent the vision of great founders. Beneath the surface is the ecosystem of venture capitalists, universities, research institutions, and a culture that encourages risk-taking and idea-sharing.

Google famously started in a garage. That garage was rented out to a young Larry Page and Sergey Brin by Susan Wojcicki, the landlord who would later join the company as employee number 16 and, in the course of a 25-year tenure at Google, eventually step in as CEO of YouTube. This is the kind of eclectic serendipity that runs deep in the Valley.

These connections create unlocks—moments where a door suddenly opens, revealing possibilities you hadn't imagined before. It might be a chance conversation that sparks a new idea, an introduction that leads to a crucial partnership, or advice that helps you navigate a critical challenge.

Take the story of Airbnb. The founders were struggling to gain traction and running out of money. It was a connection to the startup accelerator Y Combinator, facilitated by a chance encounter at a party, that provided the mentorship and funding they needed to refine their concept and scale their business. Without that connection, Airbnb might have remained a quirky idea that never took off.

Or consider J.K. Rowling's journey with Harry Potter. Yes, her imagination and writing skills were crucial. But it was her connection to a literary agent, Christopher Little, that got her manuscript in front of publishers after multiple rejections. And it was an eight-year-old girl, the daughter of Bloomsbury's chairman, whose enthusiasm for the first chapter convinced the publisher to take a chance on an unknown author.

These stories highlight a crucial truth: success is rarely, if ever, a solo journey. It's about who you know, who knows you, and how effectively you can leverage those relationships.

But these powerful connections don't just happen by chance. They're cultivated, nurtured, and strategically developed over time. You can't just collect business cards or rack up LinkedIn connections. You have to get serious about building genuine relationships, adding value to others, and positioning yourself at the intersection of different networks.

More Precious Than Gold

Some people's worlds are governed by their bank balance. Some, instead, measure their wealth in the strength and quality of their relationships. In reality, those two worlds overlap significantly, whether you realise it or not. The bank balance of your relationships often makes the difference between success and failure in the long run. Sociologists refer to this invisible ledger of favours, trust, and mutual benefit as 'social capital'.

Why should people help you? What makes someone decide to open a door for you, make an introduction, or go out of their way to support your endeavours? The answer lies in understanding the nature of social capital and how to cultivate it.

Social capital is about reciprocity. Not in the direct, transactional way you might think—not keeping score or expecting an immediate return on your 'investment', but creating a general atmosphere of goodwill and mutual support.

Think of it like tending a garden. You can't plant a seed and immediately expect a fully grown plant. You nurture it over time, and eventually, you reap the rewards. Likewise, building social capital requires consistently adding value to your relationships without expecting immediate returns.

This might mean sharing your expertise freely, making introductions without being asked, or simply being a supportive presence in someone's life. You must become the person who others know they can count on, even for small things.

Adam Grant is a widely respected and highly popular organisational psychologist. Early in his career, Grant made a habit of helping his students and colleagues without expecting anything in return. He would spend hours reviewing resumes, making introductions, and offering advice. This generosity didn't immediately translate into career advancement, but over time, it built a network of people who were eager to support him when he needed it.

When Grant published his first book, 'Give and Take', this network sprang into action. Former students and colleagues, remembering his past kindness, went out of their way to promote the book. This groundswell of support helped propel the book to bestseller status, kickstarting Grant's career as a public intellectual.

Building social capital doesn't just mean being nice. You'll have to be strategic and genuine in your interactions, understanding what you uniquely bring to the table and how you can use that to add value to others.

If you're well-connected in your industry, you might focus on making thoughtful introductions. If you have specialised knowledge, you might offer mentorship or advice. If you're an excellent writer, you might offer to review important documents for your contacts.

The key is to approach these interactions with authenticity and a genuine desire to help. People can sense when you're being transactional, and it quickly erodes trust. On the other hand, when you consistently show up as someone who's willing to help without expecting immediate payback, you build a reservoir of goodwill that can pay dividends in unexpected ways.

And when those dividends pay out, they can be worth more than gold. Social capital, in times of crisis, can be the rarest and most valuable resource you possess.

Building a Network From Scratch

The prospect of building a network from nothing can seem daunting. You might have moved to a new city, switched careers, or simply realised that your current circle isn't aligned with your ambitions. Whatever the reason, the task of creating a robust network from the ground up can seem like both an art and a science. And few mastered it quite like Gertrude Stein.

In 1903, Gertrude Stein arrived in Paris. She was 29 years old, armed with a medical education she never intended to use and a passion for art and literature. Stein had flunked out of medical school after four years, having failed an exam and eventually losing interest in the profession. She knew virtually no one in Paris when she arrived, but within a few years she would become the nucleus of one of the most influential artistic and literary salons of the 20th century.

Stein's salon at 27 rue de Fleurus became a crucible of modernism, frequented by the likes of Pablo Picasso, Henri Matisse, Ernest Hemingway, and F. Scott Fitzgerald. But how did she do it? How did this American transplant transform herself from an outsider to the centre of Parisian avant-garde?

First, Stein positioned herself at the intersection of multiple worlds. She didn't limit herself to just writers or just painters. She cultivated relationships across disciplines, creating a unique space where artists, writers, and thinkers could cross-pollinate ideas. Stein was genuinely curious about others. Stein didn't just collect famous names; she took a real interest in the work and ideas of those around her. This genuine engagement made people want to be in her orbit.

Second, she added value consistently. Stein didn't just host parties; she provided genuine support to the artists in her circle. She bought their paintings when they were still unknown, offered criticism and encouragement, and used her fledgling connections to promote their work.

Third, she created a space for connection. The Saturday evening salons at her apartment became a ritual, a place where newcomers and established figures could mingle freely. By providing this platform, Stein made herself indispensable to the Parisian art scene.

Stein wasn't just focused on building her own network; she actively introduced people she thought would benefit from knowing each other. This made her salon a valuable place to be, even for established figures.

Finally, Stein was unafraid to champion the new and controversial. She supported cubist painters when their work was still derided by the establishment. This willingness to back bold new ideas made her salon a magnet for innovative thinkers. Stein was an early supporter of Pablo Picasso and Henri Matisse when they were still unknown artists. By backing emerging talent, she built lasting loyalty and positioned herself at the forefront of new movements.

The lesson here isn't that you need to start hosting lavish parties or become a patron of the arts. It's that building a network from scratch requires a combination of openness, consistency, and the courage to stand for something.

Start by identifying the intersections in your field. Where do different disciplines or interest groups overlap? Position yourself there. Then, think about how you can add value consistently. Can you connect people? Share knowledge? Offer support or resources?

Create opportunities for connection, even if it's just organising a monthly coffee meetup for people in your industry. And finally, don't be afraid to have a point of view. Supporting new ideas or approaches can make you a magnet for innovative thinkers in your field.

Stein didn't gravitate to the centre of Parisian modernism overnight. It took years of consistent effort, genuine interest in others, and a willingness to take risks on new ideas and people. But the network she built changed the course of art and literature in the 20th century.

The Art of Adding Value

Nobody cares about your success as much as you do. But people care immensely about their own success. Master the art of helping others succeed, and you'll never lack for allies.

This is less about blind altruism than it is, strategic generosity. Every interaction is an opportunity to add value, to be the person who makes someone else's life easier, better, or more interesting. Don't just be nice, be necessary. When everyone's fighting for attention, the quickest way to stand out is to be the person who makes things happen for others. Here's how:

First, become a resource. Knowledge is currency. Cultivate expertise in your field, but don't stop there. Be curious about everything. The broader your knowledge base, the more likely you are to have the answer someone needs. Read voraciously, ask questions incessantly, and curate information like it's your job. Because in a way, it is. When you're the person who always has a relevant article, book recommendation, or industry insight to share, you become indispensable.

Connect the dots. Remember that people and ideas are like raw materials. They'll occasionally stumble into each other and a reaction occurs, but you can be the alchemist who intentionally combines them to make gold. Always be thinking, "Who should know each other?" or "What idea could solve this person's problem?" A previous co-founder of mine was an expert at this, to the point he would introduce other founders to investors in our pipeline before they'd even signed our term sheets. I wouldn't say this was prudent for business, but it was certainly effective for networking.

Woody Allen said 80% of success is showing up. In relationships, it's closer to 100%. Be there when it counts. Remember important dates. Follow up. Your reliability is your calling card. It's okay to be close to the bottom of the list of people your friends call for a random night out, if you're also at the top of the list of people they call when it counts. Help when you have the capacity to help, and offer resources and referrals when you don't.

I've banged the drum of active listening a few times already and I'll bang it again now. Most people listen with the intent to reply. Train yourself to listen with the intent to understand. Try to get below the surface of what's being said. Ask probing questions (where appropriate). Reflect back what you've heard. People will tell you everything you need to know to help them, if you let them. But also be aware that some people don't want immediate help, and just giving them the space to be listened to can be a powerful support.

Anticipate needs. This is where you level up. Don't just solve the problems people bring to you. Anticipate the problems they'll have tomorrow.

One last thing – celebrate others' successes. My memory fails me all the time. I'm not always great at keeping in touch, or being sociable. But I aim to be among the first to congratulate, share, and amplify others' wins. Be a shameless cheerleader when you see others do well. Not because they might one day do the same for you, but because you deeply want to see others win. It's a virtuous cycle. Success begets success. Show an interest, ask questions, take inspiration, keep the cycle going.

A challenge:

This week, for every person you interact with regularly, write down one thing you know about their goals or challenges. Then, do one small thing to help them progress. It could be as simple as sending a relevant article, making an introduction, or holding them accountable. Track the results.

The art of adding value isn't only in grand gestures. It can be achieved simply through consistent, thoughtful action. Master this, and you'll never worry about networking again; people will come to you.

Never Follow Orders

When I returned to the UK from Shanghai, having officially dropped out of university, I landed a graduate job with a consultancy focused on risk and governance. I was part of the new business team, specialising in compliance and financial crime. It should have been a dream start, but there was one significant hurdle: my boss seemed to hate me.

The root of this animosity traced back to my final interview. Aware that my lack of a degree would put me on the back foot, I'd given a slightly unconventional presentation, which had impressed four out of five of the company's directors. The one dissenting voice ended up being my new boss. To make things worse, the director who had championed me through the hiring process left the business shortly after I joined, leaving me without an ally in senior management.

My unconventional style quickly became a point of contention. The boss had a strict quota for daily calls, emphasising quantity over quality. I'd get to the office early, often around 7:30 AM, and hit my quota by the end of the day. But this wasn't enough.

One day, the boss slapped our team call logs on my desk, barking about the length of my calls. It turned out, my conversations were twice as long as some of my peers. I was averaging 20 minutes compared to their 10. Although I was generating more leads than many of them, he saw my approach as inefficient. And, naturally, I refused to back down. I knew that my longer, more personal conversations were building stronger connections.

This battle of wills came to a head during a call with a bank director at HSBC who I'd been courting for a while. He was moving on to a new role, which meant he had valuable insider knowledge about which banks were expanding their compliance practices. In our previous conversation, I hadn't gleaned any useful leads. But I had learned about his family, his children's sports activities, and his daily routine.

This time, armed with that personal knowledge, I planned my call on a day I knew he'd be leaving work early to take the kids to football practice. This would hopefully mean he'd be open to a more frank and productive conversation while he was away from his desk. We spoke while he was on the sidelines. I pulled on every thread of information he gave me, turning what could have been a brief, transactional call into a goldmine of leads.

That same week, following up on one of those leads, I nabbed my first new client: Bank of Tokyo-Mitsubishi UFJ. It was a sign that my relationship-building approach had merit, and I doubled down. By taking the time to get personal with people, I learned enough about the team structures at different banks that I could engage in detailed conversations with new prospects, even at institutions that weren't yet clients. I might be speaking to you for the first time, but if I had your org chart memorised it would sound like you were the only person in the building I hadn't yet worked with.

I'd willingly trade information with prospects and they lapped it up. You would tell me how teams are laid out at Barclays Capital and I'd tell you about the restructuring at Lazard Asset Management. Tell me how they're navigating MiFID II regulations at Goldman Sachs and I'd tell you who they're bringing in at Deutsche Bank.

It only took a few of these conversations, making careful note of all the names and teams, and suddenly I sounded like a seasoned advisor who knew the sector like the back of my hand. In reality, I was just a 20-year-old in a second-hand suit making phone calls so long that my boss wanted me dead.

The results, however, soon spoke for themselves. I brought on seven new mandates from four new clients in my first five months—something previously unheard of for a new hire. And then there was the time I closed three different teams at JP Morgan in a single day.

My boss was livid. My success flew in the face of his hack-and-slash, transactional methods, but there was nothing he could do about it. The numbers didn't lie.

My JP Morgan coup did blow up in my face though. Two weeks after getting three different teams on board, someone in Business Services there woke up and remembered that they had an axe to grind. It turns out that one of my boss' previous disciples had mangled a prior engagement so badly that the bank had sworn they'd never work with us again. I'd managed to get three different senior executives to bypass an internal blacklist, one that our company was previously warned about (although it was never mentioned to me), and for my sins, I was summarily dismissed. Fired in an instant.

It was okay in the end – I interviewed for a better-paying job at a competing firm three hours after being thrown from my office, but I'll tell that story in another chapter.

This experience still taught me a valuable lesson about the power of unconventional networking. While others were focused on hitting arbitrary call quotas, I was building genuine relationships. I wasn't just collecting contact information; I was learning about people's lives, their challenges, their aspirations. This deeper level of engagement not only led to more business but also to more fulfilling professional relationships.

Effective networking doesn't come from following a prescribed set of rules or meeting metrics. The quality comes from genuine human connection. You have to be willing to invest time in conversations that may not have an immediate payoff. You have to remember that the person on the other end of the phone isn't just a potential client, but a human being with a life outside of work.

This approach may not always be the quickest or the easiest. It may not fit neatly into a manager's idea of efficiency. But in the long run, it builds a network of contacts who are more likely to trust you, open up to you, and ultimately, do business with you.

The Friends of Your Friends

The power of a network isn't just in who you know—it's in who *they* know. This ripple effect of connections can open portals in brick walls, allowing you to get where you need to go without getting lost in a maze of monsters and gatekeepers. Perhaps no story illustrates this better than a pivotal moment in Starbucks' history, when a friend of a friend saved the company's future.

In 1987, Howard Schultz was on the verge of realising his dream. He had joined Starbucks five years earlier as director of marketing when it was just a small chain of coffee bean stores. Inspired by the espresso bars of Italy, Schultz had left Starbucks to start his own coffee shop chain, Il Giornale. Now, the original Starbucks owners were looking to sell. Schultz saw his chance to acquire the company and implement his vision on a larger scale.

There was just one problem: he needed to raise $3.8 million in 90 days.

Schultz threw himself into fundraising efforts. He spoke to 242 investors over two months, facing rejection 217 times. By the second month, he had only raised about half the money needed. The situation was dire.

Then came a moment that could have derailed everything. Jerry Baldwin, one of the original Starbucks owners, informed Schultz that one of Schultz's own investors had gone behind his back, making an all-cash offer to buy Starbucks outright. This would have left Schultz out in the cold, his dreams of transforming Starbucks evaporating like steam from a latte.

Feeling desperate, Schultz confided in his friend Scott Greenberg while playing basketball at the Seattle Club. Greenberg, an attorney at a prestigious firm, made a suggestion that would change everything: "You should meet with our senior partner, Bill Gates Sr."

The next morning, Schultz donned a suit and nervously made his way to meet Gates Sr., the father of Microsoft's founder. Schultz laid out his predicament, holding nothing back. Gates Sr. asked just two questions: "Is everything you told me true?" and "Have you left anything out?" Schultz confirmed the veracity and completeness of his story.

An hour later, Gates Sr. took Schultz on a walk to see Sam Strum, the investor threatening to scupper Schultz's plans. Gates Sr., an imposing figure at 6'7", leaned over Strum's desk and delivered a message that was as brief as it was effective: "I don't know what you are planning, but whatever it is, it's not going to happen. Howard Schultz is going to acquire the Starbucks coffee company and he's never going to hear from you again."

That was the entire conversation. As they left, a bewildered Schultz asked Gates Sr. what had just happened. The reply was simple: "You're going to buy Starbucks coffee company, and my son and I are going to help you."

With the support of Bill Gates Sr., Schultz raised the money and acquired Starbucks. This pivotal moment set the stage for Starbucks to become the global coffee empire we know today.

Perhaps most tellingly, in the many social interactions Schultz had with Gates Sr. afterwards (over 100), Gates Sr. never mentioned or took credit for what he had done. This level of humility and discretion in wielding influence is a lesson in itself about how to navigate and leverage networks effectively.

Years later, when Schultz recounted this story at a Microsoft CEO summit, Bill Gates (Jr.) approached him, saying he had never known about his father's role in the Starbucks acquisition. Gates Sr. had never even told his own son about his pivotal role in establishing Starbucks.

What's remarkable about this story isn't just the outcome, but the way it unfolded. Schultz's direct network - the 242 investors he initially approached - couldn't solve his problem. It was a friend of a friend, someone he hadn't even met before that crucial day, who provided the key to his success.

A fundamental truth about networking is that your network is far larger and more powerful than just the people you know directly. It extends to the people they know, and the people those people know. In network theory, these are often referred to as "weak ties", and they can be incredibly powerful.

Weak ties often provide access to information and opportunities that aren't available within your immediate circle. They bridge different social groups, exposing you to new ideas, perspectives, and resources. In Schultz's case, a weak tie provided access to influence and capital that changed the course of his career and, indeed, the world as a whole. I've personally visited over 50 countries now and the one thing almost all of them had in common, in cities from Shanghai to Riyadh, is a branch of Starbucks.

Don't underestimate the power of your extended network. Cultivate relationships not just for what they can provide directly, but for the doors they might open to other connections. Be open about your goals and challenges—you never know when a casual conversation might lead to a life-changing introduction.

Moreover, be generous with your own network. Making introductions and connecting people who might benefit from knowing each other not only helps them but also strengthens your position as a valuable node in the network.

Navigating Different Social Circles

When you step outside your usual circle, you expose yourself to new ideas, perspectives, and ways of thinking. This cognitive diversity can be transformative. It allows you to spot patterns and opportunities that might be invisible to those confined to a single domain. But beyond that, it enables you to bring fresh insights from one field to another, often leading to breakthrough innovations.

Principles of design thinking, originally developed for product design, have revolutionised business strategy. Concepts from evolutionary biology have informed algorithms in computer science. These cross-pollinations of ideas don't happen by accident—they're the result of individuals who've cultivated diverse networks and learned to translate insights across domains.

The benefits of cross-domain networking extend beyond idea generation – it can also provide a competitive edge in your primary field. By understanding the languages, cultures, and challenges of different domains, you become a valuable bridge—someone who can translate between worlds and facilitate collaborations that might otherwise never happen.

In 2011, Nasir Jones, better known as the rapper Nas, made an investment that would change the trajectory of his career. He put money into a fledgling San Francisco startup called Dropbox. This wasn't a random bet – it was the result of a deliberate strategy to break into the tech world.

Nas's journey into tech investing began in 2009 when he joined forces with a young music manager he'd met in a hotel lobby three years earlier, Anthony Saleh, who would become his business partner and confidant. Saleh, who had connections in both the music and tech industries, saw potential in marrying Nas's cultural cache with the booming tech scene.

Their first tech investment was in a streetwear e-commerce site called 12Society. While the venture ultimately failed, it provided valuable lessons and connections. Through 12Society, Nas met Ben Horowitz, co-founder of the venture capital firm Andreessen Horowitz.

Horowitz, a hip-hop enthusiast known for peppering his blog posts with rap lyrics, hit it off with Nas immediately. This connection became Nas's entry point into Silicon Valley's inner circle. Horowitz introduced Nas to the founders of Dropbox, leading to that pivotal 2011 investment.

But Nas didn't rely solely on introductions. He immersed himself in the tech world, attending conferences like TechCrunch Disrupt and South by Southwest. He read voraciously about technology and business, often sending articles to Saleh at 3 AM with ideas for potential investments.

In 2013, Nas and Saleh formalised their partnership by founding QueensBridge Venture Partners, named after the public housing project in Queens where Nas grew up. Their investment strategy was unique, focusing on companies that specifically resonated with Nas' background and interests.

One of their early successes was Ring, the smart doorbell company. Nas saw its potential not just as a convenience but as a security tool for neighbourhoods like the one he grew up in. QueensBridge invested in Ring's Series A round in 2014, and the company was acquired by Amazon for over $1 billion in 2018.

Nas's tech portfolio quickly grew to include companies like Lyft, Coinbase, and Robinhood. His investment in Pluto TV, a free streaming service, paid off when Viacom acquired the company for $340 million in 2019.

What set Nas apart in the VC world was his ability to bridge different social circles. He brought cultural insights from the hip-hop world to his tech investments. For example, his early backing of Genius (formerly Rap Genius) was based on his understanding of fans' desire to decode complex lyrics, including his own.

Conversely, Nas brought his tech knowledge back to the music industry. He was an early advocate for streaming services and advised other artists on how to leverage technology in their careers.

By 2020, Nas had invested in over 100 companies across various sectors. His success in tech investing has been so significant that by most estimates, his returns from these investments have far outstripped his earnings from his music career.

Nas's journey from Queensbridge to Sand Hill Road demonstrates the power of navigating different social circles. By authentically connecting across diverse groups and leveraging the unique perspective gained from each circle, Nas positioned himself at the intersection of culture and technology, spotting opportunities that others missed.

The Art of Burning Bridges

There are times when severing ties might be necessary or even beneficial. But there's an art in knowing when to burn a bridge, how to do it without causing unnecessary damage, and understanding the potential long-term consequences.

In the 1990s, the Chicago Bulls were the most dominant team in basketball history. Led by Michael Jordan, Scottie Pippen, and head coach Phil Jackson, they won six NBA championships in eight years. Behind the scenes, however, tension was brewing.

The Bull's General Manager Jerry Krause, despite his role in assembling this legendary team, felt under-appreciated. He famously declared, "Players and coaches don't win championships; organisations win championships." This statement, perceived as downplaying the contributions of Jordan and his teammates, created a rift that would never heal.

Krause's relationship with the team's stars deteriorated further due to contract disputes and his desire to rebuild the team prematurely. His treatment of Phil Jackson was particularly contentious. Despite Jackson's unprecedented success, Krause announced that the 1997-98 season would be Jackson's last, regardless of the team's performance.

This decision effectively signalled the end of the Bulls' dynasty. Jordan had stated he wouldn't play for any coach other than Jackson. After winning their sixth championship in 1998, the team broke up. Jordan retired (for the second time), Pippen was traded, and other key players left.

The consequences of Krause's bridge-burning were severe and long-lasting. The Bulls entered a prolonged period of mediocrity, not reaching the conference finals again for 23 years. Krause's legacy, despite his earlier successes, was tarnished. He became a villain in basketball lore, his achievements overshadowed by his role in breaking up one of the greatest teams in sports history.

Krause's story illustrates the dangers of burning bridges unnecessarily. His actions, driven by ego and a desire for recognition, ultimately harmed not only his relationships but also his own legacy and the organisation he sought to prioritise.

Not all bridge-burning is detrimental. Sometimes, severing ties can be necessary for personal growth, ethical reasons, or to escape toxic situations. The key is to do so thoughtfully and professionally. But sometimes, even when a relationship seems tenuous, not burning through a bridge in haste can prove to be a blessing.

An Animated Kinship

When Bob Iger became CEO of Disney in 2005, he was inheriting a potentially fraught relationship with someone who could be mercurial and spiteful, or a gentleman in equal measure – Pixar CEO Steve Jobs. The relationship between the two companies had been strained due to repeated conflicts with Iger's predecessor at Disney, Michael Eisner. Iger had a choice. The beef would need to end one way or another. He could bury the hatchet or use it to behead his supposed enemy.

Instead of continuing the antagonistic relationship with Jobs, Iger reached out to repair the situation. He recognised the value of maintaining a positive relationship with both Pixar and Jobs, even in the face of past conflicts. Before his first day on the job, Iger called Jobs personally in advance to inform him of his appointment as CEO, a gesture that surprised Jobs given the history of tension.

Iger then arranged a one-on-one meeting with Jobs. During this meeting, Iger shared his vision about the future of digital media, including the idea of films being available on handheld devices. Jobs, recognising a kindred spirit, would later show Iger an early version of the iPod Video once he'd returned to the helm of Apple. And when Jobs asked if Iger would be willing to put Disney films on the device, Iger agreed without hesitation.

This moment marked the beginning of a strong professional relationship and personal friendship. Iger's willingness to embrace new technology and think creatively aligned well with Jobs' innovative approach.

The rebuilt relationship bore fruit when Iger eventually proposed the idea of Disney acquiring Pixar. Despite initial scepticism, Jobs was open to the discussion. Iger's respect for Pixar's culture and his commitment to maintaining its independence were crucial in convincing Jobs to consider the deal. And none of this would be on the table if Iger hadn't first extended the olive branch.

The acquisition was successful, making Steve Jobs Disney's largest individual shareholder and a board member in the process. But more than that, it was the start of a deep personal connection. Jobs confided in Iger about his cancer diagnosis, one of the few people he told early on. Iger became a trusted advisor to Jobs, and Jobs often provided insight and guidance to Iger on Disney's strategic decisions.

Their relationship continued until Jobs' death in 2011. At Jobs' small, private burial, Iger was one of only about 25 people present.

The contrast between these two examples highlights a crucial point: while standing your ground is sometimes necessary, it's often more beneficial to find ways to maintain relationships, even in difficult circumstances.

By approaching Steve Jobs with openness, respect, and a willingness to embrace new ideas, Bob Iger not only secured a crucial business deal but also gained a valuable mentor and friend. With the right approach, even the most damaged professional relationships can be repaired and transformed into powerful alliances.

Even when the beams seem worn, cracked and crumbling, before burning a bridge, carefully consider the long-term implications.

Ask yourself:

1. Is this conflict truly irreconcilable, or is there room for resolution?

2. Is this conflict a reflection of real differences or simply the result of partisanship and competition?

3. What are the potential future costs of severing this relationship? And what might be the second-order effects (the consequences of those consequences)

4. Am I acting out of temporary emotion or a reasoned, long-term perspective?

If you do decide that ending a relationship is necessary, do so with grace and professionalism. Avoid public confrontations or disparaging remarks. Be clear about your reasons, but remain respectful. Remember, industries are often smaller than they appear—your paths may cross again in the future. And never underestimate your ability to do the opposite—to build an alliance with benefits that could compound for years to come.

Moreover, even when a professional relationship ends, it's possible to maintain a degree of cordiality. You never know when circumstances might change, making a former adversary a potential ally.

The art of burning bridges is really about knowing when not to. Develop the wisdom to see beyond current conflicts and the maturity to handle disagreements without permanently damaging relationships. If you believe that your network is your net worth, don't squander your wealth by letting pride and ego make you blind to your riches. Preserving connections should always be the default. Only in rare, carefully considered circumstances should bridges be burned. And even then, it's worth leaving a small boat nearby, just in case you need to cross that river again someday.

Adversity

PART III

Adversity

Adversity

Life isn't smooth, predictable or formulaic – it's a bubbling, vibrant force of motion. Despite your knowledge, skill, and best-laid plans, the tide can turn at any moment. Things won't always go your way. They won't always go to plan. You won't always understand why the chips fall as they do.

In the face of challenges, setbacks and unexpected obstacles, you will always have the choice to turn back. To seek safety. To cower in the comfort of consistent complacency. Adversity says to ambition: "How badly do you want it?"

Most people crumble in the face of difficulty. They see obstacles as signs to retreat, to lower their expectations, to accept defeat. But the sovereign see adversity differently. They recognise that the path to greatness is paved with challenges, that diamonds are formed under pressure, that steel is forged in fire.

Fear isn't a weakness. It's a natural evolutionary response. But it doesn't have to dictate your actions. What makes the distinction between being refined by pressure and burned by it, is your ability to stand fast under fire, stare through the flame, and withstand the heat.

Resilience doesn't avoid hardship, it embraces it. It stands firm when others would flee. It pushes forward when every instinct screams to retreat. It transforms pain into power, setbacks into comebacks, and failures into fuel for future success.

Without adversity, we remain untested, our potential unrealised. History's greatest achievements were born not from comfort, but from struggle. The most inspiring stories are those of individuals who faced seemingly insurmountable odds and emerged victorious. Not because they were exceptionally gifted or lucky, but because they refused to be defeated.

Adversity strips away pretence and reveals your true nature. It forces you to confront your weaknesses, to question your assumptions, to dig deep and discover whatever reserves of strength had lain dormant awaiting provocation.

Embracing adversity doesn't mean seeking out hardship for its own sake, but simply approaching challenges with a mindset of growth and opportunity. It means viewing setbacks not as failures, but as feedback. It means understanding that while the path may not be smooth, traversing it is always worth the journey.

David Elikwu — Raging Bull, 2025

27

LEARN TO TREAD WATER

"The world breaks everyone, and afterward many are strong at the broken places."

— Ernest Hemingway

Some of the best lessons you learn in life are the hard ones. When those revelations arrive on your doorstep, they are rarely cute and small and neatly wrapped like fortune cookies in a Chinese restaurant. Instead, you open the door, and the mailman smacks you in the mouth. The mailman is the universe, and you'll accept this package whether you like it or not:

No one is coming to save you; that's possibly one of the most powerful lessons I've learned. This doesn't mean you should walk around with a cold snarl and a chip on your shoulder. It also doesn't mean you should cry yourself to sleep, resigning yourself to perpetual victimhood. You just need to learn the difference between swimming and thrashing.

When we're lost in life's vast ocean and being tossed violently by waves, our immediate reaction is to thrash. Deep down you know that you can't beat the water into submission, but you try it anyway, attempting anything to survive. But you can't thrash for too long. Once your energy is spent, you'll drown. You have only two options: swim, or tread water.

Swimming means putting one hand in front of the other. Kicking your feet. Trying to generate rhythm. It doesn't matter if you're swimming in the wrong direction at first – as long as your body is under control. You'll have the peace of mind to notice that you're off track and adjust accordingly. Most people don't. They're too busy panicking.

The other option is to tread water. It's one of the first things you're taught when learning to swim. It's a skill that can save your life. Maximise energy conservation and keep your head above the water. Make slow, smooth movements. Analyse your surroundings. Buy yourself time to determine your next actions. In moments of panic, don't thrash, tread water. It makes the difference between life and death.

My entire time at Google felt like the last scenes of The Titanic. I was standing on the world's biggest and most beautiful ship, surrounded by decadence, all while knowing the ground was shifting beneath my feet. I was still desperately trying to keep my dream alive. My dream of becoming a lawyer. But with each tilt of the ship, I could feel the odds waning. In retrospect, it's easy to draw the scene. I can hear the music playing. The symphony shining above the noise. But in that moment, all I heard was chaos.

My first-year grades at university weren't great. I'd been skipping class either to spend more time at Google, to watch Friends re-runs, or to loaf around with a girlfriend who went to school in another city. I was playing two sports. I was on multiple societies. I was having a good time.

Someone had told me that your first-year grades don't matter. I took that advice as liberally as you can imagine. Turns out they lied, or I was deceived by my own ignorance. Either way, I'd only just realised how much those grades might impact my odds of getting a summer internship, let alone a training contract with a top law firm. Now, I was looking for a way out. Scrambling for a lifeboat. I desperately needed to hear someone tell me everything was going to be okay.

But I didn't know any corporate lawyers. I didn't even know anyone who had actually received an offer to train at a top firm. I had never come across someone who had made it, against the odds, as I would need to.

So when I approached a director at Google in the midst of a swanky soiree, I was standing on the deck of the Titanic and asking the band to play one last song. I was searching for affirmation—a refrain to soothe my nerves. I cornered him between finger food and champagne, under the pretence of getting another drink.

I told him my story. I'd previously been invited to dozens of law firms, investment banks and wealth managers. But office tours and free biscuits weren't the same as job offers, and I couldn't shake the fear that those would never come. I asked for advice. I asked if he could mentor me. I was asking for directions to the nearest lifeboat.

"I'm sorry," he said. "I can't help you".

I'm not abridging the script here for brevity. I talked for five minutes, he talked for five seconds. Those were the only words that man said to me before turning around and walking away. Back to the party.

His words crawled under my skin, passing right through my bones and out of my body before being absorbed by the thrum of the crowd behind me. I had no idea if the music was still playing. All I could hear was chaos. It was my last night on the Titanic, and it had only just dawned on me that no one was coming to save me. I reeked of desperation, and you could smell it coming from a mile away.

I did a pretty miserable job of stifling my tears. Lesson learned. I'd never put my destiny in someone else's hands again. Instead of floundering in uncertainty, I took a momentary step back to consider my options and find another path forward. A few months later I'd paused my degree and was on a plane to Shanghai with a business visa to work for a law firm there.

My first-year grades might have been an issue for white-shoe firms in London, but I'd previously taken the International Baccalaureate, and my English grades were in the top 0.06% globally. I'd taken both English Language and English Literature, and only dropped a single mark across both final exams. Halfway across the world, for all my troubles, that made me an asset to a Pan-Asian law firm looking to increase their global presence.

28

TAKE THE MASK OFF

"There is no passion to be found playing small—in settling for a life that is less than the one you are capable of living."

— Nelson Mandela

I'm going to tell you a story that you must promise not to replicate. It's about a little boy who almost got stabbed on the bus. It was me. I was about 14, and on my way home from school.

I'll give you a brief set of facts that might provide some illumination regarding my environment and state of mind at the time:

1. I got into a fight on my first day of secondary school, before the morning bell had even rung. I didn't start the fight, but I wasn't going to lose it either.

2. The first time I saw someone get stabbed, I was twelve, and just arriving at a pre-arranged fight between kids from two schools. The fight had nothing to do with me, but you had to show up to these things so that other kids would return the favour if you ever got into trouble yourself. Luckily, I was late and didn't have to fight, because I had double-detention that day.

3. I went to the kind of school which had an assigned local police officer who had his own office in the building. I don't

think it was a particularly bad school, it was just a particularly bad point in time. One of the kids in my class got laughed at because his parents bought him a knife-slash-proof school uniform. It was that kind of time.

So I'm on the bus home from school. Not the one I mentioned above – by this point, I'd been forced to transfer schools after racking up 386 incident slips in two and a half years at the first one. Nothing serious, I'd just crack a lot of jokes in class and come up with silly ways to make money, like stealing confiscated balls from the school storeroom at lunchtime and selling them back to the kids who had lost them that morning.

A man gets onto the bus and sits next to me, near the back. Weathered skin. Beard in grizzled, peppercorn patches. Smelling faintly like alcohol. I'm holding my LG flip-phone in my left hand, by the window. Out of nowhere, he grabs my right hand forcefully, wrenching it below the view of neighbouring passengers. His grip is cold and vice-like. He squeezes close to me, and in his other hand, half out of his hoodie, I see the dull grey of a small, serrated chopping knife.

Under his voice and stinky breath, he growls at me to hand over the phone. I could feel his fist full of fingers clamping down harder, threatening to snap my small wrist as I tried to hold the phone away from him. My arm hurt so much that I almost dropped the phone.

I had nowhere to run, so I said something. I don't remember exactly what I said, but I had a smart mouth as a kid. In my panic and anger, I just raised my voice and started insulting him. It was strange, the way he instantly shrank back. So I kept going. It was as though he had been possessed by a demon, and through the heat of our connection, his hard arm on my weak one, the demon had transferred from his body to mine. I wasn't shouting or yelling. I just told him that he wasn't having my phone, and a few other things I won't print here. And he fled, like the thief he was, elbowing his way off the bus as it approached the next stop.

I don't know what got into me that day. I'd never do that again, and you shouldn't either, but it was interesting to realise how half-hearted even the worst criminals can be. They want easy targets because they still fear shame. The last thing they expect is a little kid to talk back at them like he has nothing to lose, and lambast them in front of a crowd of strangers. Once he saw that I was sufficiently serious, and realised that he himself was not, he scarpered. In retrospect, while I'm grateful to not have lost my life because I was ignorant of its value, I appreciate that I can now see that pattern play out everywhere I look.

At school, at work, at home, and everywhere else, seriousness scares people. Earnestness is a threat to anyone who hasn't sat down to ruminate on their resolve. When a hardened sword comes across a hasty one, the latter breaks into pieces. Once you understand this, it becomes easier to navigate life, as long as you can remember to hold on to your earnestness. The world would love, more than anything, to strip it away from you.

What Does Your Mask Look Like?

Society flinches at earnestness. It recoils from the unmasked ambition of those who dare to take themselves seriously. This is the kind of truth you'll notice everywhere once you start looking for it. It starts with the ceremonial bullying of the kids who enjoyed homework at school, the ones who proactively raised their hands during class, the ones who adopted niche interests and devoted hours to their hobbies. It ends with the gawks and awkward glances at work, the whispered "*Who does she think she is*" when you develop an interest in improving the standard of your work, or your taste and sense of style.

Most people get their opinions the same way they get their furniture. Their thoughts come like new kitchens—pre-designed, flat-packed, delivered and assembled by others in a matter of days. When everyone around you has pre-fab opinions, developing individual taste feels dangerous. Developing niche interests feels vulnerable. Earnestly and obviously going after the things you want seems slimy. But to pursue and take hold of your deep desires, you'll have to take your mask off.

Over time we're taught to play it cool, to hide our passions behind a veneer of ironic detachment. God forbid someone catch us caring too much. Fitting in feels good, until you realise it's a trap. You won't feel awkward if you make yourself bland, the corrective inner voice says. But if there are ambitious things you want in life, you'll have to unplug yourself from the mainstream aversion to sincerity in order to achieve them.

Think about the last time you shared a dream with someone. A real, audacious goal that you'd quietly held on to and tried to nurture. When you finally said it out loud, did you preface it with a self-deprecating joke? Did you downplay its importance, just in case it didn't pan out? That's your mask at work. They are the shields we use to protect ourselves from the potential sting of failure or ridicule.

But that mask, that protective barrier, it doesn't just shield you from pain. It suffocates your potential. It muffles your voice. It dims your light.

Taking off your mask won't be as simple as becoming humourless or obsessive. It will require you to find the courage to stand naked in your ambition, and to pursue your goals with a ferocity that makes others uncomfortable. You'll need to be willing to look foolish, to be laughed at and dismissed – all in service of a vision that others can't yet see.

This is the hidden superpower of the unapologetically serious; of the Sovereign. When you refuse to dilute your passion, when you approach life with the intensity of a zealot and the focus of a monk, you become a force of nature.

When the people around you are accustomed to half-hearted attempts and casual indifference, the person who dares to care deeply becomes almost terrifying in their power. They shake others from their stupor, reminding them of their complacency. They challenge the status quo with the vigour of their commitment.

Think again about the shape of your mask – those habits you have built to hide your passions and smooth over the sharp edges of your personality. What would happen if you took the mask off? If you pursued your goals not with the timid, tepid hope of the quiet dreamer, but with the unwavering, white-hot conviction of the possessed? As though a force of heaven were guiding your steps. What mountains could you move? What empires could you build? Find out now, or you'll die never knowing.

The Birth of a Beast

In 2020 a video titled "Hi Me in 5 Years" was published to YouTube. It went viral instantly for one reason alone: it had been recorded and scheduled to upload five years earlier by a 17-year-old Jimmy Donaldson. Jimmy had decided to call his own shot, sending a message into the future predicting his success.

Four years before that, in 2012, 13-year-old Jimmy had uploaded his first YouTube video under the username "MrBeast6000." It was nothing special – just a recording of him playing Minecraft, a popular video game. But Jimmy had a goal that wouldn't stay secret for long—it would soon become his singular obsession. He didn't just want to become a professional YouTuber. He wanted to be great at it. The *greatest*.

Over the next four years, young Jimmy experimented with various content types, searching for his first viral hit. He made reaction videos, compilations of funny clips, and estimates of other YouTubers' wealth. Progress was slow, but steady. By mid-2016, he had amassed about 30,000 subscribers.

He'd rush home from school, lock himself in his room, and make videos until the early hours of the morning. His mother would find him, bleary-eyed at 3 am, still editing. When she fretted about his grades slipping, he made her a promise: "I'm going to be the biggest YouTuber in the world." She thought he had lost his mind.

Later when, just a few weeks into college, Jimmy decided to drop out of East Carolina University to pursue YouTube full-time, his mother was livid. She kicked him out of the house, and he crashed on a friend's couch, living on his share of YouTube's ad revenue.

But Jimmy wasn't just throwing videos up with a wish and a prayer. Each one was the product of meticulous studying. Donaldson obsessed over analytics – he and a group of friends would spend hours each day on a Skype call watching successful YouTubers and dissecting their videos, monitoring the growth of their channels. He'd figure out what worked for YouTube's biggest stars while simultaneously experimenting with new content ideas, applying the patterns he'd learned from others into his own videos.

He would read the entire dictionary on camera, critique other YouTube videos, and bury himself alive for views. While other kids at school were playing for fun, Jimmy was playing to win. He was decoding the levers of viewer retention and click-through rates by iterating on thumbnail designs and mastering the dark art of clickbait. He was playing Moneyball with video impressions.

His big break finally came in 2017. Donaldson had pivoted to creating videos featuring challenges, experiments, and extreme stunts. One of his first viral hits was a video where he counted out loud to 100,000—a bizarre stunt that took over 40 hours to complete. It was the kind of thing that people would watch because they'd never attempt it themselves. A kid just like them was willing to grind out hours of mind-numbing work simply because he was committed to creating a rare artefact. It was a product of intense earnestness, and it marked the beginning of what became his signature style: endurance challenges, extravagant donations, and high-concept stunts that pushed the boundaries of what YouTube content could be.

As his channel grew, so did the scale of his productions. Jimmy was offered $5000 as his first sponsorship deal, and he asked the company to double it so that he could simply give the money away. He made that the entire premise of the video. It went viral. Then he started doing that in every video. He'd give away large sums of money, cars, and even houses. Just like a regular YouTuber, he'd collaborate with brands and sponsors. But unlike anyone on the platform, instead of pocketing the money, he poured it all back into creating even more ambitious content. He only had one goal, and he'd put everything on the line for it.

When the "Hi Me in 5 Years" video was finally released in October 2020, it revealed how dramatically Donaldson had exceeded his own expectations. 17-year-old Jimmy had predicted he would hit one million subscribers with 5 years of focused effort. Instead, he had amassed over 45 million subscribers. Most people forget their New Year's resolutions after five weeks. Jimmy not only predicted he could stay focused on a single goal for half a decade, but he blew past his own eccentric estimations. In a few short years, he had established himself as one of the most influential creators on YouTube. And he didn't stop there.

Jimmy revealed that he had previously recorded more videos for his future self, including ones set to be released 10, 20, and 50 years into the future. He was prepared to devote his life to this singular goal.

He looked insane at first, but in retrospect, his seriousness was obvious from his approach to content creation. He became known for spending months planning a single video, obsessing over every detail to maximise engagement. His videos eventually cost hundreds of thousands or even millions of dollars to produce. When the Netflix series "Squid Game" became a worldwide sensation, Jimmy recreated every set from the multi-million dollar program and brought hundreds of random subscribers to his campus in North Carolina, to battle it out for a $456,000 prize. Jimmy spent $2 million on the set and production, with another $1.5 million for various cash prizes.

The YouTube video he eventually uploaded showcasing his take on Squid Game cost $134,600 per minute of final screen time to produce, while the original show cost Netflix approximately $43,500 per screen minute across 9 episodes. Jimmy's video went on to break YouTube's record for the most views in a day for a non-music video, racking up 42.6 million views in 24 hours, and over 100 million views in 4 days.

Netflix, by contrast, later made their own version of the fictional reality show, which is only fair considering they own the IP. The debut episode of Netflix's 'Squid Game: The Challenge' hit 2 million views after 5 days. Despite their size, they couldn't come close to beating MrBeast at his own game. Amazon saw the gulf in popularity play out and immediately offered Donaldson $100 million for the opportunity to create his own game show on their competing platform, Amazon Prime Video. The show will have 1000 contestants and feature a $5 million cash prize. That's the power of being serious.

In 2024, MrBeast has over 250 million subscribers across six different channels. He's given away millions to charity, planted 20 million trees, and cleaned up 30 million pounds of ocean trash. He's launched successful side ventures like MrBeast Burger and a snack company called Feastables. Jimmy Donaldson makes over $700 million dollars a year and will be YouTube's first billionaire.

Donaldson's journey from a 13-year-old making Minecraft videos to a modern media magnate shows the power of unwavering focus and relentless self-improvement. Every time conventional wisdom suggested he tone down his early ambitions or pursue a "real job", he doubled down instead. He didn't just take off the mask of cool indifference; he discarded it entirely, embracing a level of dedication that many still find hard to comprehend.

The Proof is in the Poison

Barry Marshall was a young doctor at Royal Perth Hospital in Australia. In 1982, he and his colleague Robin Warren thought they had stumbled upon something extraordinary: spiral bacteria living in the stomachs of patients with ulcers and gastritis. This flew in the face of established medical wisdom, which held that only stress and lifestyle factors caused ulcers.

Marshall and Warren weren't just idly curious. They were convinced these bacteria, later named Helicobacter pylori, were the real culprits behind ulcers. But the medical community wasn't buying it. Prestigious journals rejected their papers. At conferences, their presentations were met with scepticism, even mockery.

Most people would have given up in the face of such overwhelming opposition. But Marshall wasn't most people. He didn't just believe in his theory; he was willing to put his own health on the line to prove it.

In 1984, after his research proposals involving human subjects were repeatedly rejected, Marshall decided to become his own guinea pig. He drank a broth teeming with H. pylori bacteria cultured from a patient's stomach.

This wasn't a rash decision made in the heat of the moment. It was a calculated risk, born of frustration with the scientific community's intransigence and a deep-seated belief in the importance of his work.

Marshall knew that if he was right, he was on the verge of revolutionising the treatment of a condition that affected millions worldwide.

Within days, Marshall developed symptoms of gastritis. Endoscopy revealed severe inflammation in his stomach lining. He had successfully given himself an acute case of H. pylori infection, proving that these bacteria could indeed colonise a healthy human stomach.

He was willing to give himself a stomach ulcer to prove a point, and his self-experimentation provided the irrefutable evidence needed to convince the sceptics. But it didn't happen overnight. Marshall's seriousness made people take a closer look at an idea everyone thought was outlandish, and it still took years for the medical community to fully accept the bacterial theory of ulcers.

Throughout it all, Marshall remained unwavering in his conviction. He continued to research, publish, and advocate for his theory, even as many of his peers dismissed him as a crackpot.

It wasn't until the mid-1990s that the medical community finally accepted Marshall and Warren's findings. In 2005, over two decades after downing that poisonous pint, Marshall and Warren were awarded the 'Nobel Prize in Physiology or Medicine' for their discovery.

Marshall's story isn't just about scientific breakthrough. It highlights the power of unapologetic seriousness in the face of ridicule and rejection. When the entire medical establishment told him he was wrong, he didn't back down. He didn't try to soften his stance or hedge his bets. Instead, he doubled down, risking his own health to prove his point.

This level of commitment might seem extreme, even reckless. But it's this very intensity that allowed Marshall to overturn decades of medical dogma and improve the lives of millions worldwide.

The Crucible of Cringe

It's unlikely that you'll ever have to knock back a vicious beaker of bacteria just to be taken seriously, but everyday earnestness often carries a penalty that seems just as harsh: being cringe.

No one really wants to be 'cringe'. The phrase signifies a social taboo, a label slapped on those who seem awkward, embarrassing or unrelatable to the cool kids. But being cool is a crutch, and a cage if you try and optimise for it too early in your journey. Nothing will kill your progress faster than the desire to be cool. The laxity of sprezzatura can't be forced.

As a teenager, I had the strange blessing of recovering from a plague of childhood asthma and becoming strong and mildly athletic. During the years that followed, I played football, and then basketball, and eventually American football. But throughout school, I'd occasionally disappear at lunchtime, and nobody had any idea where I was. I was actually in the library living my second life among fellow nerds, writing Lord of the Rings fan fiction and drawing anime characters. And yes, I realise I'm essentially admitting that I lived the plot of High School Musical (I even sang in a choir at the Royal Albert Hall). But I wasn't the only one.

The star of the Creed trilogy and Marvel's Black Panther, Michael B. Jordan, got bullied for carrying his headshots to high school as an aspiring actor. It was cringe then, but decades later he was interviewed on the red carpet of a star-studded premiere by one of the girls from his school who used to bully him. Kids used to call him corny and laugh at his name being the same as basketball legend Michael Jordan. Now he's a legend in his own right, and they have to call him actor, director, and Hollywood mogul Michael B. Jordan.

At Princeton, Jeff Bezos was the head of the space society. What a cornball, his classmates laughed. It was cringe. He had to change his major from Physics to Computer Science because he found the math too hard. He didn't become an astronaut when he graduated, he became a boring banker. But he rose through the ranks quickly.

After a few years, Bezos quit banking. He took the money he made as a financier, raised a little more, and built a weird company – an online bookstore. Another cornball move, it seemed, in 1994. He was a laughing stock once again. That is, until that tiny little company, the one which used old doors as its first desks in a cramped office, the one whose stock lost 80% of its value in the dot com crash, the one he was going to call Relentless.com before he settled on Amazon.com , went on to surpass everyone's wildest expectations. Everyone's except Jeff's.

That company made him, for a while, the richest man on the planet. And then Jeff took the money he made building Amazon and built a new company—a spaceship company called Blue Origin—and Bezos took himself to space. An astronaut without a physics degree.

It can take a while for things to come full-circle. Bezos did everything he said he was going to do, and nobody believed it until it was inevitable. Then suddenly, when his success was obvious, in the eyes of many, he became cool.

> Greatness is deviance. It requires being distinct from the good and the ordinary. It requires hitting a target nobody can see. And the number of people who can truly become great is only limited because deviance is socially discouraged.

What people won't tell you is that nobody achieves greatness without passing through the crucible of cringe—without caring about something, believing in something, when consensus doesn't.

Leonardo DiCaprio's first film scored 4/10 on IMDB. Brad Pitt's first role was as an uncredited extra on a film that scored 5/10. Things might suck. People might laugh. But trust that it is only part of the process. If you push through the cringe, holding steadfastly to your earnest truth, consensus will eventually shift.

Embrace the cringe. Hold on to your obsession. Let them laugh, then let them watch.

29

KEEP YOUR SHOULDER OFF THE MAT

"Life's not fair. It never was, it isn't now, and it won't ever be."

— John F. Kennedy

I owe much of my success to a massacre in my hometown. It is a terrible and costly truth. Growing up, my father told me stories of his experiences during the Nigerian civil war. What I didn't learn from him, I could pick up from novels like Half a Yellow Sun. But the clear weight of its consequences didn't hit my chest squarely until the day I had to draw my extended family tree for a school project. While researching, I stumbled upon a local memorial in my hometown of Asaba, listing the dead. There, line by line, I read the names of over a dozen direct relatives—casualties of Nigeria's troubled history.

The acrid smell of war still clung to my grandfather's clothes when he arrived in London. This was 1967, and civil war was tearing his homeland apart. He left behind a wife and three children, my father the youngest among them. Their fates hinged on his simple mission: find work, save money, and bring his family to safety, one by one.

By the time my father, the last to arrive, landed on British soil, he found he was no longer the family's baby. In the years it took to secure safe passage for everyone, he'd become a middle child of six. Three more siblings had joined the brood. Now, he wasn't just finding his way in a new country, he was finding his place in a family that had grown in his absence.

Settling in at school was hard enough. In the span of mere months, he'd gone from evading bombs in the bush, to dodging fights in the kind of school that would later become a juvenile detention centre after being closed and relaunched numerous times due to poor performance. The local newspaper which announced the school's final shuttering ran the headline: "It's all over for the school of no hope." A few relaunches earlier, when it came time for my father to take his O-level exams, he'd hit a wall. The school administration had ruled that he wasn't fit to take mathematics. A teacher had decided that he wouldn't be able to cope with it, and that was the end of that, they thought.

The problem is, my father is more stubborn than I am. He hadn't survived a war and crossed an ocean just to let some petty pedagogue prevent him from going to university. If they wouldn't let him take math at school, he'd find another way.

He enrolled in a separate night school, determined to spite them. What should have taken two years, he crammed into one. It was a gruelling schedule, but he persevered. His efforts paid off when he secured acceptance to the University of East Anglia. Perhaps not the world's most prestigious university, but it was a foot in the door they had tried to close on him.

Once there, things changed fast. It didn't take long for professors to realise his aptitude for mathematics, and he spent the rest of his twenties with full rides at whichever institution he chose to attend. First, a master's degree at the London School of Economics. Then offers to do further research at both Oxford and Imperial College.

It seemed bananas to me, at first, that he chose Imperial instead of giving me a ticket into the nation's elite by attending Oxford. Especially considering that he'd deferred a lucrative job offer as an actuary in order to stay in academia. And doubly so, considering he later dropped out of the maths department and returned to Nigeria, after finding faith and deciding he preferred purpose to pedigree and profit.

Somehow, in Lagos, he ended up marrying a PhD dropout who had similarly postponed parasitology research to pursue church and charity work, and that's how I ended up being a first-generation immigrant once-removed, the only person in my family with no degrees, but still the first one to actually get a corporate or graduate job.

When Life Says No, Don't Listen

While I was at school, my father enrolled me in judo and karate. Because somewhere along his own improbable path, between escaping civil war and becoming a math prodigy, he'd also managed to become a regional champion in both judo and karate, with a black belt in the latter. When I eventually asked how he managed the feat, especially considering his diminutive frame, his answer was characteristically understated: "It was easy once I realised judo was just village wrestling."

Training with my father was the kind of gruelling labour that I can only appreciate in retrospect. The push-ups and sit-ups on Saturday mornings, the grappling, the headaches after spending half an hour practising rolls and throws in the living room.

There's a single line he drilled into me that I later internalised as a life philosophy:

> *"Keep your shoulders off the mat."*

There are only a few ways a judo match can end:
1. **Ippon**: The match ends immediately when one competitor performs a throw or technique with such force, control, and precision that the opponent's back (both shoulders) touches the mat. An ippon can also be awarded for a successful submission or hold-down lasting 20 seconds.
2. **Waza-ari**: A waza-ari is awarded for a throw or technique that is almost perfect but doesn't fully meet the criteria for an ippon. Two waza-ari scores equal one ippon, thus ending the

match.

3. **Submission**: The match ends if a competitor successfully applies a choke or joint lock that forces the opponent to submit by tapping out or verbally indicating defeat.

4. **Penalty**: The match can end if a competitor receives a disqualification (hansoku-make) or accumulates enough penalties to lose. This results in a win for the opponent.

5. **Timeout**: If time expires, the competitor with the highest score wins. If scores are tied, the match may go into overtime, known as "golden score" (where the first point scored in overtime wins the match).

So, barring disqualification, for as long as the clock is still ticking, keep your shoulders off the mat. Life will try to pin you down, to stop you, to pressure you into submission. You might be knocked off your feet, thrown head over heels, and find yourself on the ground, battered and bruised. But the match only ends once both shoulders touch the mat.

As long as you can wriggle and writhe, and keep one shoulder in the air, refusing to accept defeat, you're still in the fight.

When life had said no to my father, he simply refused to listen. He rejected that reality and crafted his own. This, I have learned, is the only way to live. It is the only way to truly persevere, and build the life you want.

Life can throw whatever it wants at you. You won't always have a choice between standing tall and falling.

Sometimes your momentum is snatched away from you, and past victories disappear as you find yourself disoriented, plunging violently to the ground. But your choice comes in refusing to stay down, in demanding to stay in the fight, and in maintaining the presence of mind, in the midst of chaos, to keep your shoulder off the mat.

Don't Come Home Empty-Handed

One day I got fired. It happened quite suddenly, and I remember the details viscerally. It was dress-down Friday, and I was wearing a slightly more avant-garde outfit. A white t-shirt with black graffiti, a black bomber jacket, jeans, and a fake pair of all-black Nike Huaraches, which I'd picked up from a market while working in China.

I had every reason to think work was going reasonably well, hence the outfit. I'd brought on 7 deals with 4 new clients. And on that particular day, the directors had given my colleagues in the new business team a challenge to see who could get the most leads by midday. We hit the phones. I don't remember what the prize was, I just remember that I was winning. Before I went to lunch, the director from the oil and gas division came to my desk and gave me a high-five for knocking the ball out of the park that morning.

By the time I returned from lunch, my world had turned upside down.

My boss, the director of financial services, called me into a meeting room. He was there with the COO. The specifics of what they said are a blur, but the sensation is etched in my memory—it felt like my head was in a food processor, being violently cut and crushed and turned into mulch. We were on J.P. Morgan's blacklist. I shouldn't have tried to get one deal with them, let alone closing three. And my boss still hated that I spent too long on each of my outbound calls.

They told me not to touch my computer. Not to pick up my notebook. Just pick up my bag and walk. I was tossed to the street and out into the wilderness.

I was thoroughly discombobulated. And ashamed. And angry. So angry. I couldn't lose this job – we were only a few years removed from a financial crisis that saw master's degree graduates working as baristas, and I didn't even have a degree to lean on. I'd gotten my graduate job due to a stroke of good fortune and because someone was prepared to take a bet on me. There was no guarantee that it would ever happen again. I couldn't be jobless again. So I decided, in that moment, that I just refused. I flat-out refused. I rejected the premise. This couldn't be it. This couldn't be the end. I couldn't have left my house that morning with a job and come home without one. I couldn't come home empty-handed. I'd burn the street down before I let that happen.

I paced the block, turning life over and over in my head until something clicked. A few weeks earlier, I'd received a message on LinkedIn that I'd ignored completely. It was from the director of financial services at a competing firm. The equivalent of my boss. He hadn't said much or made me any offer. He'd only generically indicated that he wanted to connect. I'd ignored it at the time because I knew my superiors scrutinised our LinkedIn pages and would sniff it out instantly. But now, that unanswered message was a window. A chance. A narrow slice of light on a rapidly darkening horizon.

So I googled their offices, and I walked there. I didn't send any email or message—I couldn't afford to waste a second. I just turned up in their lobby and said I was there to see him. He came down, rather confused, to find a Black boy in street clothes on his doorstep. He didn't quite know what to do with me, but I was adamant he give me a chance. He was just on his way out, he explained, for a meeting with the Ministry of Defence. But if I came back in two hours, he'd meet with me.

Sighing relief that I'd somehow managed to grab hold of a lifeline in a storm, I sat down on a garden bench behind an old church and let my body process what had happened earlier. I had, so far, been operating completely on autopilot, out of a stubborn inability to accept defeat. I let myself breathe for a moment, and then I wiped my face dry. I only had two hours to get ready for an impromptu interview. And the first thing I had to do was get out of those clothes.

Now—I wasn't being paid much, and was only a few months into the job. I'd spent a good chunk of my money on work clothes, but still lived with my parents – too far away from the city to go home and change. I checked my bank account. I had a little over £200. That would need to be enough.

I found my way to a T.M Lewin store and exchanged meagre savings for some dignity. An hour and a half later I returned to the director's office with a new suit, shirt, tie, tie clip, cuff links, and a pair of fake black Nike Huaraches from a market in China. I'd run out of money before I could buy new shoes, but it would have to be enough. I'd blown all the money I had to increase my odds of converting this one opportunity. It would have to be enough.

I had the interview. It went well. He was impressed that I'd made the effort to change, considering the short notice. He told me they'd be prepared to pay me 25% more than my previous job had, subject to another interview with a senior executive. And that evening I could go home and tell my father that I'd lost my job, but was about to get another one.

In the span of a few hours, I'd been thrown to the mat with crushing force. But I didn't hang my head and accept defeat. I'd blindly, stubbornly, wrestled back to my feet, turning a devastating setback into a hopeful opportunity.

That story has since been as useful to me as reading any biography of a great leader or businessman. Not because I did something great, or because I found another job, but because I proved to myself that no matter how hard life hit, I could always find a way to keep fighting. These people couldn't kill me.

If you almost drown once but find a way to survive, you're no longer as scared of the water. So going forward, every time I found myself in a tough spot, there was a new story I could tell myself: I am the kind of person who bounces back. I am the kind of person who finds a way. I am the kind of person who wrests victory from the jaws of defeat. This is something I now knew to be true, because I had proved it, and I would fight to the death to maintain that narrative.

If you haven't yet found that to be true for yourself, you can simply decide otherwise at any moment.

You can make that decision right *this* very moment. Win, or fight. Fight, and win.

You Can't Beat a Boulder

Imagine the weight of a thousand pounds pressing against your arm, crushing it against solid rock. The pain is excruciating, but it's nothing compared to the dawning realisation that you're trapped, alone, in a remote Utah canyon. This was the reality Aron Ralston faced on a sunny April afternoon in 2003.

Ralston, an experienced 27-year-old outdoorsman, had set out for a day of canyoneering in the vast wilderness of Canyonlands National Park. As he descended through a narrow slot canyon, a dislodged boulder, larger than a refrigerator, came crashing down. In a split second, Ralston found himself pinned to the canyon wall, his right arm crushed between the immovable rock and the unforgiving sandstone.

The initial shock gave way to frantic attempts to free himself. Ralston pushed, pulled, and heaved against the boulder, his free hand scrambling for purchase on the smooth rock face. But the boulder didn't budge. Not an inch. Not a millimetre.

As the sun began to set, the gravity of his situation sank in. He had told no one his exact whereabouts. He had limited food and water. And he was stuck fast in a crevice barely wider than his body, 100 feet below the desert surface.

The first night was the hardest. The temperature dropped to near freezing, and Ralston, unable to sit or lie down, shivered uncontrollably. Sleep came in fitful bursts, interrupted by the searing pain in his arm and the gnawing fear in his gut.

Day two brought renewed determination. Ralston rigged up a pulley system with his climbing rope, hoping to shift the boulder. Hours of straining and sweating yielded nothing but exhaustion and disappointment. He began to chip away at the rock with his multi-tool knife, producing little more than a small pile of dust.

By the third day, Ralston's water was gone. Thirst became an all-consuming obsession. He resorted to drinking his own urine, gagging at the warm, acrid taste but knowing it might keep him alive a little longer.

On day four, hallucinations set in. Ralston's mind, addled by dehydration and lack of food, conjured visions of family, friends, and a future he might never see. In a moment of clarity, he used his video camera to record goodbyes to his loved ones, his voice cracking with emotion and desperation.

As the fifth day dawned, Ralston knew he was dying. His trapped arm, long since numb, had begun to decompose. The stench of rotting flesh filled the narrow canyon. In what he believed might be his final act, Ralston picked up his multi-tool and began to carve into the sandstone wall. With painstaking effort, he etched his name, date of birth, and what he presumed would be the date of his death: April 27, 2003.

After this, he recorded one final message, asking that his family cremate his body and spread his ashes. He'd said a quiet prayer and made peace with the world. On that tape, he left what he thought would be his last words: *"So again, love to everyone. Bring love and peace and happiness and beautiful lives into the world in my honor. Thank you. Love you."*

But even in this moment of apparent surrender, a part of Ralston refused to give up entirely. It was then, staring at his own presumed date of death, his epitaph etched in stone, that he had his epiphany. His precious arm was no longer a part of him—it was the thing keeping him from life. The more he tried to hold on to the identity of his whole self, the more he was doomed to perish. In that moment, Ralston chose to fight on, to stay alive, even if it meant leaving a part of himself behind. He knew what he had to do.

With trembling hands, Ralston began the gruesome task of amputating his own arm. The first cut into his flesh sent shockwaves of pain through his body. But he persevered, sawing through skin, muscle, and tendons with his dull knife. When he reached bone, he had to use the torque of his trapped arm to break it, the crack echoing off the canyon walls.

After an hour of unimaginable pain and determination, Ralston was free. But his ordeal wasn't over. Weak from blood loss and days without food, he still had to rappel down a 65-foot wall and hike seven miles through the desert before chance brought him face-to-face with a Dutch family who called for rescue.

Resilience often demands sacrifice. It requires us to adapt, to problem-solve, and sometimes to let go of something we thought was essential.

When life pins you down, when all seems lost, remember that as long as you're breathing, as long as you're willing to accept your conditions, adjust your plans, and sacrifice your ego, you're still in the fight. You still have a chance to write a different ending to your story.

Ralston was ready to die, but determined to live. He had fully accepted and internalised the difficulty of his situation. He wasn't under any delusion that there would be some magical way to escape unscathed. But despite carving his presumed date of death into the wall, Ralston never fully gave up hope in survival.

Even when you're pinned down by circumstances that seem impossible to overcome, you always have a choice. There may not be any way to escape unharmed. Survival isn't always free—it can carry a cost that most people aren't willing to pay. Ralston wanted to live more than he wanted an arm. A precious limb. A part of him.

> When the odds are stacked against you, and there is truly no way out, you can still find a way to survive if you're willing to cut off any part of your ego that's holding you back.

Eye of the Tiger

At the peak of his career, Tiger Woods was more than just a golfer; he was a cultural icon, a prodigy who had rewritten the record books and changed the face of his sport. But in November 2009, his carefully crafted image came crashing down. A late-night car accident outside his Florida home sparked a series of revelations about marital infidelities, leading to a very public divorce and the loss of several lucrative sponsorship deals.

The scandal was just the beginning of Woods' troubles. His body, long pushed to its limits, began to break down. Between 2014 and 2017, Woods underwent four back surgeries, including a spinal fusion. The pain was so severe that there were days when he could barely walk or sit up straight. His world ranking plummeted to 1,199th. Many pundits declared his career over, suggesting that the once-great Tiger Woods would never compete at the highest level again.

In May 2017, things reached their nadir. Florida police found Woods asleep at the wheel of his car, his speech slurred and confused. Toxicology reports revealed a cocktail of painkillers in his system. The mugshot from his arrest, showing a bloated, bleary-eyed Woods, was a far cry from the fist-pumping champion the world once knew.

At this point, it would have been easy for Woods to accept defeat. He had already achieved more than most athletes could dream of. He had a fortune in the bank and a seat secured in sporting history. Many in his position might have decided to rest on their laurels, to accept that their time in the spotlight was over.

But Woods refused to let both shoulders touch the mat. Despite the pain, despite the humiliation, despite the chorus of voices saying he was finished, he kept fighting. He underwent yet another back surgery. He committed to a gruelling rehabilitation process, slowly rebuilding his body and his swing.

The road back was long and fraught with setbacks. There were tournaments where he could barely finish, where his once-mighty drives were outstripped by journeyman pros. But Woods kept showing up, kept working, kept believing when few others did.

In September 2018, Woods won the Tour Championship, his first victory in five years. But he wasn't done. He had his sights set on a bigger prize: one more major championship.

April 14, 2019. Augusta National. The final round of the Masters. Woods, wearing his signature Sunday red, was in contention, but few truly believed he could win. As he stood on the 12th tee, the ghosts of his past failures seemed to loom large.

But this was a different Tiger. One who had been forged in the crucible of public humiliation, physical pain, and personal demons. As his competitors faltered, Woods remained steady. When he tapped in the winning putt on the 18th green, the roar from the crowd was deafening. Tiger Woods, at 43, had done the impossible. He had won his fifth Masters and 15th major championship, a full 11 years after his last major victory.

As he embraced his children by the 18th green, in almost the same spot where he had hugged his own father after his first Masters win 22 years earlier, the magnitude of his achievement was clear. This wasn't just a sporting comeback; it was a redemption story, a testament to the human spirit's capacity to endure, to persevere, to resist submission when it feels like the entire universe has conspired to pin you down.

> The road back from hell is a long one. Sometimes 'bouncing back' won't feel like being launched from a springboard. It may instead be a slow climb, a strenuous marathon, the herculean effort of dragging yourself, soaked and heavy, from the deep well you were drowning in—the pit that even your most ardent supporters might have consigned you to.

Persistence isn't just about the rapid counterstrike. You must be willing to play the gruelling long game.

Comebacks are rarely linear. They're messy, filled with setbacks and moments of doubt. But if you refuse to accept defeat, if you keep showing up and putting in the work, you give yourself a chance at redemption, at rewriting your own story. Even if it takes a while.

In your darkest moments, when the world has long written you off, remember Tiger Woods on that Sunday in Augusta. In life, as in golf, it's not over until the last putt drops.

30

KEEP YOUR WHEELS SPINNING

"Luck is not a chance, it's toil; fortune's expensive smile is earned."

— Emily Dickinson

There are fates more cruel than mockery, and rejections more grating than ridicule. There is, after all, the haunting isolation of invisibility. You may go completely unnoticed, regardless of your outcomes. At least the barbs from disbelievers and the swelling spite from those who spurn you can fuel you. But what happens when you are out in the field, breaking your back, straining your soul, pushing the limits of expectation, stretching the boundaries of belief, on the verge of changing the world, or rebuilding your life, and nobody seems to care?

Being willing to sacrifice up-front for some later reward is commendable. Working in spite of disbelief is worthy of applause. But it can be even harder to commit to a process when you're not sure if there's a light at the end of the tunnel. The problem with those stories of great painters who are posthumously celebrated, is that they're dead. Most of us would rather collect our flowers in person than have them laid at our graves.

If you're committed to doing great work, you'll have to accept that it may often require working in silence and solitude. Not because you chose an alienating path, but because the path itself is alien. Not everyone will realise that the voyage is more valuable than the promised treasure at its end. Your belief in the inherent value of the path might require you to walk alone even if no one walks with you.

I started travelling solo because I couldn't convince friends to come with me to far-flung places. Eventually, I just went alone and found it wasn't so bad, so I kept doing it. And then I started taking photos, and people started taking interest. Suddenly thousands of strangers were willing to pay just to travel with me, and I built a business travelling at least once a month with strangers from around the world.

Most people like treasure more than they like adventure. Few are willing to wander in the wilderness when there is no promise of great bounty. But once a path has been proven, people flock to it.

If there is a goal you want to achieve, or some outsized outcome that you're aiming for, you must be willing to do the work when the outcome isn't obvious. **Start when everything hasn't already fallen into place. Build when others sleep. Sleep when others play. Work when no one is looking. Commit when no one cares.**

Toil by Torchlight

The mental toll of invisibility can be immense. Humans are social creatures, wired for external validation. We crave recognition, appreciation, and the nods of approval from peers. When that validation is absent, our hard work seems to disappear into a void, and it can be tempting to question everything. Are we on the right path? Is this worth the effort? Should we just give up and do something—anything—that people will notice and appreciate?

Transformative progress happens in this invisible space. The foundations of both great personal and public breakthroughs are often laid in obscurity. World-changing ideas are nurtured by those willing to work without applause, and persevere without recognition.

Keeping your wheels spinning in these circumstances requires a special kind of resilience. It demands faith in your vision, trust in your process, and the fortitude to forge forward when every external signal suggests you should stop. It takes finding motivation not in the cheers of the crowd, but in the quiet satisfaction of everyday progress.

This is the challenge that separates dreamers from doers, and dabblers from the dedicated. It is a test of will, conviction, and self belief. But for those who can endure it, who can keep their wheels spinning in the face of indifference, the rewards can be extraordinary. Because when the world finally catches up, when the spotlight finally finds you, you won't be scrambling to get ready. You'll be ready to seize the moment you've been preparing for all along.

Two bicycle mechanics from Ohio changed the world one day in 1903, and it took almost half a decade for people to realise it.

On December 17, 1903, on a wind-swept beach in North Carolina, human flight became a reality. Orville Wright piloted the first powered, controlled, sustained flight in history. It lasted 12 seconds and covered 120 feet. He and his brother Wilbur would fly another three times that day, iterating quickly on the magic they'd discovered. By nightfall they'd achieve their longest flight so far—Wilbur Wright flew for 59 seconds over a distance of 852 feet. This was the culmination of years of research, experimentation, and perseverance. It was, by any measure, one of the most significant technological achievements in human history.

Their first flights received little coverage at the time, even in local papers. J.M. Cox, publisher of the Dayton Daily News, agreed to cover the boys briefly, but privately admitted, "Frankly, none of us believed it." Meanwhile, the editor of the Dayton Journal famously quipped that even if it was true, 57 seconds was not long enough to be a news item. The rest of the world remained oblivious to the fact that human flight had been achieved.

For years after their groundbreaking flight, the Wright brothers continued their work in relative obscurity. They refined their designs, improved their techniques, and pushed the boundaries of what was possible in the air. The few eyes that did eventually glance their way were loaded with scepticism, indifference, and mockery. The prestigious Scientific American magazine dismissed their claims of flight as a hoax as late as 1906. Yet, the Wright brothers persisted. They knew the value of their work, even when others didn't. They understood that real progress comes from toiling by torchlight rather than standing in spotlight.

It wasn't until 1908, nearly five years after their first flight, that the Wright brothers finally gained widespread recognition. Wilbur Wright's public demonstrations in France that year left spectators and journalists in awe. Suddenly, the world woke up to the reality of human flight, and the Wright brothers were catapulted from obscurity to international fame.

The crucial point is that those five invisible years were not wasted time. Wilbur and Orville didn't stop innovating simply because no one was paying attention. Their resolve was steadfast, and their pace was unbroken. For five years they kept on refining their designs, improving their piloting skills, and preparing for the moment when the world would finally take notice. By the time their work was widely known, it was that much harder to ignore.

Stay Ready

Success occasionally seems to come out of nowhere, like a meteor hurtling into Earth's orbit, striking a single lucky soul and imbuing them with fame and otherworldly talent. The reality is more mundane. Success is a process, and the shiny outcomes are usually just symptoms of dogged performance and persistent preparedness.

Whether you're running towards victory or fleeing near-certain defeat, the secret to reproducible success is staying prepared, on your toes, ready to strike, even when opportunity seems distant or unlikely.

Readiness means more than just waiting. Patience and passivity are not the same. You must commit to continuous improvement in every moment, even when there's no obvious path forward. When the road ahead seems blocked, hone your skills and expand your knowledge. Summon opportunity to meet you where you stand. Let the target move into the path of your waiting arrow, rather than scrambling to get it in your sights.

The athlete maintains good conditioning in the off-season. The artist sketches while paint dries. The public speaker writes and rehearses lines they can call upon at a moment's notice. The scientist engages in frequent discussions, poking at the unknown.

Catalogue Your Ideas

While working in law, I nurtured an itch for entrepreneurship, even when I had no time to actually run a business. I developed a habit of running business-idea sprints in my spare time, where I'd sit down with my notebook and try to come up with a business idea, sketch out a logo, flesh out the business model, and design a basic landing page in two weeks. I had a bunch of ideas in this way, and got lots of reps quickly putting the design elements together. After the two weeks were up, it was up to me if I wanted to continue exploring the idea.

Most of those businesses didn't go anywhere – they weren't intended to. I just did it to maintain the practice of being creative at pace. Eventually I started a travel business which saw some success and enabled me to travel the world for a while. Around November 2019, I cancelled a trip for the first time in over two years of operation. We were meant to be going to Thailand, but I kept hearing reports of people getting sick there. No one really knew what it was, but I didn't want to risk dealing with refunds or insurance issues if people got sick on my watch.

A few short months later, I had a second trip cancelled. This time, to Mexico, and the choice was completely out of my hands. Mexico City had gone into lockdown due to the coronavirus pandemic, which quickly swept over the world. All non-essential travel was paused indefinitely. I had a lot of friends in the travel industry—many of our businesses were completely wiped out in the months that followed due to Covid restrictions and fresh waves of the virus, which spread faster than experts predicted. There were only so many times you could cancel and postpone trips, and there wasn't any sign of things changing soon. It was a bloodbath.

KEEP YOUR WHEELS SPINNING

Travel was paused whether I liked it or not, and there wasn't anything I could do about it. But I still needed money. I'd quit corporate law the year before, in order to focus on business interests and consulting for early-stage startups. So I turned to my notebook, which at this point had nearly five years' worth of half-baked business ideas. Some, more fleshed out than others.

There was one old idea that was already creeping to the front of my mind—I'd called it Democratic Republic of Coffee. The idea was to sell coffee grown across Africa in order to support local farming communities, and tell stories about the origins and history of coffee in Africa. It was perfect.

I already had a logo, and I'd previously taken the time to source and negotiate with farming cooperatives in Kenya, Ethiopia and Tanzania, as well as with a roaster in the UK. I'd just been too busy to take the idea any further. I quickly sent a few emails to confirm prices and availability with various partners. I'd first had the idea in 2018 but, two years later, was ready to pick it up and run with it.

On 25 July, I sent a tweet announcing that we'd be launching in one week, on August 1st. This bought me a little time to get assets ready and collect emails. When we launched, I still didn't have a single bag of coffee on hand. The launch was for pre-orders only, and for exactly ten days. Why? Because the Shopify trial period was 14 days. That gave me 3 days to set up a website before we went live, and 10 more days to make money before the first bill came due. I didn't want to pay for anything until I was sure the business would work. Luckily, I'd had a lot of practice with two-week sprints. I designed labels for the bags myself and mocked them up with free Photoshop templates I found online.

With a trial-period website full of mockups, Canva designs, and street photos I'd taken while travelling around Africa, I launched and made enough from pre-orders to cover all my initial costs. There was even enough left over to hire an award-winning African artist to design better labels than the one I'd cobbled together years earlier. We moved fast, changing labels three times and packaging twice between the initial orders placed and the first bags being sent out. In the first month,

I shipped bags to customers in six different countries and four U.S. states.

We went on to sell thousands of bags before expanding into biodynamic wine imported from Tuscany and rebranding as a sustainable drinks company. I ran the same playbook again – pre-orders based on mockups to fund the stock, which shipped a few months later. Our audience grew, and eventually, we got the opportunity to launch a physical space store in the heart of central London.

But none of this would have been possible if, at each stage, I had sat on my hands and waited for the path to reveal itself. I jumped the gun every time, preparing far in advance, even when the next step wasn't apparent.

Fortune favours the prepared mind. Harvest accrues to the patient hand. Destiny falls to the decisive.

> Opportunities rarely announce themselves in advance. Staying ready doesn't just make room for your chances—it actively creates the conditions for your future success.

Till the soil. Lay the bedrock.

The Grocery Bag Baller

At Regis High School in Cedar Rapids, Iowa, a young Kurt Warner showed flashes of promise as a high-school quarterback, but not enough to turn any heads. He was solid, dependable, but far from extraordinary. Becoming a starter in his junior and senior years, scouts and college recruiters overlooked him. The University of Northern Iowa (UNI) was the only school that gave him a chance.

Northern Iowa played in Division I-AA, a tier below the major college football schools, and even there he was benched for three years, playing behind a more experienced quarterback. Warner's senior year finally brought him the starting role, but by then, he was already largely forgotten by the wider college football world. There were no headlines, no recruiters beating down his door. He was invisible.

After graduating, Warner put himself forward for the NFL draft. He was ignored by every team, in every round. He couldn't even get a spot on a practice squad as a punching bag defenders could get reps with. He went undrafted, and the one goal he had dreamed of his entire life, to play in the National Football League, seemed impossibly distant.

Fresh out of college with no other prospects, Warner was forced to stock shelves at a Hy-Vee grocery store in Cedar Falls, earning $5.50 an hour to support his young family. He was a father of two, living in his mother-in-law's basement, but for some reason, every day after work, Warner kept training. He ran drills in the empty parking lot, occasionally throwing balls to his wife, imagining that one day the call would come.

It didn't. But Warner wasn't ready to give up. He took a chance on the Arena Football League (AFL), a second-tier league with a fraction of the audience and a fraction of the pay. The AFL was hardly a stepping stone to the NFL. The game was faster, more chaotic, played on a smaller field, with less time to make decisions and more chances to fail. But Warner thrived in the chaos, leading the Iowa Barnstormers to back-to-back ArenaBowl appearances and earning a reputation as one of the best quarterbacks in the league. The AFL didn't provide much in the way of fame or fortune, but it sharpened Warner's skills in ways that would later serve him well.

After his successful stint in the Arena Football League (AFL), Warner caught the attention of the NFL's St. Louis Rams and was picked up, but only as a backup option. He was shipped off to the Amsterdam Admirals in NFL Europe, a league designed to develop potential players for the NFL. Playing for the Admirals in 1998, Warner led the league in passing yards and touchdowns, demonstrating his ability to perform under pressure, even if the audience was small.

Despite his impressive statistics in Europe, Warner still returned to the NFL as an unknown. The Rams signed him as a third-string quarterback, buried in the depth-chart, with little expectation that he would ever start a game. But at least he was finally in the league.

He spent the 1998 season on the bench, watching and learning, while the Rams continued to struggle. Even then, Warner's commitment to preparation was unyielding. He was often the last to leave practice, staying behind to work on his throws and study the playbook, quietly readying himself for an opportunity that might never come.

Fate intervened in 1999 when the Rams' starting quarterback, Trent Green, suffered a season-ending knee injury during the preseason. The Rams were in disarray, and Warner was suddenly thrust into the starting role—a position few believed he was capable of handling. The team, the fans, and the league at large had low expectations.

But Warner was ready. In Week 1 of the 1999 season, he took the field and immediately defied all odds. Warner executed the Rams' "Greatest Show on Turf" offence with pinpoint accuracy. His remarkable play led the Rams to a 13-3 regular-season record. Warner threw for 4,353 yards and 41 touchdowns, winning the NFL Most Valuable Player (MVP) award in the process.

The Rams' Cinderella season culminated in a trip to Super Bowl XXXIV, where Warner cemented his legacy. He passed for a then-record 414 yards and two touchdowns, including a 73-yard game-winning strike to Isaac Bruce in the fourth quarter. The Rams won the Super Bowl 23-16, and Warner was named the Super Bowl MVP.

Warner's journey from stocking shelves, to obscurity in the AFL and NFL Europe, to the pinnacle of the NFL, was nothing short of extraordinary. It was only possible thanks to his relentless dedication, his belief in himself, and his readiness to seize the moment when it finally arrived.

But that's only half the story.

It's Not Over Because You Win

After his meteoric rise in 1999, Kurt Warner's career continued to be a rollercoaster of highs and lows, underscoring the resilience that had defined his journey up to that point.

Following the Super Bowl victory, Warner led the Rams back to the playoffs in 2000 and again in 2001. The 2001 season was another standout year; Warner threw for 4,830 yards and 36 touchdowns, earning his second NFL MVP award. Not bad for an undrafted shelf-stacker. The Rams returned to the Super Bowl, but this time they were defeated by the New England Patriots in a game that marked the beginning of Tom Brady's legendary career.

The next few years were tough for Warner. Injuries began to take their toll, and his performance declined. In 2002, Warner suffered a broken hand, and by 2003, he had lost his starting job with the Rams to Marc Bulger. Warner's career seemed to be on the downswing, and in 2004, he was released by the Rams.

Warner signed with the New York Giants, but his time there was short-lived. He started the first nine games of the 2004 season before being replaced by rookie Eli Manning. It seemed like Warner's time as a starting quarterback in the NFL was over.

But Warner's story had one more chapter. In 2005, he signed with the Arizona Cardinals, initially as a mentor to younger quarterbacks. Somehow, by 2007, Warner had won the starting job, and took to the field as their number one option. The 2008 season marked an almost unheard of resurgence in a league where many careers are cut short due to age and injury. Warner led the Cardinals to an improbable Super Bowl appearance, where they narrowly lost to the Pittsburgh Steelers in a thrilling game that came down to the final seconds.

Warner's performance during that 2008 season was nothing short of remarkable. He threw for 4,583 yards and 30 touchdowns, leading a franchise that had long been considered a perennial loser to within inches of a championship. His play earned him yet another Pro Bowl selection, and his leadership was widely praised.

Warner played one more season with the Cardinals before announcing his retirement in January 2010. He left the game as one of the most accurate passers in NFL history, holding the record for the three highest passing yardage totals in Super Bowl history at the time. His post-football life has been marked by his work as a broadcaster, philanthropist, and motivational speaker.

In 2017, Warner was inducted into the Pro Football Hall of Fame, cementing his legacy as one of the greatest quarterbacks of all time.

The game isn't over when you win—it's over when you stop playing. Many meteoric rises are followed by similarly steep crashes into obscurity. But when you're playing infinite games instead of finite ones, playing for the love of the game and a willingness to better yourself instead of being obsessed only with accolades and competition, you might find that you can stay on the path far longer than others would expect. You might realise that the path itself is more valuable than the treasure.

Keep your chin up. Keep your wheels spinning. Stay ready. Play the long game.

31

STAY IN THE POCKET

> *"Cowards die many times before their deaths;*
> *The valiant never taste of death but once.*
> *Of all the wonders that I yet have heard,*
> *It seems to me most strange that men should fear;*
> *Seeing that death, a necessary end,*
> *Will come when it will come."*
>
> — William Shakespeare (Julius Caesar)

In Buddhist teaching, there is a commonly used metaphor of two arrows.

The first arrow is an event—unexpected, often painful, and beyond your control. It could be a scathing email from your boss, a sudden market crash, or a friend's betrayal. This arrow stings, but you may survive it. It's the second arrow that kills you.

The second arrow is your response. It's the panic, rage, and despair that floods your system in response to that first hit. While the first arrow is shot by unexpected circumstances, we notch and release the second one ourselves. It's this self-inflicted wound that ultimately causes the most damage.

You know the pattern. Something happens which catches you off guard. Your heart rate spikes. Your blood pressure rises. The voices in your head become an anxious, angry, cacophonous chorus, distracting you. And suddenly your better senses are overcome by the heat of rage, the fog of war, the disorienting waves of anxiety and fear.

> The key to long-term survival is realising that the first arrow can't always be dodged. Even if you plan patiently, work diligently and execute perfectly, life has a funny way of reasserting itself. Your best made plans can be undone in a heartbeat.

You grind and save for years to buy a home, and then your mother gets sick. You relocate for a dream opportunity and then get made redundant. You make every sacrifice to please your partner and suddenly get divorced. If only real life were as predictable as our inner fantasies.

Once you accept that you cannot dodge the first arrow, you must realise that your long-term life outcomes will be entirely dependent on whether you can avoid the second one. You will live or die by your ability to avoid shooting yourself in the foot in a flash of self-sabotage, or succumbing to the depressing belief that all paths lead to certain defeat.

Can you stay composed in a moment of crisis, absorb the heat, stare into the fire, and allow the pain to roll over you?

In Frank Herbert's Dune, Paul Atreides recites a 'Litany against fear' to steel his mind when tested in circumstances of excruciating and overwhelming agony. It is relevant here:

> *"I must not fear.*
> *Fear is the mind-killer.*
> *Fear is the little-death that brings total obliteration.*
> *I will face my fear.*
> *I will permit it to pass over me and through me.*
> *And when it has gone past, I will turn the inner eye to*
> *see its path.*
> *Where the fear has gone there will be nothing. Only I will*

remain."

— Frank Herbert (Dune)

Paul Atreides knew that fear was inescapable, but it doesn't have to control you. It doesn't need to dictate your actions. You can accept the first arrow and persist, moving forward regardless. Pain is inevitable, but suffering is a choice. You need not shoot yourself with a second arrow.

Find Poise in the Pocket

I've had the opportunity to play American Football at some of the highest levels available to me in the UK. I played at the university level for the few years I was enrolled, and then at adult level with a team in Division 1 and the Premiership. It's a far, far cry from what it would be like to even play at the level of college football in the US, but enough to learn a few lessons.

In American Football, the offensive line falls back into a protective pocket around their quarterback (QB), giving him room to make the perfect pass. Their job is to keep the other team's defensive line away from the quarterback. In an ideal world, your offensive line will be stronger and more skilled than the other team's defensive line, and the defensive players swarming towards the quarterback can be held at bay indefinitely, or at least long enough for the QB to get the ball out of his hands. But reality is rarely so clear-cut.

At some point, the offensive line cracks, and a defender breaks through, ready to crush the QB. The QB now has a choice. Stay composed, staring downfield, using the final second or two he has to find an open receiver to pass to, or drop to the ground and protect his body and the ball. There is, however, a third choice—to scramble. The quarterback can leave the pocket voluntarily, making himself even more vulnerable to attack, but perhaps buying himself extra time to make a play. And that's where the next problem begins.

Some QBs default to protecting themselves. They don't want to get injured, and they don't want to get hit. Once their original plan falls apart they drop to the ground, curled up in a ball. Other QBs panic too early – as soon as they feel the pocket collapsing they scramble wildly, hoping some better outcome emerges. The best QBs are often the ones with pocket-poise. They can hold on for just an extra second. They feel the heat of a defender bearing down on them. But they stare right through them, keeping their eyes downfield on their target. Sometimes there's no pass to be made, and they eventually must scramble. But often enough, they can make a game-winning pass right as they're being pancaked by a defender.

In the moments that matter most, victory often goes not to the person who never gets hit, but to the one who can take a hit and stay focused. The one who can let the wave of fear or anger wash over them without being swept away. The one who can stay in the pocket until the final moment, and still make the right call.

Check Your Poker Face

A word commonly used in poker parlance is "tilt"—a term used to describe a state of emotional frustration or anger that negatively affects a player's decision-making, throwing them off their game. A player is described as being "on tilt," when they are observed to make irrational bets, chase losses with overly aggressive moves, or make poor strategic decisions because they're playing based on emotions rather than well-thought-out theory, logic and analysis.

Tilt often occurs after a player experiences a bad beat (losing a hand despite having the statistical advantage), a series of unlucky events, or a significant mistake. The psychological impact of these events can cause the player to deviate from their usual, disciplined strategy, leading to even more losses—a vicious cycle that can spiral out of control.

Phil Hellmuth, one of the most successful and well-known poker players in history, crashed out of the 2005 World Series of Poker by getting tilted and being unable to recover quickly.

In the main event Hellmuth was holding pocket aces, the best starting hand in poker. Confident in his hand, he made a large bet. Another player, whose hand was much weaker, decided to call the bet and stay in the hand. The flop (the first three community cards dealt face-up) didn't seem to help the other player, and Hellmuth was still in a commanding position.

However, as the turn and river cards (the final two community cards) were dealt, Hellmuth's opponent miraculously completed a straight, an unlikely hand given the initial cards. Hellmuth lost the hand, and his frustration was palpable. He couldn't believe his bad luck and began berating his opponent, accusing them of playing poorly and getting lucky.

This bad beat triggered Hellmuth's tilt. Over the next few hands, instead of playing with a typical level of discipline, he started making increasingly aggressive bets and calls, driven by anger and a desire to win back the chips he had lost. His decision-making deteriorated and he continued to lose, eventually getting eliminated from the tournament much earlier than expected.

When you let your emotions rule you, you become your own worst enemy. When you feed your inner beast, it will eventually consume you. Don't release the second arrow out of anger—you'll only end up chasing a loss with a loss.

Your emotions might be unavoidable, but you're allowed to feel them and release them without letting them direct your actions. Step back in the moment, reign in your wild and wicked thoughts, let the wave of your emotion rise in its towering ferocity, then crest, soften, and eventually dissipate. As long as you can stay poised in the pocket without scrambling, you're still in control of the outcome, or at least whatever portion of the outcome you ever had the power to control in the first place.

The Sniper's Breath

A sniper's greatest weapon isn't a high-calibre rifle, it's their breath. In the chaotic heat of battle, a sniper must find stillness. Their success—and often their survival—depends on their ability to steady their aim despite the turmoil around them. They achieve this with the magic of breath control.

As a sniper prepares to take a shot, they enter a state of hyper-focus. They slow their breathing, often using a technique called "box breathing" – inhaling for four seconds, holding for four, exhaling for four, and holding again for four. This controlled breathing does more than just steady their aim; it calms their mind, slows their heart rate, and allows them to enter a state of composed readiness.

In the moment before they pull the trigger, many snipers employ a final, crucial technique called respiratory pause. They take a partial breath, filling their lungs about halfway, and then hold it. They stay in the pocket, resisting the urge to rush or second-guess. This half-breath creates a momentary stillness in their body, eliminating even the slight movement caused by breathing. In this momentary window of calm, they squeeze the trigger.

In all things, you must be a marksman. Ready to capitalise on a fleeting chance. Ready to take action when the time is right. Ready to take control of life as it charges at you, horns bared, even if the best you can do is to stem the bleeding of a wound which came from nowhere.

In any high-pressure situation, your breath can be your anchor. When the bullets are flying, when your instincts scream at you to panic or lash out, you can create a pocket of calm. Control your breathing. Carve out the one crucial moment you need to assess, to aim, to make the right decision instead of a reflexive one.

This mastery of breath isn't just an exhibition of physical control—it characterises mental discipline, and the connection between mind and body. Achieving this requires that you learn to create a buffer between stimulus and response, a space where you can choose your reaction rather than being propelled by passion, moved only by instinct or emotion. In that space, in that pocket of calm you create, lies the potential of every possible outcome.

To act rashly is to roll the dice, to let the roulette wheel spin simply because the rush of motion feels good, even if it makes your outcomes harder to predict and more precarious to plan for. By taking a half-breath, fully owning the brief moment before you act, you can craft paths out of thin air, creating other options for yourself where there previously seemed to be only one.

Sharpshooting Through Chaos

On October 8, 1918, in the dense Argonne Forest of northeastern France, Corporal Alvin York found himself in a situation where panic seemed not just reasonable, but inevitable.

York and a small detachment of 17 American soldiers had been tasked with taking out a heavily fortified German machine-gun nest that had been wreaking havoc on Allied forces. As they manoeuvred through the forest and into enemy territory, they stumbled upon a much larger force than anticipated – over 70 German soldiers. Their platoon was ambushed and pinned down, suddenly finding themselves under a siege of enemy fire. Nine Americans were shot down almost immediately, leaving York effectively in command of the seven remaining men.

The immediate instinct would be to retreat; the natural response, to surrender, to scramble for cover, to do anything in desperation to escape the deadly hail of bullets. But York didn't scramble. He didn't panic. In the face of overwhelming odds, he lingered in the pocket, standing fast as fear washed over him.

Under heavy fire, with his comrades either dead, wounded, or unable to move, York assessed the situation with remarkable clarity. He knew that returning fire indiscriminately would only waste ammunition and potentially give away his position further. He understood that any rash action could spell certain doom for himself and the remaining men.

York happened to be a hunter by trade. He'd honed his focus for years in the hills of Tennessee, and as he stared into the chaos, he noticed a pattern in the flash of muzzles spraying bullets towards him.

The cluster of flashes gave away the enemy positions. The timing of their shots indicated that the German machine gunners, positioned on the ridge above, had to stand up to fire down at his men in the valley. This exposed them, if only for a moment.

York made a decision. Instead of retreating or blindly returning fire, he would point his gun toward the hail of bullets. He began to pick off the German gunners one by one, with the precision of a sniper. He recalled later, "Every time I seed a German I jes teched him off." He ignored the shells raining down around him and his platoon, and waited for the next German head to pop up in the gap between long rounds of fire.

His composure was so complete that when six German soldiers leapt from a trench and charged him with fixed bayonets, York calmly shot them in order from back to front, so that those in front wouldn't realise their comrades were falling behind them and scatter.

York's incredible display of marksmanship and calm under fire eventually led to the surrender of the entire German unit. By the end of the engagement, he had killed at least 25 enemy soldiers and captured 132 more, including four officers.

York didn't allow the chaos around him to dictate his actions. He didn't give in to the fear that must have been flooding his nervous system. Instead, he created a moment of calm in the midst of battle, assessed his options, and took decisive action.

When everything around you is falling apart, resist the urge to panic. By staying in the pocket even as danger closes in from all sides, a disastrous defeat can be turned into an extraordinary victory.

Your path won't always be smooth or straightforward. Your ability to stay calm and focused under fire can make all the difference. Life will never require you to be fearless. Complete fearlessness is the sole domain of the reckless and psychopathic. Instead, feel the fear and take action anyway. Acknowledge your feelings and outlive them. Appreciate the pressure you're under and fortify your position, assessing your odds with clarity and moving forward with purpose.

32

KEEP THE DREAM ALIVE

"In the middle of the journey of our life I found myself within a dark woods where the straight way was lost."

— Dante Alighieri

Where do legends come from? I have a theory that every success story is a little less successful than you'd imagine. Heroism and success are coloured lenses that change the way we see the facts. If you take a big bet and it pays off, you're a visionary. If you tank, you were drunk on grand delusions.

The stories we hear in the wild are also coloured by survivorship bias. Everyone wants to be a startup founder because the people that give talks and tell stories are the ones who won the game—the founders that survived. The ones that failed either went back to JP Morgan and McKinsey or are on a soapbox on ProductHunt evangelising about their latest punt.

Lots of people are similarly fascinated by the ancient world. People obsess over Ancient Rome and read books on Ancient Greece. We love the heroes—the characters—so much so that we gloss over the rough patches in their journeys and only seem to remember the highlights.

Take the Spartans, for example. Famous warriors. Ferocious badasses who bred hardship into their children to make them strong and fearsome in combat. The problem is, that wasn't always the case.

Three Hundred Brave Losers

In the Archaic period (c. 800-500 BC), Spartan power increased largely by virtue of sheer numbers. They didn't spend much time learning to fight, but every man was required to, and Sparta had about 8000 men. They were one of the biggest political communities at the time, but there was nothing to mark them out as particularly skilled fighters. Individually, they were actually comparatively weak, as there was no standing army.

Most of the surviving records from that period confirm that Sparta was hardly noted in any military regard. War songs of Tyrtaios report of conflict with the Messenians, but say nothing of any military institutions or practices that were developed later on. Meanwhile, the choral songs of Alkman spoke of pretty girls, flowers, and bees. Hardly the stuff of legend.

That all changed after the Battle of Thermopylae (480 BC). Popular tales of this battle focus on the 300 men of Sparta. This is largely the result of sensational propaganda, because everyone seems to have forgotten the rest of the Greeks present. 7000 hoplites were deployed to hold the mountain pass. Xerxes and the Persian army arrived sooner than expected and were winning the battle faster than expected. At this point, most of the Greeks elected to flee. Except, of course, for the 300 brave men of Sparta... and 400 Thebans... and 700 Thespians. The Spartans only made up a fifth of the men who stood to fight, but it was their king who first gave the order to stand, so they got the credit for the decision.

And that's disregarding the important fact that this famous battle was a losing one. The group of brave soldiers who stayed back to fight was absolutely annihilated, and the battle was a complete loss in every sense of the word. But the courage of the men who stood despite tough odds gave Spartans a moral victory, and they were immortalised as legends. They lost, but they didn't run scared. And then, the word started to spread. Stories, rumours, tall tales of their bravery. Enemies began to fear them. This state with zero prior record as a competent fighting force was suddenly spoken of in whispers and hushed tones.

After the Archaic period, gone were the songs of birds and bees, the leisure-class and luxury that Sparta was previously known for. These gave way to a new obsession with living up to their reputation as hard nuts. Suddenly other sources through the Classical and Hellenistic periods are waxing lyrical about Sparta's political stability and military skill.

Spartan culture bred strict obedience, which made their men more reliable in battle than other hoplites. The biggest conduit to their success was basic formation drills. They were the only Greeks that subdivided armies into platoons led by individual officers who could give their own commands. They taught their men to march to the sound of flutes and could change direction instantly without needing an individual general shouting at the top of his lungs. This made them incredibly versatile in battle, and their tactical superiority won them several notable battles. Individually they were weak, but in units they became fearsome.

This simple tactical edge, combined with a reputation that was founded on a losing fight in which they were the smallest force, led to the Spartans being undefeated in a pitched battle for over 100 years. It was the ultimate self-fulfilling prophecy.

Up and to the Right

Our stories, like our legends, are seldom clean-cut. Often we're defined by tiny slices of history, which are pulled together in retrospect to form a coherent narrative.

When we look back, we tell stories with linear progression. How did you get to where you are today? *'I did x and then y and then z.'* What we neglect to mention is that in the moment, none of it was scripted or intentional. We may have had self-belief, but no certainty of the outcome. The narratives we spin often omit our moments of confusion and disillusion—the valleys of despair.

Straight lines are boring. Human progression is rarely linear. There are always ups and downs. There is fluctuation in every decision. We waver, falter, and fall flat on our faces. The chart doesn't just go up and to the right.

When we look at stocks and cryptocurrencies that are hugely successful or disruptive on a macro level, we see momentous success, but zooming in on any three-week slot can highlight the turbulence of market corrections. The moments where focus and clarity abandoned us. Moments when you would have sold.

If you were watching your life on a chart with no idea of what was to come next, speculating on your own success, would you bet on yourself in every moment? Possibly. But I'm going to guess there are at least a few occasions where you thought it was the end of the world but things ended up okay. Even if it was just when you were six and got rejected by your first crush.

No speculator is prescient. What makes stocks worth sticking with are the higher highs. You only hold on through a drought when you know your pick will bounce back. And most of the time, you have no such knowledge—only hope.

You will frequently see people regurgitate banal takes like "$1000 invested in [Tesla/Amazon/Bitcoin] in 2009 would have been x amount today". These narratives seem painfully easy when you're looking in the rearview mirror, but how many of us know the future? How many believers have the resolve to stay the course?

Success is built when you capitalise on opportunity; legend is built when you survive long enough to tell the story.

The Power of Curved Lines

In English counties like Suffolk, you may come across waved walls which bend back and forth every few metres but otherwise cover a straight line. They're known locally as 'crinkle crankle walls.'

At first glance, they look weird, but they're cooler than you might imagine. Walls like this only require one layer of brick to be stable, whereas straight walls require two. The inherent peaks, troughs, and fluctuations make them more resilient, using fewer materials than what you might require going the conventional path.

Many eventual successes will be preceded by hesitation, doubt, and despair. It's a wavy line, and we learn things both in the trenches and at the peaks. Your ability to learn from failures and bounce back is what determines ultimate success, and surviving is what helps cement a legacy.

You don't need to have been the best—you just need to last long enough to tell a great story.

It's the crinkles in our stories that let us stand the test of time. You don't need to worry when things don't go smoothly, or when you're wrestling through the turbulence of finding your path. It's okay for your line to be wavy. The truth is, we're stronger for it.

What Stands in the Way Becomes the Way

Drew Lynch is a comedian with an intriguing story. A single game of softball changed his life forever. At 20, Drew had dreams of becoming an actor. But fate had other plans.

During a casual softball game with friends from work, Drew lunged to catch a ball. It struck the ground, bounced unpredictably, and smashed into his neck.

Losing his balance, he toppled over, his head violently meeting the ground. He came to, unaware of the severity of his concussion, and went home to sleep it off. Drew slept deeply, but woke up the next day with a pronounced stutter—a result of untreated brain damage. His acting aspirations suddenly seemed like a pipe dream.

With the damage to his vocal nerves irreversible, Drew found solace in comedy. His newfound passion led him all the way to the finals of America's Got Talent. Although he didn't clinch the title, the experience became a turning point. A few years later, now with over two million followers and an inspiring TED talk under his belt, Drew's journey has been nothing short of extraordinary.

In his talk, he shares a profound lesson:

"We often see missed opportunities as roadblocks, but what if they're actually guardrails guiding us towards the path we were meant to take all along?"

Drew's story exemplifies the unexpected detours that can propel us to greater heights. Success is rarely linear. Holding on to a perceived identity that may no longer serve you will only become a limitation on your possible trajectory. Not gripping too tightly to labels allows you to remain open to exploration and tactically adjust your plans and goals for maximum impact.

Nassim Nicholas Taleb, in his book *"The Black Swan"*, emphasises the importance of embracing randomness and uncertainty. He posits that life's most significant opportunities often arise from unforeseen events and serendipitous encounters, rather than meticulously planned strategies.

Detours can be the most rewarding part of the journey. Things that look like obstacles could actually be pathways to a better destination, even if it doesn't look the way you'd imagined. Removing our reflexive attachment to titles, labels, and fixed identities allows us the flexibility to chart our own course and redirect on the fly.

Drew was echoing the words of the great Roman emperor, Marcus Aurelius.

> *"Our actions may be impeded . . . but there can be no impeding our intentions or dispositions. Because we can accommodate and adapt. The mind adapts and converts to its own purposes the obstacle to our acting. The impediment to action advances action. What stands in the way becomes the way."*
>
> — Marcus Aurelius

For those willing to accept difficulty with open arms, and by embracing it learn to navigate it, the things that block your path will become the path. What stands in the way becomes the way.

As long as you adapt to your obstacles, there will always be a path forward.

33

The Final Chapter

"You could not prevent a thunderstorm, but you could use the electricity; you could not direct the wind, but you could trim your sail so as to propel your vessel as you pleased, not matter which way the wind blew."

— Cora L. V. Hatch

Tsutomu Yamaguchi stood in a field just outside Nagasaki. It was early morning, hot and humid, and the August sun climbed higher into a grey sky. The sun seemed to prick at the recently bandaged burns which wrapped around the left side of his body. But those burns didn't come from any ordinary fire.

For the last three months, he had been on a business trip 400km away in another city: Hiroshima. On the very last day of that trip, he had been transported to hell; ferocious, indescribable, and all-consuming.

Yamaguchi and his two colleagues had been on their way to the train station, finally heading home after the prolonged work engagement, when he froze in realisation. He'd left his identification stamp at work. He couldn't leave the city without it. Yamaguchi turned, telling his colleagues that he'd meet them at the station, and he ran back alone towards the docks.

That's when it happened. He saw the plane—about 3 kilometres away, flying low over the city centre, too far to recognise immediately as an American B-29 bomber. But he saw two small parachutes unfurl from it. And then it came—the flash. A white-hot burst of searing light that stole his eyesight, if only for a moment. And in the reeling disorientation, there came a wave of sound. Like the bark of 10,000 wild dogs and the roar of great machinery. An explosion malevolent enough to burst his eardrums in an instant, throwing him back, off his feet, in a tumble to the ground.

After recovering enough sense to gather himself, his body still shell-shocked and stinging in the heat of radiation burns, Yamaguchi ran to find his colleagues. Fortunately, they too had survived. The three of them spent that night in the city, cowering in an air-raid shelter, and fled home the following day.

That was two days ago. Now, home in Nagasaki, despite still being heavily bandaged, bald from burns, and unable to hear in his left ear, Yamaguchi would have to report to work. He had lived in this city all his life, and made his living as an engineer. He arrived at the Mitsubishi shipyard early, as always, with a feeling in his bones that he'd used up all his luck.

It was 10am on the 9th of August. Yamaguchi had no idea that 200km away, halfway between Hiroshima and Nagasaki, a B-29 bomber named Bockscar was circling the city of Kokura. In its belly was another beast—the plutonium bomb dubbed "Fat Man".

An American, Major Charles Sweeney of the US Air Force, was in the pilot seat, charged with delivering the second atomic bomb. Kokura was his target—a city housing Japan's largest munitions factory. But as they approached, Sweeney's heart sank.

A thick blanket of clouds obscured the city below, rendering their visual bombing run impossible. The Americans could see through the clouds in patches, but couldn't get a direct sighting on the arsenal they were aiming for.

For nearly an hour, Bockscar circled Kokura, burning precious fuel as Sweeney and his crew searched desperately for a break in the cloud cover. With each passing minute, the tension in the cockpit ratcheted higher. They had enough fuel for just one more run before they'd be forced to turn back or risk ditching in the sea.

In another world, Sweeney wouldn't have even been in this region of Japan. Hiroshima, where the first bomb had struck, was originally meant to be the second target. Kyoto had been the first. But weeks ago in Washington, a change had been made.

The Americans had two bombs ready. Little Boy, and Fat Man. The Target Committee, selected by President Harry Truman, sat down to determine which Japanese cities would receive their payloads. Four cities made the shortlist: Kyoto, Hiroshima, Kokura, and Niigata. Two of them would receive a bomb fearsome enough to make America's military dominance clear, and scare the Japanese into surrender.

But at that table, one man felt a twinge of unease. Not because of the tens of thousands who might be killed in order to spare multiples more, but for a slightly more personal reason. U.S. Secretary of War Henry Stimson intervened as the list was being certified, begging Kyoto be kept off the list. He remarked that the city carried too much cultural significance to be decimated. It also happened to be the place he and his wife had honeymooned years before, and a fondness for the ancient capital had grown on him.

With that stroke of sentiment, Kyoto was removed from the list. Hiroshima and Kokura were bumped up, and almost as an afterthought, a fourth-place alternative was added to the bottom. A city of some significance, but one that no one expected would come into play: Nagasaki.

Yet on that August morning, as clouds clung to Kokura and Bockscar's fuel gauges dipped dangerously, Nagasaki's position as last resort became a death sentence for thousands of its citizens.

Since Yamaguchi's arrival at his office that day, he had recounted the horrors he'd witnessed in Hiroshima to disbelieving colleagues. And at that very moment, in the skies above Japan, the crew of Bockscar was making a decision that would alter the course of history.

The clock was ticking. Yamaguchi's colleagues listened intently as he described the blinding flash he had seen in Hiroshima. "It couldn't have been a single bomb," he insisted. "Nothing could cause that much destruction."

As if in cruel response to his words, at 11:02am, the sky above Nagasaki erupted in a familiar, terrifying white light. Yamaguchi, in a twist of fate almost too incredible to believe, found himself witness to the second atomic bombing in human history.

The bomb that fell on Nagasaki that day was not meant for the city. It was a last-minute decision, the result of a series of chance events and desperate choices.

Yamaguchi, and most of the world at the time, had no idea how close Nagasaki had come to escaping this fate. As the dust settled and the horrific scope of the destruction became clear, the role of chance in Nagasaki's fate came into sharp focus. A honeymoon destination spared one city. Cloud cover doomed another. Split-second decisions made miles above the earth determined who would live and who would die.

Life really is that random. I tell this story because it illustrates the complexity of time and fate. Decisions cascade, interfacing with chance, and the outcomes ripple around the world. Each one of us acts in small and seemingly isolated ways, which collide and incrementally shape the world around us.

Tsutomu Yamaguchi, the man who survived two atomic bombs in the span of three days, would live to be 93. But things could easily have been different.

The Illusion of Control

The world doesn't unfold according to any one person's grand design. Events, at scale, don't happen because they were "supposed" to happen. They just happen.

Humans are pattern-seeking creatures, hardwired to construct narratives that make sense of the chaos around us. We tell ourselves that success comes to those who deserve it, that our triumphs and failures are solely the results of our actions. But the reality is far messier. It can be useful to think of ourselves as the authors of our own stories, carefully plotting each twist and turn. But the truth is moderately more chaotic.

If you could go back and relive your life, making the exact same decisions, would you end up in exactly the same place? Probably not. The butterfly effect of countless tiny variations would likely lead you down a different path. A train delayed by a minute, a different seat chosen in a classroom, a minor cold that keeps you home on a crucial day—any of these could alter the course of your life in profound ways.

> The precise life you've lived, the exact circumstances you find yourself in right now, intentional acts notwithstanding, are the product of an unfathomable number of variables, many of which were entirely outside your control. Your genetics, your place of birth, the economic conditions of your formative years, the random encounters that shaped your path; all of these were, to a large extent, matters of chance.

This isn't to say that our choices don't matter. They do, profoundly. But they matter in a way that's far more complex and less predictable than we often assume.

The dice won't always roll well. This is when you have a choice that changes everything. Like many, you could take the excuse to nihilistically throw up your hands, lie prostrate, and submit yourself as a victim to the whimsy of the universe. Or, you could recognise that there was never a need to control every variable.

Yes, life's ocean is vast and endless, capricious and powerful beyond your control. But in the same way that cowboys corral runaway cattle with nothing more than a horse and a rope, you can learn to channel chaos—not by wrestling with the foundations of the universe, but by learning to ride waves of chance rather than being overwhelmed by them.

Sovereignty doesn't lie in the illusion of total control, but in the ability to navigate uncertainty, seize opportunities, and make the most of whatever hand you're dealt.

Navigating Your Nature

The lottery of birth deals us all a unique hand. Some are born with perfect pitch, others tone-deaf. Some have minds wired for mathematics, others struggle with basic arithmetic. These innate characteristics, whether gifts or challenges, may determine where you start your journey, but they don't dictate where you must finish.

There is no guarantee that you will ever overcome the casualties of your birth, or the afflictions of your life. But you can still control how you rise to meet those challenges. Your sovereignty lies in whatever self-direction you can slice from the situations you encounter.

Ludwig van Beethoven, born in 1770, is widely regarded as one of the greatest composers in history. But at the height of his career, aged only 28, he began to lose his hearing. By 1811, he could no longer hear music or conversation. By 1815, aged 44, he couldn't hear at all.

The years surrounding Beethoven's peak deafness were known as his dry period. Reeling from heartbreak, marked by madness, from 1813 to 1816 he wrote nearly nothing. He grew increasingly isolated, withdrawing from social interaction as his world faded into final silence.

He could no longer perform, the love of his life was out of his grasp, he felt ill-fated to never marry, he was mired in a legal battle for his nephew Karl, who he saw as a son but was deemed to not be capable of caring for. He had lost it all. But in that terrible darkness, he found his pen again. In 1817 he began the 'final stage' of his career.

His new work was personal and philosophical. It was seen almost as an entirely new kind of music. Beethoven's style had changed so completely that the music was hard to understand and appreciate at first. In his silent years, Beethoven had been considered dead weight, and musical tastes had evolved in his absence. But in that period of quiet solitude, he had learned to hear again. Even without use of his ears, Beethoven slowly learned to feel the vibrations of music through his piano.

He used conversation books to communicate, forcing him to distill his thoughts into written form. His later works, composed in complete deafness, relying on vibration and patient practice, are among his most profound and innovative: Hammerklavier, the Diabelli variations, Missa Solemnis, and the Ninth Symphony.

Beethoven's struggle with hearing loss didn't end—it lasted until his death. But he found sovereignty in refusing to let it dictate the terms of his existence. And he wasn't the only great creator who had afflictions to overcome.

Your Unique Perspective

Virginia Woolf, one of the most influential modernist writers of the 20th century, battled severe mood swings throughout her life. Today, she would likely have been diagnosed with bipolar disorder. Woolf didn't vanquish her mental health struggles; they were a constant companion. Yet she channelled her experiences into her art, using her unique perspective to create works that revolutionised literature.

Woolf was institutionalised several times, but kept returning to her craft, wrestling against dark thoughts to find beauty in words. After completing the manuscript of her last novel, she fell into a deep depression similar to one she had experienced many years earlier.

In her novel *"Mrs. Dalloway,"* Woolf vividly portrays the inner workings of a mind grappling with mental illness. Her own struggles allowed her to write with a depth and authenticity that resonated with readers. Woolf's sovereignty wasn't in conquering her condition, but in refusing to let it silence her voice.

The Second World War broke out, Woolf's home in London was destroyed by the Blitz, her biography of a dear friend was poorly received by critics, and her mental state continued to deteriorate. Her suffering was so intense that death came to seem preferable. In the end, after writing her husband one last letter, she filled her overcoat pockets with stones and walked into the River Ouse, perishing. Her final novel was published posthumously, in the year of her death.

Sovereignty doesn't lie solely in transcending your limitations. It comes from engaging with them, wrestling with them daily. It comes from an acceptance of who you are, good and bad, and the path you have to walk. The sovereignty exhibited in the stories I've shared doesn't come from victory over conditions, but in a refusal to be defined by them.

> Your life may well include unavoidable challenges. Some persistent, some permanent: anxiety that grips you in social situations, depression that colours your world in shades of grey, a neurodivergent mind that struggles to adjust to neurotypical expectations. You can't will these away. You could overcome them with support and training, or they might still plague you. But you can always choose how you approach and engage with them. Submission or sovereignty—that's the choice.

The goal isn't to overcome the fundamental aspects of who you are. It's to navigate them, to find the unique perspective they offer you, and to use that perspective to chart a course that is undeniably your own.

The Art of Letting Go

Admiral James Stockdale was shot down over North Vietnam in September 1965. He would spend the next seven and a half years as a prisoner of war (POW), enduring torture, isolation, and brutal conditions. During that period, Stockdale became the highest-ranking naval officer held as a POW.

It was a tough ordeal. Many of the POWs didn't make it. But of those who cracked, Stockdale made a crucial observation—one which became key to his own survival. Stockdale noticed that among his fellow prisoners, it wasn't the pessimists who struggled most – it was the optimists. These were the men who would say, "We're going to be out by Christmas." Then Christmas would come and go. "Okay, we'll be out by Easter." Easter would pass. "Alright, by Thanksgiving." And so on.

According to Stockdale, these optimists died of broken hearts. Their repeated disappointment crushed their spirits. They kept moving the benchmarks and each passing date fell on their hearts like a guillotine. They eventually broke when they couldn't reconcile their hopes with the harsh reality they faced.

Stockdale, on the other hand, adopted a different mindset. A Sovereign one. He accepted the brutal facts of his current situation – that he might be imprisoned for a long time; that he would face torture and hardship. Short of escaping, he had no control over how long he was kept there. Short of being killed, he could only control how defiantly he held on to his life. Stockdale maintained an unwavering faith that he would prevail in the end, regardless of the difficulties.

This paradoxical approach—confronting the most brutal facts of your current reality, while maintaining faith that you will prevail—became known as the Stockdale Paradox. It allowed Stockdale to survive where others faltered.

He didn't pine for rescue or cling to specific dates for release. Instead, he focused on what he could control: creating a system of communication between prisoners, developing a code of conduct for prisoner behaviour, and resistance to interrogators. He found ways to lead and to maintain his integrity, even in the direst circumstances.

Stockdale was tortured over twenty times, survived wartime imprisonment for almost a decade and, in his own words, came out of the enemies' camp stronger than when he went in. The secret was letting go of what he couldn't control. What those around him didn't realise at the time, was how closely his sentiment echoed a school of ancient philosophy; a mindset shared by emperors and slaves alike, in Ancient Rome.

The Spirit of a Slave

Born into slavery around 50 CE, Epictetus had every reason to feel powerless. As a young man, he served in the household of Epaphroditus, a wealthy freedman and secretary to Emperor Nero. Despite his circumstances, Epictetus found freedom in philosophy, studying under the Stoic teacher Musonius Rufus.

One day, as the story goes, Epaphroditus was twisting Epictetus' leg in anger. Calmly, Epictetus warned, "If you go on, you will break my leg." When Epaphroditus did break it, Epictetus simply remarked, "Did I not tell you that you would break it?". He didn't retaliate. Didn't lash out in anger. The situation was internalised instantly.

The historical record here is admittedly murky—we can't be sure whether Epictetus was crippled from birth or whether it was indeed a casualty incurred in his master's care—but in either case, there was nothing he could do. Epictetus couldn't control his master's actions any more than he could control the wind. To lay a hand on Epaphroditus, a freedman, was a death sentence.

Epictetus learned that his only freedom lay in controlling his response. He would gain nothing from writhing in pain or seething in anger. A broken leg was broken – he'd have to live with that for the rest of his life. He could either accept it or be mentally tortured by something he could never change.

After gaining his freedom, Epictetus went on to teach this philosophy, which we now know as Stoicism. His teachings attracted students from all walks of life, from commoners to senators. One of his most famous students was Arrian, who would later compile Epictetus' teachings into "The Discourses," a cornerstone of Stoic philosophy.

Epictetus taught:

> *"Some things are in our control and others not. Things in our control are opinion, pursuit, desire, aversion, and, in a word, whatever are our own actions. Things not in our control are body, property, reputation, command, and, in one word, whatever are not our own actions."*

— Epictetus

This idea—focusing on what we can control and accepting what we can't—became a guiding principle for many, including emperors. Marcus Aurelius, ruling an empire beset by war and plague, found solace and strength in these teachings. In his personal writings, later published as "Meditations," he reminded himself, "You have power over your mind—not outside events. Realise this, and you will find strength."

The Stoic approach is a Sovereign one. It doesn't encourage passivity or resignation, but clear-sighted action. By releasing the illusion of control over external events, ancient Stoics found the freedom to act decisively on what truly mattered. This philosophy guided them through war, loss, exile, and even the mundane frustrations of daily life.

Make Your Own Music

Life rarely follows a clean script. In this way, it might be compared to music. Every aspiring musician wants to get things right. They obsess over the perfect outcome. They hyperfocus on hitting the right note, in the right way, at the right time. But in hunting for perfection, their focus subconsciously flows from their mind to their palm, cramping it, and ruining the music. When your grip is too tight, your rhythm becomes stiff. You lose the flow, and sour the song.

Release whatever tension you hold in your mind regarding the outcomes you seek. All you have are your actions. Let life's turbulence resolve on its own, and you'll be surprised at how often it still follows whatever beat you set.

> You can sit patiently, practicing the perfect recital, hoping for a perfect life, or you can learn to make jazz music instead. You can embrace life's naturally occurring randomness, and adopt the spontaneity that gives jazz its soul.

In jazz, every 'wrong' note is an opportunity. The great jazz trumpeter Miles Davis once said, "It's not the note you play that's the wrong note – it's the note you play afterwards that makes it right or wrong." This philosophy applies equally to life.

When we hold too tightly to our expectations, we become rigid, and unable to adapt to life's curveballs. The Sovereign learn to loosen their grip, to let the metaphorical drumsticks bounce naturally in their hands. This doesn't mean being careless or unprepared. It means being ready to improvise, to incorporate unexpected turns into your performance.

Jazz gives you the opportunity to make all music good music. It doesn't matter what cards you were dealt, what pain you have suffered, what hardship encountered. All that matters is the moment before you. Your next note, and what you choose to make of it.

Will you marry discordant notes into a melody? Carve riffs from randomness? Find novelty in noise? None of this can come from a place of passivity. You have to own your song, and make your music.

The Sovereign Choice

In the film "The Matrix," Neo is offered a choice between two pills. The blue pill would allow him to return to his life—to what he now knew was a comfortable illusion. The red pill would instead reveal the harsh truth of reality, and lead him to battle with monsters of fate. You face a similar decision now. It's not too late—you could close your eyes and pretend you never read this book. You could ease back into the comforting embrace of rules, order, and the status quo. Or you could choose the life of the Sovereign, daring to see the world as it truly is and take control of your destiny.

The blue pill life isn't bad. That's what makes the choice so difficult. Most people crave a simulated life. One where you can just be told what to do – where the good guys and gals get what they deserve, and where your needs are met simply and predictably, by the system's perfect design. This path isn't pain-free—quite the opposite. But many happily turn a blind eye to their yearnings of ambition, swallow the gnawing discomfort, and participate in the program.

However, for those who seek self-sovereignty, who aspire to remarkable lives, the blue pill isn't an option. They *must* take the red one – the path of seeing reality for what it is and finding their power within it. It's not an easy choice. Remarkable lives aren't safe. They're not simple. They're not easily replicable. They come with no guarantees of a triumphant resolution.

As you now know, becoming Sovereign starts with ambition. It requires agency, in the form of confidence, competence, and charisma. It takes overcoming adversity and the obstacles on the path. And it means accepting those things which are outside of your control, and acting purposefully on the objects within reach.

The Sovereign life isn't for everyone. It's challenging, often lonely, and fraught with uncertainty. But it offers something the simulated life never can: the opportunity to chart your path and author your story—to create something remarkable and uniquely your own.

As you close this book and step back into the world, know that you carry within you the seed of a remarkable life. You have the power to reshape your reality, to bend the arc of your life towards your deepest desires. But potential alone is not enough. Sovereignty demands action.

Will you settle for the simulation, or step into Sovereignty? Let the currents of chance carry you where they will, or learn to navigate chaos? Wait to see what life brings you, or wield intentionality and decisiveness as a sail and rudder to chart your course through the storm?

The choice, as always, is yours. Choose wisely. Choose courageously. Choose Sovereignty.

Further Reading

Below is a list of books that support the development of a sovereign mindset. (For a more extensive, categorised list of 50+ recommendations with additional commentary, including a Dramatis Personae listing all the book's characters, visit **tools.becomesovereign.com/list**.)

Aurelius, Marcus. *Meditations*. London: Penguin Classics, 2006.

Carnegie, Dale. *How to Win Friends and Influence People*. New York: Simon & Schuster, 1936.

Clear, James. *Atomic Habits: An Easy & Proven Way to Build Good Habits & Break Bad Ones*. New York: Avery, 2018.

Coelho, Paulo. *The Alchemist*. London: HarperCollins, 1988.

Covey, Stephen R. *The 7 Habits of Highly Effective People: Powerful Lessons in Personal Change*. New York: Simon & Schuster, 1989.

Dalio, Ray. *Principles: Life and Work*. New York: Simon & Schuster, 2017.

Duckworth, Angela. *Grit: The Power of Passion and Perseverance*. New York: Scribner, 2016.

Dweck, Carol S. *Mindset: The New Psychology of Success*. New York: Random House, 2006.

Epstein, David. *Range: Why Generalists Triumph in a Specialized World*. New York: Riverhead Books, 2019.

Ferriss, Tim. *The 4-Hour Workweek: Escape 9–5, Live Anywhere, and Join the New Rich*. New York: Crown Publishers, 2007.

Frankl, Viktor E. *Man's Search for Meaning*. Boston: Beacon Press, 1959.

Greene, Robert. *Mastery*. New York: Viking, 2012.

Harari, Yuval Noah. *Sapiens: A Brief History of Humankind*. London: Harvill Secker, 2014.

Holiday, Ryan. *The Obstacle Is the Way: The Timeless Art of Turning Trials into Triumph*. New York: Portfolio, 2014.

Jorgenson, Eric. *The Almanack of Naval Ravikant: A Guide to Wealth and Happiness*. Magrathea Publishing, 2020.

Kahneman, Daniel. *Thinking, Fast and Slow*. New York: Farrar, Straus and Giroux, 2011.

Newport, Cal. *Deep Work: Rules for Focused Success in a Distracted World*. New York: Grand Central Publishing, 2016.

Acknowledgements

Every week tens of thousands of people read my newsletter and blog posts, so it appears I have a wide audience to write for. But many of my earlier posts began life as long text messages to my younger sister, who—like many of you—is earnestly trying to navigate life on this earth.

Most of what I've learned has come from taking wild risks and making mistakes, and I've found that what I share with my sister is typically useful for many others. More than half a million people on my blog at theknowledge.io, to be exact. So I wrote this book with my sister in mind. If she finds it useful, it will be a success. If thousands of others find it enlightening, I will be glad.

Special thanks to Kelly for the urge to commit to this project. To Toby and Jasmine for reviewing countless cover drafts; to Esmé, Rachael, and Jeremiah for their early thoughts on positioning; and to Jenya, Jason, and Etta for engaging conversations. My gratitude also to Bob, Jenny, Ed, and Luca for their advice and encouragement, and to Tobi, Zoe, and the rest of the beta crew for proofreading at various stages.

Thanks to the many mentors and guiding hands who helped shape my career and mindset in various ways, and at various points—Kasia, Peter, Andy, Joseph, Jayne, Natalie, Gary, and more.

And finally, enduring gratitude to my closest friends, for their support, and to Efua, my love, Harry, my ball of trouble, and to my parents—giants on whose shoulders I stand.

About the Author

David Elikwu is a London-based writer, entrepreneur and strategy adviser whose career has spanned continents and industries. He started his first business importing electronics from Shenzhen at fourteen, and trained in corporate law in Shanghai and London. He's built businesses in every vertical, from African coffee to Tuscan wine, from travel services to global e-commerce, and has built growth and operations for venture-backed tech startups across Europe and Africa.

David now writes **The Knowledge**, a newsletter and podcast on ambition, agency, and decision-making, followed by more than 40,000 founders, operators, and creatives, with his essays reaching millions online. He has delivered keynotes and workshops for Google, Bloomberg, Unilever, Deloitte, Cambridge University and more.

When not writing or advising teams, he is usually travelling—50 countries and counting—running and walking through woods and backstreets, or testing his next experiment.

Newsletter: **theknowledge.io**
Speaking: **contact@theknowledge.io**

www.ingramcontent.com/pod-product-compliance
Lightning Source LLC
Chambersburg PA
CBHW010248010526
44119CB00055B/771